ROUTLEDGE LIBRARY EDITIONS: WW2

Volume 18

THE MONTGOMERY LEGEND

THE MONTGOMERY LEGEND

R.W. THOMPSON

LONDON AND NEW YORK

First published in 1967 by George Allen & Unwin Ltd.

This edition first published in 2022
by Routledge
2 Park Square, Milton Park, Abingdon, Oxon OX14 4RN

and by Routledge
605 Third Avenue, New York, NY 10158

Routledge is an imprint of the Taylor & Francis Group, an informa business

© 1967 George Allen & Unwin Ltd.

All rights reserved. No part of this book may be reprinted or reproduced or utilised in any form or by any electronic, mechanical, or other means, now known or hereafter invented, including photocopying and recording, or in any information storage or retrieval system, without permission in writing from the publishers.

Trademark notice: Product or corporate names may be trademarks or registered trademarks, and are used only for identification and explanation without intent to infringe.

British Library Cataloguing in Publication Data
A catalogue record for this book is available from the British Library

ISBN: 978-1-03-201217-9 (Set)
ISBN: 978-1-00-319367-8 (Set) (ebk)
ISBN: 978-1-03-204534-4 (Volume 18) (hbk)
ISBN: 978-1-03-204535-1 (Volume 18) (pbk)
ISBN: 978-1-00-319366-1 (Volume 18) (ebk)

DOI: 10.4324/9781003193661

Publisher's Note
The publisher has gone to great lengths to ensure the quality of this reprint but points out that some imperfections in the original copies may be apparent.

Disclaimer
The publisher has made every effort to trace copyright holders and would welcome correspondence from those they have been unable to trace.

The Montgomery Legend

BY

R. W. THOMPSON

BOOK I

'If the art of war consisted
merely in not taking risks,
glory would be at the disposal of
very mediocre talent.'

NAPOLEON

ILLUSTRATED

London
GEORGE ALLEN & UNWIN LTD
RUSKIN HOUSE   MUSEUM STREET

FIRST PUBLISHED IN 1967

This book is copyright under the Berne Convention. Apart from any fair dealing for the purposes of private study, research, criticism or review, as permitted under the Copyright Act, 1956, no portion may be reproduced by any process without written permission. Enquiries should be addressed to the publishers.

© *George Allen & Unwin Ltd., 1967*

PRINTED IN GREAT BRITAIN
in 11 pt. Baskerville type
BY C. TINLING AND CO
PRESCOT

ACKNOWLEDGEMENTS

The extracts from *The Mediterranean and Middle East*, vol. iii by Major-General I. S. O. Playfair; from *Grand Strategy*, vol. iii, part ii, by J. R. M. Butler; from *Grand Strategy*, vol. v by John Ehrman, are quoted by permission of Her Majesty's Stationery Office; from: George F. Howe, *North West Africa: Seizing the Initiative in the West*, United States Army in World War II (Washington, 1957), published by the Office of the Chief of Military History, Department of the Army, by permission of the Chief of Military History, Washington, D.C.; from *The Hinge of Fate* and *Closing the Ring*, vols. iv and v, *The Second World War* by Winston S. Churchill, by permission of *The Daily Telegraph*.

I owe special thanks to Capt Sir Basil Liddell Hart for making private papers available for me from his archives, and for his kindness in reading the first four chapters of this book in manuscript before leaving England to take up an appointment in the USA. My debt to vol. ii, *The Tanks*, The History of the Royal Tank Regiment, will be obvious to all who may read this book.

I have a debt to the late John Connell for his steadfast encouragement over many years, and for the insights gained from his work, particularly his biography, *Auchinleck*. I record with gratitude, and a deep sense of my inadequacy, my thanks to Major-General and Mrs Eric Dorman O'Gowan for inviting me to work in their home during part of my long convalescence, and for making private papers and their military library available to me. I thank Brigadier John Stephenson for his careful reading of my book, and for his forthright and valuable criticisms, and the Librarian of the Royal United Service Institution for making many books available to me over a long period.

I acknowledge gratefully the works listed in the bibliography, all of which, whether referred to in the text or not, have added to my pleasure and knowledge.

None of which is to say that anyone but myself agrees with or approves in the smallest degree a single word that I have written.

Finally, without the generous aid of Dr J. A. Linnell and The Royal Literary Fund; without the courage of my wife, and the patience and kindness of my three youngest children, it would have been impossible to have written this book, or to have survived as a writer.

R. W. THOMPSON
Belchamp Walter
Suffolk
March 1966

CONTENTS

INTRODUCTION	page	15

PART I: THE INHERITANCE
ONE	Churchill's Agony	23
TWO	Redemption	38
THREE	Catharsis	52

PART II: THE INHERITORS
FOUR	The General	75
FIVE	Alam Halfa: the general and the battle	95
SIX	The 15th September	107

PART III: ANATOMY OF A LEGEND
SEVEN	2nd Alamein	119
EIGHT	2nd Alamein II	137
NINE	The Triumphal March	156
TEN	On to Tunis!	174

PART IV: UNDER TWO FLAGS
ELEVEN	The Allied Command	197
TWELVE	'Husky'	214
THIRTEEN	Fortress Europe	229
FOURTEEN	A Soldier's Farewell	245

NOTES	253
READING LIST	263
INDEX	266

ILLUSTRATIONS

1. "All the talents" on the lawn of the British Embassy, Cairo, August, 1942. *facing page* 80

2. General Sir Alan Brooke, chatting with Major-General Dorman Smith at El Alamein, August, 1942.
   facing page 81
   Mr Winston Churchill with Major-General Dorman Smith during his visit to the Western Desert.
   facing page 81
   Mr Churchill giving the 'V' sign to Australian troops, August, 1942. *facing page* 81

3. Lieutenant-General Montgomery talking with officers of the 22nd Armoured Brigade. *facing page* 96
   The Army Commander looking at a wrecked German tank. *facing page* 96
   General Montgomery and the Padre, December, 1942.
   facing page 96

4. The Army Commander speaking to junior officers of the 1st Armoured Division. *facing page* 97
   Lieutenant-General Montgomery announcing the destruction of the Afrika Korps to war correspondents.
   facing page 97

5. General Montgomery in his famous hat. *facing page* 128

6. General Montgomery inspecting men of the 5th Brigade, N.Z. Division. *facing page* 129
   Outside Homs. General Montgomery talking to the B.G.S. Brigadier Erskine. *facing page* 129

7. General Montgomery with Marshal Messe.
   facing page 144
   Italy: December 1943. General Montgomery after his farewell address. *facing page* 144

8. General Eisenhower decorating General Montgomery with the Legion of Merit. *facing page* 145
   General Montgomery addressing war correspondents, 1943. *facing page* 145

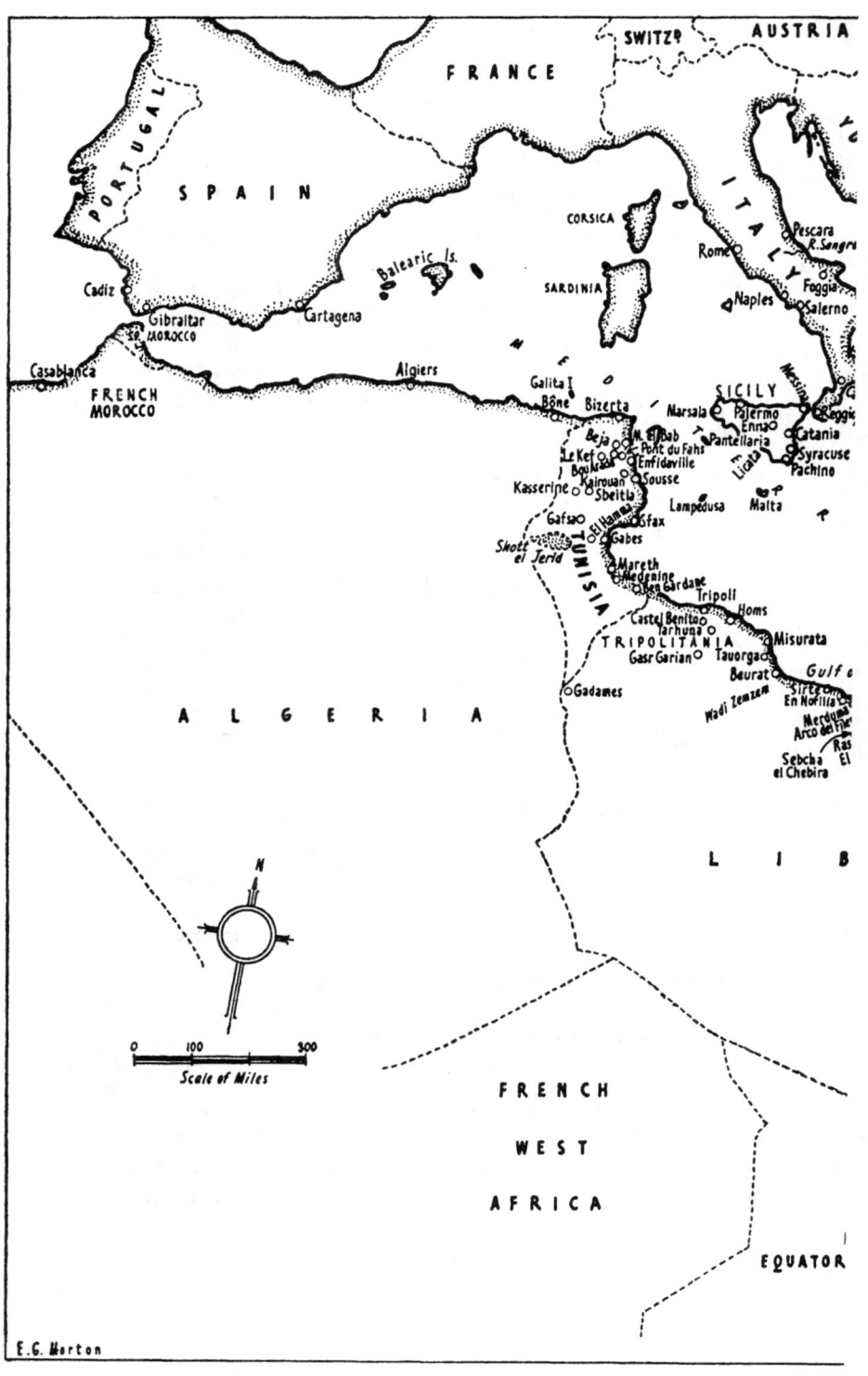

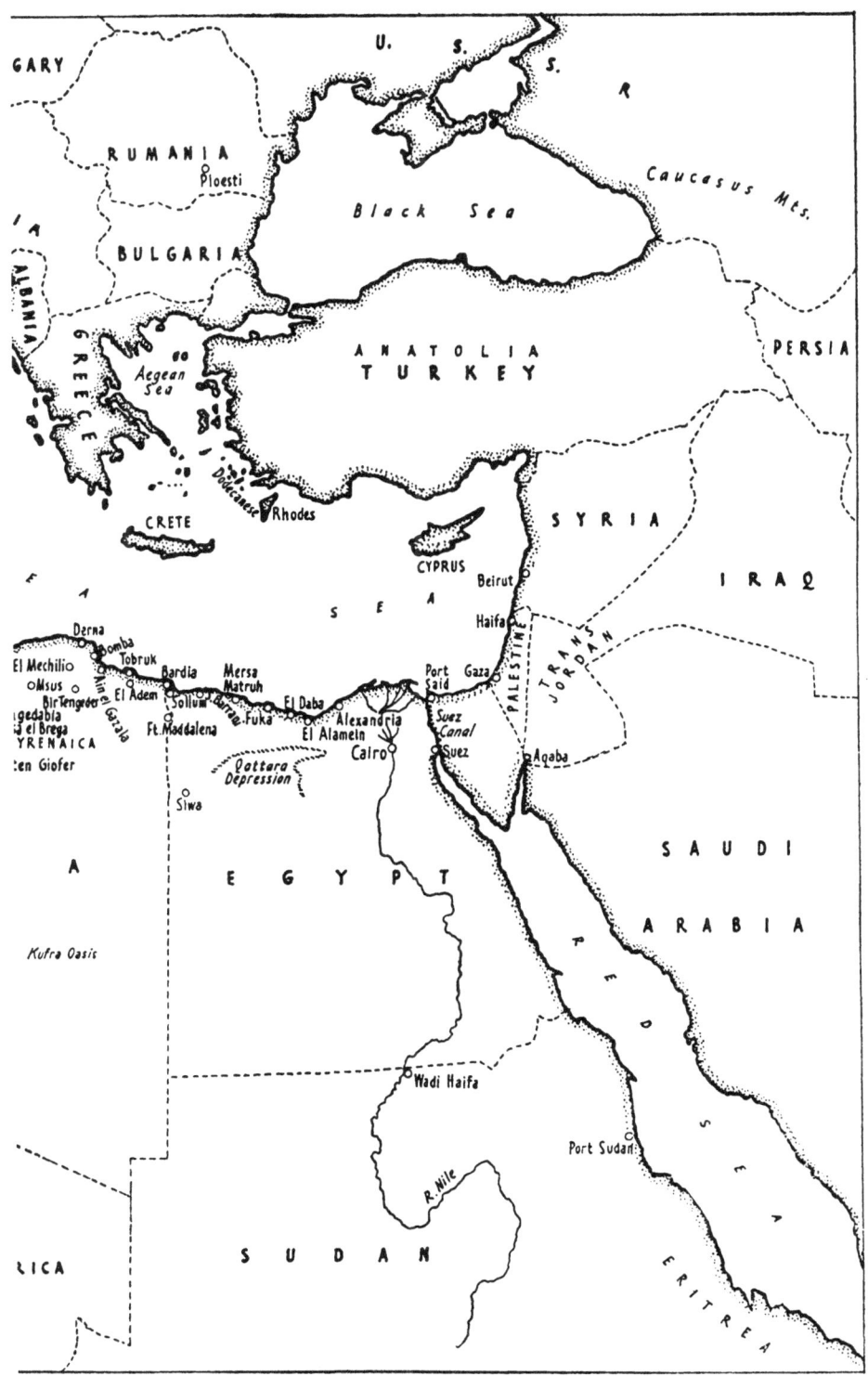

Introduction

CONTEMPORARY history is dangerous stuff. It has been always so. It is doubly dangerous to attempt to discover the substance of famous personalities, especially when such personalities have become the symbols of myth and legend.

We live in an age of highly skilled 'image' makers, the masters of a wide range of techniques, and with the means to project their images upon the screens of our minds. Soon they may contrive to plant their images while we sleep.

The events I have attempted to set down took place more than twenty years ago in the days when image making was in its infancy, and perhaps now that much of the dust has settled it may be possible to achieve some tranquillity of heart, mind and spirit. Perhaps now we can bear to look a legend squarely in the eye; strive to 'see' the man and events of its substance, and even dare to glance for a moment into the 'tomb' beneath the monument. For no monument stands upon nothing, marking nothing.

I have reflected a great deal on this subject, on the towering figures of a more remote past, and on the few larger-than-life figures of our own times. I find it difficult to share humanity with 'Sacred Cows'. I want to render unto Caesar the things that are Caesar's, and unto God the things that are God's. Thinking on these things it seems to me that we have always found it difficult to forgive truly great and noble men their nobility. They do not fit comfortably into the world of prevarication and compromise in which we live. They are, perhaps, too grave a reflection on ourselves.

Christ was nailed to his Cross; Socrates drank his hemlock; Belisarius (though some deny it) came to his rags and his begging bowl. Such men in their various ways were too good for us.

In our own times we sweep the deeds of our great men of noble stature 'under the carpet of history', while extolling the virtues of lesser men. We no longer shoot our 'Byngs' or condemn our scapegoats to begging bowls, but it might be less cruel, more human, a more true reflection of our inner disgust with ourselves, to do so.

It is no less a disservice to our great men and to ourselves to elaborate myths, and to strive with every means at our command to harden myths and legends into facts. Mass communications, the manipulation and control of innumerable channels of propaganda, many of them subtle, all of them gaining access to millions of unsuspecting minds, enable images of men and events to be projected to suit the needs of 'The Powers that be.' These needs may seem reasonable at the time, politically expedient, even absolutely necessary. I beg leave to doubt that 'brain washing', even in the midst of war, is ever justified.

Myths and legends are always signs of weakness. In an ailing society they are dangerous. A myth having been created and nurtured is not easily observed for what it was. Moreover, 'Hero' figures once projected often tend to develop a momentum of their own, startling even to their sponsors. Emperors, poorly clad, or stark naked, strut about on the stage of life, and there may be very few to remark their nakedness, or the quality of their garments.

We live in an incessant uproar of violence about violence, and are in danger of knowing almost nothing about almost everything; and that 'almost nothing', false. The un-event has begun to be preferred to the event, the fiction to the fact. We strive to escape from a reality which terrifies us, and are beset by dangers from which our ancestors—even our grandfathers—were relatively free. We have come to value the meretricious above the meritorious.

But there is—there must be—truth, even if there are two or ten sides to it. And we must seek it without fear. There must be something that is not a lie.

History is as alive as we are ourselves, and if we do not seek to know and to challenge the truths and falsehoods of our times, we mock the past, build the present upon insecure foundations, and undermine the future. We not only falsify our own lives, we poison the wells from which those who come after us must drink. Today is the product of yesterday, and tomorrow will be a product of today. History is now.

The physical facts of history, the bare bones of what is happening, and what has happened, are difficult to discover, and to quote certain episodes out of their context may be as bad, or worse, than to lie. Events and people are parts of each other, and to attempt to evaluate the performance and achievement of any man in the framework of the events which he made, and which made him, is a formidable and daunting task. When such an individual is the keystone and substance of a powerful legend, the task is even more formidable. One is confronted with the truth that no man is an island. We are unescapably a part of each other, sharing life and death, good and evil, guilt and innocence, honour and dishonour, triumph and disaster. We wash our hands of our involvement at our peril.

When we decide to attempt an assessment of a great public figure, a 'Hero', we do more than examine an individual, we examine a society.

Moreover, not only are individuals a part of each other, and of all mankind, but events also are a part of larger events, each one sending its ripples to the ends of the earth and back. Events do not occur in a vacuum. Chinese box reveals Chinese box, but not *ad infinitum*. There must be an ultimate box, and we must dare to open it when we find it.

All this would be portentous stuff if it were merely the preamble to the simple exploration of a man and his legend, and perhaps in the process to uncover certain injustices and grievous wrongs, grave and even disastrous to the individuals concerned, but of little importance in the life and history of a nation. There are bound to be casualties in the rough and tumble of our times, and not even an Anthony may hope to heal great Caesar's wounds, nor breathe one spark of life into that poor bleeding piece of earth.

This book hopes to be more than that. In studying the substance of a legend it draws attention to some of the political undercurrents of a crucial year in this century of crucial years. It is the year in which the tide of war, and the tides of history turned together, and the seeds of a new future were sown. It is the year in which Britain found herself virtually caught between two kinds of 'civilization', and striving not to commit herself to a choice, she finally drifted into a position from which she has never recovered. She is neither European nor American.

One begins to understand why Britain earned the sobriquet—Perfidious Albion! Our geographical position made us great, and now it makes us small.

My book does not go deeply into these things, but it does, I think, reveal that they are there, and that some of them have been obscured by this legend of Montgomery. Legends always hide more than they reveal.

In the summer of 1942 Britain needed a Champion in the field. She needed a 'Victory' and a 'Conqueror' plain for all to see and to acclaim. It was politically necessary. It meant the manipulation of 'history', and the adjustment in time of certain events. It meant the 'sweeping under the carpet' of the substance of many brave and anxious days. In the end, inevitably, the hours and days which were there, and are there still, must be revealed. There is always a 'clue'; some small piece of 'evidence' overlooked.

Old champions, old armies, were banished out of sight, and, it was hoped, out of memory. Even the brave struggle of the Fourteenth Army in the steaming jungles of Asia was 'forgotten'. There was one General and one Army, and nothing in the way. Upon this man, this army, and this place attention was focused.

The champion Britain chose, quite fortuitously, and even by accident, was General Montgomery. We needed a bold champion, and a glamorous man, and General Montgomery was neither bold nor glamorous. The choice once made could not be easily changed, and from the military point of view it seemed unlikely to matter. There is a limit to the number of generals even a Churchill may sack with impunity, and in the midsummer of 1942 Churchill had reached that limit. Probably he had exceeded it.

It is one of the ironies of history that Montgomery should have been the man in that hour. A few months earlier, had he been called to that same theatre of war, he would have been an almost certain casualty of Churchill's frustration, anger and impatience. There was no time then, no patience. Generals either got on or got out. They even got out when they got on. It was a time of desperate urgency for Britain, and for the Prime Minister. His crisis, Britain's crisis, and what may be seen as a European and a world crisis, all coincided in the summer of that fateful year.

And no man ever made General Montgomery hurry; no man ever induced him to attack until his strength was such as to ensure victory. These conditions could not have been met before the late summer of 1942.

Apart from being an instrument of great affairs, a pawn in a power game of great complexity, Montgomery became a unique prototype for the 'image' makers in their 'primitive' days. The decks, as it were, were cleared, and the success of the operation of projecting Montgomery was phenomenal. It was almost 'magic', like an invention arising astoundingly out of some commonplace routine chore, tinkering with a kettle, or a kite.

Whatever one may think about Montgomery's generalship there is no room for doubt about his success as a Conquering Hero figure. The virus took instantaneously, and millions were inoculated with him.

But what kind of a 'Conquering Hero' was he?

In this book I have examined General Montgomery's generalship with all the faithfulness of which I am capable, and in so doing I have attempted also to discover the man behind the hero, as well as the facts behind the legend.

General Montgomery's success was so great that when this book ends at his farewell to the Eighth Army on the Sangro River, he had already become an 'Old Man of the Sea'. He had a stranglehold on his sponsors. His faith in himself was absolute, a military Messiah.

For better or for worse he was Britain's general and champion to the end.

Belchamp Walter,
December 16, 1965.

PART I
THE INHERITANCE

CHAPTER ONE

Churchill's Agony

I

IN his preface to the fourth volume of his autobiographical account of the Second World War, Churchill wrote: 'For the first six months of this story all went ill; for the last six months everything went well. And this agreeable change continued to the end of the struggle.'[1]

The year was 1942, the year of decision. At the half-way mark it was clear that the tide of war had turned in favour of the Western Allies. The first half of the year marked a period of grave crisis for Britain, the Commonwealth, and for the Prime Minister personally. Politically Churchill was at his lowest ebb, reaching his nadir at the end of June. A fearful series of disasters had befallen British arms in every theatre of war, and a shudder seems to pass through Churchill as he looked back upon these events. From the Mediterranean to the Indian Ocean major disasters had been in part the results of his megalomania. The loss of Singapore, and of the capital ships *Prince of Wales* and *Repulse,* stemmed from his negligence. In the Mediterranean his fatal insistence on the expedition to Greece had resulted, not only in the loss of Crete, but had been the means of establishing the German General Rommel and the Afrika Korps in the Western Desert, with the loss of all that we had won, and of all that we might have won. Churchill had put Britain's stake upon strategic bombing. He had announced that the Air Force would be the means of victory, the Navy a poor second, could lose the war, the Army an almost contemptible also ran. 'The Navy can lose us the war, but only the Air Force can win it.'[2] 'On 6th March he had issued one of his periodical directives, in which he instructed us to proceed upon the assumption that the army would never play a primary part in the defeat of the enemy.'[3]

[1] *The Hinge of Fate,* vol. iv., R.U. edition, Preface.
[2] Memorandum September 3, 1940. Winston Churchill, *Their Finest Hour* (The Second World War, vol. ii, R.U. edition).
[3] Maj.-Gen. Sir John Kennedy, *The Business of War,* pp. 96-7. London, Hutchinson, 1957.

This decision, dominating British industrial capacity, starved the navy of landing craft, and the army of armour. It deprived them also of the support aircraft vital to the full performance of their roles. There were, of course, other factors dating back to the 1930s.[1] At a time when the three arms of the services should have been welded into a single fighting instrument, he divided them into three separate parts. In May 1942 the first 1,000-bomber raid upon the city of Cologne underlined futility. In the Mediterranean and Middle East the Navy and the Army were fighting almost for survival, short of almost everything.

It was indeed remarkable, as the Prime Minister himself commented, that he was not dismissed from power. He had no illusions: 'I should then have vanished from the scene with a load of calamity on my shoulders, and the harvest, at last to be reaped, would have been ascribed to my belated disappearance.'[2]

Ironically, Churchill's dismissal at this stage of the war would have made very little difference for good or ill in the march of events. No man may be wholly blamed or wholly praised for the triumphs and disasters of war, but there can be no doubt that Churchill's personal responsibility for a long train of disasters was very great. He had gathered the great offices of Prime Minister and Minister of Defence into his own hands, making of himself a 'Supreme Commander'.

It has been said that Churchill never acted directly against the advice of his Chiefs of Staff. It is true that if they were adamant, if their resolution—and their confidence in their own rightness—was strong, if they could withstand his violence, he would, brooding and silent, at last give way. But it would be an ordeal few men cared to face. More often than not the Prime Minister's will prevailed. In conserving his prodigious energies he was ruthless. He imposed his long nights upon the long days of other men, and assaulted them with the violence of his rhetoric. While he fortified himself with brandy and wreathed himself in the blue smoke of his cigars, his advisers propped their eyes and ears open, strove to keep alert, and longed for respite. The dawn heralded a new day for them, but not for him. Everyone, from the

---

[1] Maj.-Gen. I. S. O. Playfair, *The Mediterranean and Middle East*, vol. iii, Appendix 8. London, H.M.S.O.

[2] *The Hinge of Fate*, vol. iv, R.U. edition, p. 445.

C.I.G.S. down to the least of his servants, would conform to his timings. He had reduced Sir John Dill to impotence, browbeaten his emissaries, and harried his commanders in the field, and out, with remorseless energy. Wavell, who had produced a vast base out of the desert sands, and organized the defence of the Middle East from Libya to the Caucasus, from the shores of the Caspian to the Indian Ocean who had conducted operations on four fronts, and enabled General O'Connor to win his resounding victories, had been sacked.

By the end of 1941 certain changes had become evident in Churchill. He had conserved his energies, but had shed much of the exuberance, at times an almost boyish enthusiasm, that had made him tolerable, even likeable, to his close political and military associates. Friendship with him, always difficult, became impossible save for those few possessing his own 'pirate-potentate' characteristics; such men as Beaverbrook and Baruch. Their dice was loaded in similar fashion. They understood the 'game'. I think it is true to say that by the end of 1941 Churchill's exuberant irresponsibility, often fascinating, at times attractive, invariably dangerous, had been replaced by a megalomania that was menacing. It frightened the highly experienced Lords Hankey and Chatfield, and gravely disturbed well-informed Members of the House of Commons. Mr Churchill quotes 'one of the ablest and most important of the Dominion High Commissioners: 'The emotional value of Mr Churchill is no doubt very great, but . . .'[1]

The implication is clear that the writer is doubtful whether the Prime Minister's emotional value outweighs the perils of his physical running of the war.

The rumblings of a larger discontent were becoming evident by the end of 1941, but the Prime Minister made it abundantly clear that he would not 'consent to the slightest curtailment of (his) personal authority and responsibility'. His self-assurance had become inordinate, his total identification with the country and the struggle, less clear and certain. The terrier had become a mastiff. He was a towering magnate, immensely formidable, a pike among minnows, resolved not to shed one mite of his power, to 'slay or be slain'. Afterwards there would be scapegoats sacrificed to preserve his image, and it was not difficult to foresee

[1] *The Hinge of Fate*, vol. iv, R.U. edition, p. 445.

that his 'night of the long knives' would be staged in the Middle East.

II

The Japanese attack upon Pearl Harbour and the immediate entry of the United States into the war had brought Churchill his hour of elation and relief. One kind of struggle was at an end, a new kind had begun. Soviet Russia had withstood the first tremendous assaults of the enemy deep into her territory, and it was a reasonable hope that she would sustain a second shock. Now the immense potential of the United States was added. If victory remained far off, defeat had become a virtual impossibility. General de Gaulle, waging his own brave struggle within the embrace of his powerful allies, striving to protect French interests against the devious machinations and assaults of friend and foe alike, perceived that certain simplicities had become enmeshed in new complexities: there were now three wars, if not four. The Allies were not fighting for the same reasons, nor for the same ends.

A change of temper is discernible from this moment, not only in the Prime Minister himself, but in the British people. They liked to be alone, responsible for their own fate. They clung to a kind of amateur status in an increasingly professional world, and were happiest—and at their best—with their backs against the wall. It seldom occurred to them seriously to consider that they might be beaten. They were content to lose all battles but the last. It was, perhaps, a hangover from Edwardian and Victorian times. Mixed, therefore, with their relief in the total involvement of the United States in the struggle, was a sense of resentment. They might even have to play second fiddle, not only in the Pacific and in the Far East, where their one-time Empire appeared to be about to tumble like a house of cards, but also in their own back-yard. Their heroic days were over, and they gravely needed a period of transition.

To no Englishman was this more evident than to Churchill. With an almost indecent haste he requested an immediate conference with the Americans, and caused the imperturbable President Roosevelt to raise his eyebrows. Surely, the President said, a conference could wait until the New Year? It could not.

On December 11, 1941, four days after Pearl Harbour,

Churchill reported to the House of Commons, and was heard in grim silence. The record was bad and would assuredly get worse before it might be expected to improve. But that it would improve there could not be doubt.

The House, Churchill wrote, 'seemed to hold its judgement in suspense'.

Three days later the Prime Minister and his entourage embarked upon the battleship, *Duke of York,* for the crossing of the dangerous Atlantic Ocean, perhaps the most truly decisive 'battlefield' of the Second, as also of the First, World War. On the voyage the Prime Minister produced a personal summary of the state of the war, and his plan[1] for the future. It was a masterly piece of work. It inspired General Ismay to remark that 'in his grasp of the broad sweep of strategy—"the overall strategic concept"—as our American friends called it—he stood head and shoulders above his professional advisers'.

Here was the man who, given 'brakes', as Lloyd George had understood, would be a mighty asset to a nation at war. He was about to answer to the 'brakes' put upon him by his powerful ally, but there were no adequate brakes for him at home.

In producing his plan Churchill made his bid for the European war to be fought in a European way. It was a brave effort, and it was largely successful. Churchill perceived that it was vital to Britain to gain control of the North African coast, including French North-West Africa, to clear the Mediterranean, and to unite the split power of Britain in the Western hemisphere.[2] The realization of this plan was the pre-requisite for an entry into the mainland of Europe, wherever or whenever it might take place. Mr Churchill visualized such an entry as possible in 1943, but he would have had no doubts about the difficulties to be overcome. Whatever the Americans, or the Russians, might think of it, the North African and Mediterranean strategy would constitute a genuine 'second front'.

Unfortunately, the United States and British concepts of strategy were diametrically opposed. Whereas the United States' Joint Chiefs of Staff saw problems in plain black and white, and regarded it as a simple truth applicable to military

---

[1] J. M. A. Gwyer, *Grand Strategy,* vol. iii, Part I, p. 325 (iii) *et seq.*, H.M.S.O., 1964.
[2] The British Forces in the United Kingdom and the Middle East were not complementary while the Mediterranean remained closed.

action that a straight line is the shortest distance between two points, the British approach was necessarily devious and indirect. It was a tribute to American vision that, in spite of the devastating assault the Japanese had launched against them in the Pacific, they could still see clearly that the Atlantic remained the prior theatre of war. Germany, they affirmed, remained the major enemy. It would be Germany first, but it swiftly became evident that they were in no mood to waste time on what they regarded as dangerous diversions. They had the manpower to confront the enemy head on. Britain was the base for an attack against the German enemy, and a cross-channel assault was the shortest route. It must be mounted at the earliest possible moment, and it was not much use to argue about when that might be. An assault code-named 'Sledgehammer', must be planned for 1942. It would become 'Round-up' planned for 1943, and would be launched finally as 'Overlord' in 1944.

Inevitably, Churchill's Mediterranean plans were met with suspicion by the American Joint Chiefs of Staff, but aroused the guarded support of the President. It would be necessary to proceed with caution, paying lip-service to 'Sledgehammer' and leaving events to take care of the timings. Nevertheless it would be dangerous to forget that in American hearts and emotions the Pacific was uppermost, and if their suspicions of British intentions were over-aroused, their war effort might be switched. Such a switch remained a possibility for a very long time, and teetered more than once on the edge of probability.

When Churchill returned to London in mid-January 1942 he believed that his North African plan, code-named 'Gymnast', would prevail. It must depend on the survival of Malta, on the course of the struggle in the Middle East, and particularly upon the struggle with the German Afrika Korps in the Western Desert. In November 1941 the personal intervention of General Auchinleck, Commander-in-Chief Middle East, in the great battle called 'Crusader',[1] had turned imminent defeat into victory, and the Eighth Army had discovered new inspiration in his leadership. There was no doubt that Auchinleck's presence had stimulated the troops, and that he had proved himself a match for the German General Rommel. But the Commander-in-Chief's place was in Cairo to attend to the incessant demands

[1] See notes on Crusader and 2nd Alamein.

of the vast areas it was his duty to defend. Prematurely, perhaps, Auchinleck returned to his post, leaving the command of the Eighth Army in the hands of General Ritchie, a protégé of his own and General Brooke's, the C.I.G.S. It was a tragic choice, for Ritchie quickly proved too junior and too inexperienced for the task. His virtues as a staff officer were not evident in command in the field. He tended to consult his corps commanders, and to arrive at decisions by 'committee', resulting in compromise. Auchinleck watched anxiously from afar, unwilling to hamper his general unduly while finding his feet. Ritchie's command was woolly and lacking in inspiration. Victory had not been consolidated. Rommel had withdrawn his battered army to Agheila, and with convoys reaching Tripoli unopposed he was swiftly reinforced to launch a counter-stroke. By mid-January the hopes of late November had disappeared.

A chapter of disasters was about to begin, and it was a chapter the Prime Minister would refuse to read in depth. The position for the Prime Minister and for Britain was very little short of desperate. Time was short and the urgency was great. Malta was gravely threatened, and must surely fall if the enemy concentrated upon the task. Control of the Mediterranean was lost. The Eighth Army, poorly equipped in many departments, and even starved of petrol by the use of a wretched container that spilled as much of the vital fluid into the desert sand as into the tanks and vehicles,[1] was heavily beset. Above all, it was out-generalled.

Worse probabilities loomed with the coming of spring. In the Far East Malaya was over-run, and India gravely menaced. The renewed German offensive in Russia might well threaten the Caucasus. An advance through Anatolia was a dangerous possibility. Abadan and Persian Gulf oil would be in jeopardy. If these things happened; if the German Afrika Korps reached the Nile Delta; if a German and Japanese link-up became not only a possibility, but a reality, an abyss of disaster threatened Britain. Doubtless the Island would survive. That was all.

These threats were clear to the Commander-in-Chief Middle East, and to Wavell in India. The responsibility for the defence of Persia, Iraq, Syria and the whole Northern front, as well as the Western Desert devolved directly upon Auchinleck. The loss of

[1] See Notes.

Abadan would be a dire calamity, greater even than the loss of Egypt. And Egypt also was his responsibility. These were the sharp horns of his dilemma, holding him at his post in Cairo while the Prime Minister hungered for him to take command of the Eighth Army in the field.

It is difficult not to sympathize with the Prime Minister. In Auchinleck Britain possessed an army commander capable of rising to supreme heights, but it was not his role to command an army. It is certain that Auchinleck would have been happiest in that role. It was the task for which he was born. One of his close associates in battle wrote:

> It was Auk, in spite of his total misjudgement of Ritchie, who really saved us all. The British have never contemplated the abyss which yawned before the allies in June/July 1942, and so do not appreciate the man who hauled everyone else back to safety. But nobody likes to think that such a situation had ever arisen.[1]

Auchinleck liked to live rough with his troops. He stimulated them to their best, and they him. His offensive spirit was supreme and undefeatable. Instead he bore the immense burden of the Middle East upon his shoulders at the supreme crisis of the war.

Churchill knew this. He knew, whatever he might say, that our equipment left much to be desired; that we lacked armour-piercing shell caps; that our new Crusader tanks were mechanically suspect and often death traps. Doubtless he knew the whole dismal story. But in the first months of 1942 we had to fight as best we could with the tools to hand. These months were certain to be decisive, not only in the Middle East, but in the Far East, and in Russia. It needed no great prescience to know this clearly. And for Churchill these months would bring also his greatest personal crisis. He had returned from the Washington Conference optimistic that his plans for North Africa would be fulfilled. He had also no doubts that the supreme direction of the war in Europe would move out of his hands. He had become '1st Lieutenant' to the President of the United States, and time was very short if British arms were to restore his 'image' and the Nation's prestige. Inevitably, we should be rescued by the

---

[1] Personal Correspondence. Maj.-Gen. Dorman (Smith) O'Gowan.

United States in due course, but let us not be floundering in defeat when that moment came.

Let the Chiefs of Staff argue the immense difficulties, and spell out the priorities. They were right, of course. But to Churchill the only right was to win, whatever the gamble.

At the end of January Churchill sought and gained an overwhelming vote of confidence in the House of Commons. His majority was 464 to 1. It showed, comments the Official History, 'that there was no desire—at least none that dared express itself for a change in leadership'. In fact, there was a desire, a growing undercurrent of criticism and unease. The Prime Minister had not hesitated to mislead the House. 'He had assured them that our troops in the Middle East had met the enemy for the first time on the whole with equal weapons'. With Rommel in retreat, Auchinleck had sent home a full report on the inadequacy of our armour, weapons and equipment, and much else besides. Captain Lyttelton, Minister of State, had informed the Defence Committee that the loss of faith in their equipment 'had had its effect on tactics', as it was bound to do.

Armed with his vote of confidence, the Prime Minister focused his massive attention upon the Western Desert. Here was the battlefield, the only battlefield. It was a terrifying simplification, and of course he knew that as well as his advisers. He revealed in these months all his vices and his virtues. Here was the man who had left his seat of First Lord of the Admiralty to go off and direct operations in person at Antwerp in 1914. Let Auchinleck do likewise, ignoring his orders from Whitehall, ignoring the growing threats to his Northern front, ignoring everything but Rommel.

It has been written that Churchill could not understand the 'Chain of Command'. General Brooke, the C.I.G.S., laments and wrings his hands. I think Churchill understood well enough. He had simply reduced everything to an ultimate simplicity, refusing to see any trees, even denying them, even forgetting the 'wood' itself in order to concentrate on the hard core of action.

Disaster followed upon disaster in the Far East at alarming speed. Hongkong had gone. Malaya and Singapore were easily over-run. Burma was urgently menaced; the Dutch East Indies must go. The French, striving to hold an end up in Indo-China, were ignored. The Indian Ocean was dominated by the

Japanese. Troops that could not be spared were sent to India from Auchinleck's improverished Middle East. In a sense very little could be done. The faults lay in the past. We had failed our Empire, failed shamefully to protect all those people who had looked to us for protection. It was all a very long way away, 'in the twilight of his mind', the Prime Minister once wrote. Wavell, Slim and a dozen generals whose names would be little known and seldom sung, would hold out as best they could with their 'forgotten army'.

Nothing impressed or disturbed the British people more in the midst of these catastrophes than the sudden break-out from Brest of the German battle cruisers, *Scharnhorst* and *Gneisenau*, and the cruiser *Prinz Eugen*. Almost unscathed, these powerful ships ran the narrow gauntlet of the English Channel to join the *Tirpitz* and the *Bismarck* in the North, and to harass the Murmansk convoys. The failure of the Navy to prevent this insult was due in the main to the lack of reconaissance aircraft. The public was profoundly shocked, and the feeling grew that 'something was very wrong at the top'.

The chain of events in the Middle East through January makes sad reading, and all that Auchinleck had won was lost. Bardia, Sollum and Halfaya had surrendered by the time Churchill arrived home from Washington.[1] On the day of his vote of confidence Benghazi had been evacuated, and the Italians could sail across the Mediterranean unchallenged to reinforce Rommel. There was not at that time a British ship in the Mediterranean completely seaworthy. Malta was starved and hanging by a thread. It was doubtful if it could be held if the Eighth Army failed to hold Cyrenaica, or if the enemy decided upon a major assault.

At this time Admiral Raeder was urging upon Herr Hitler that there was a 'golden opportunity' for an attack upon Egypt and the Suez Canal. Fortunately, Hitler's attention was focused almost exclusively upon Russia and the Caucasus. Malta precariously survived, while in the Desert General Ritchie stabilized the Eighth Army on a line, Gazala-Bir Hacheim.

Early in February General Auchinleck warned Ritchie that:

> If, for any reason, we should be forced to withdraw from

[1] They had been taken from the axis in the Crusader battle. After Auchinleck had returned to Cairo, they were lost.

our present forward positions, every effort will still be made to prevent Tobruk being lost to the enemy; but it is not my intention to continue to hold it once the enemy is in a position to invest it effectively. Should this appear inevitable, the place will be evacuated, and the maximum amount of destruction carried out in it, so as to make it useless to the enemy as a supply base.[1]

This instruction was passed to Whitehall and agreed on the highest level. Without naval command of the Central Mediterranean, Tobruk could not be held, nor was there much point in holding it. By acting against these orders, with the consequent sacrifice of the garrison of Tobruk, General Ritchie drove a dagger into the Prime Minister at a terrible moment. It is an essential incident in a tragic story.

III

For three months there was a lull in the Western Desert, with both sides preparing for major action. The Prime Minister, whose furious concentration on the Middle East had finally destroyed Wavell, had now become obsessed. There were a thousand other things occupying the perimeter of his mind, but at the fiery heart was the Desert. He had stripped the whole Middle East Command down to a simple contest with the German General Rommel. In this contest Auchinleck must be his champion, casting his vast commitments aside to command the Eighth Army in the field.

From the beginning the Prime Minister liked to spend some hours alone in his Map Room, next to his sleeping quarters in 'The Hole', the shelters beneath the Cabinet Offices. There he could square up to the battle map and survey the theatres of war. He longed to smash a left hook to the North, 'Operation Jupiter', while slamming in a devastating right to pulverise the enemy in North Africa, to open up the 'soft underbelly' to body blows. 'Jupiter' and 'Torch'[2] in unison remained his dream.

Studying war maps on such a scale is a dangerous pastime, even for brilliant amateurs. The galaxies of headquarters flags dotting the immense areas of the Middle East spoke to Churchill of a power that was not there. He could not, or would not,

[1] Playfair, *The Mediterranean and Middle East*, vol. iii, p. 197.
[2] The final code name for 'Gymnast'.

understand what all those troops were doing. Why were they not fighting? He had raged against Wavell. Now he raged against Auchinleck. In a sense Churchill failed to wrench himself away from old-fashioned warfare. The Official History puts the position clearly:[1]

> ... an undeveloped region which becomes an important theatre of war becomes also a bottomless pit. Setting up the bases and armed forces in the Middle East was like gradually transplanting a complete modern society with all its complicated needs. Almost every activity known in ordinary life was being carried out there by someone in uniform. There was therefore a constant demand for men to fill the establishments of many sorts of units, some newly created, and others of longer standing which had been reduced by various causes.

That was what 'all those men were doing out there'. They were also dealing with many hostile or unpredictable peoples whose friendship or tolerance was precarious. They were also fighting. Between November 1941, the great 'Crusader' battle, and August, 1942, there were over 100,000 casualties, and it was not until September, 1942, that it was possible to embark upon 'a programme of rigorous training'. By that time also the deficiencies in equipment, armour, artillery and ammunition had been made good overwhelmingly in the British favour.

But in the early part of the year this happy outcome was a long way off. Throughout all February, March and April, Auchinleck withstood the constant hammering of the Prime Minister with quiet courtesy and reason, reporting faithfully on the condition of his troops, their equipment and weapons and his plans. In March the Commander-in-Chief resisted the Prime Minister's request to return to England for consultation. He conceived it his duty to remain at his post. In a fury Churchill ordered Sir Stafford Cripps to study conditions on the spot, and report back before going on to India. He did so and reported that he thought Auchinleck's attitude was correct. At the same time General Nye, the V.C.I.G.S., made a detailed study of Auchinleck's problems on the spot, confirmed his reports and assessments and stressed the need for training. This verdict was

---

[1] Playfair, *The Mediterranean and Middle East*, vol. iii, p. 372

accepted by the Chiefs of Staff, but it was a distasteful one for Churchill.

The German threat to the Caucasus caused the Chiefs of Staff to spell out the priorities in the Middle East to General Auchinleck. The Germans had reached the Don on a wide front about Rostov and we had no idea whether the Russians had enough reserves to check an advance through the Caucasus.[1] The loss of Abadan and Bahrein would be 'calamitous', a loss of thirteen and a half million tons of oil a year to be found elsewhere, and demanding an estimated tanker fleet of 270 vessels to carry it. Moreover, the loss of Persian oil would mean the loss of Egypt, the command of the Indian Ocean, and would put India and Burma in terrible danger.

The C.I.G.S. knew that a false move by Auchinleck could 'lose Egypt in five minutes'. In the 'worst possible case', if it came to a choice, the Northern front and Persian oil must hold at the cost of Egypt.

Such was the appalling situation with which the Commander-in-Chief lived, and for which he had to plan. This was the nature of his task. No man would ever again be asked to shoulder such a burden. The decisive hours of the war were striking, and Auchinleck stood between Britain and a disaster which must spell the end of her power, whatever else might befall. The Battle of the Atlantic was going badly, and the sinkings of Allied ships exceeded the building rate. The Italians were running convoys across the Mediterranean to reinforce Rommel. The future of Malta and much else seemed to hang upon the thread of a victory for Britain in the Western Desert.

Auchinleck had only one overwhelming thought in his mind; that he must and would win. But he dared not risk the destruction of the Eighth Army. Whatever happened it must be kept in being as an army. Patiently, Auchinleck assured the Prime Minister that it was his intention to destroy the enemy, but to attempt to do this prematurely would be disastrous. Moreover, his weakness in tanks and artillery made it improbable that the Eighth Army could withstand a renewed offensive by the enemy. The long lull had been in their favour.

Nevertheless, on May 10 Churchill persuaded the War Cabinet to order General Auchinleck to attack by the end of the

[1] Kennedy, *The Business of War*, p. 258.

month, and only a profound sense of duty prevented the Commander-in-Chief from acceding to Churchill's request for him to take personal command. The Official History puts it simply:[1]

> The outcome of the Desert fighting was a matter of such supreme concern to General Auchinleck that he must often have been tempted, and was in fact pressed from London, to go and command the Eighth Army himself. What held him back was the fact that his post was at the centre of affairs in the whole Middle East.

Elsewhere the Official Historians comment:[2] 'It was only from Malta that the sea-traffic to North Africa could be attacked to good purpose, so the longer Malta was without adequately supplied striking forces the stronger would General Rommel become.'

If Auchinleck could recapture Western Cyrenaica the pressure on Malta would be relieved. 'Cause and effect were thus chasing each other in a circle.'

Thus, in a sense, there was no choice but to fight, even if to fight meant to lose all. It was a hideous situation, for all Auchinleck's instincts urged him to take personal command and fight, while his reason told him that to launch an offensive at this time would be madness, and his own duty lay at the hub of his Command, to save, not Malta, nor the Nile Delta, but Abadan oil. Above all, since this would be impossible otherwise, to 'save' the Eighth Army.

The story of these months is fundamentally one of the desperate need to achieve victory in the field, while at the same time the Prime Minister was involved in a personal struggle to retain power, to preserve his plans for the Anglo-American landings in North Africa, and to gain a victory plain for all to see before the arrival of the Americans inevitably removed the direction of the war from his hands.

On May 26th, before Auchinleck had reached his deadline, Rommel attacked the Eighth Army in the Gazala-Bir Hacheim positions. Ten days later the British armour met disaster. Contrary to Auchinleck's advice for an indirect assault, Ritchie had

[1] Playfair, *The Mediterranean and Middle East*, vol. iii, p. 286.
[2] *Ibid.*, p. 197.

squandered his armour in futile frontal attacks. He failed to concentrate his strength at any one point or time to overwhelm the enemy, and permitted the enemy to out-manoeuvre him consistently. 'Besides being too deliberate and too direct, the offensive was delivered in too piecemeal a way,' wrote Liddell Hart.[1]

'In a moment so decisive,' Rommel commented, 'they should have thrown into the battle all the strength they could muster. What is the use of having overall superiority if one allows each formation to be smashed piecemeal by an enemy able to concentrate superior forces on every occasion at the decisive point'.[2]

In the withdrawal that followed, Ritchie continued to ignore the orders of his Commander-in-Chief, and at times to prevaricate. On the morning of the 14th Auchinleck told Ritchie: 'Even if you have to evacuate Gazala you should hold Acroma, El Adam and to the south, while I build up reinforcements on the frontier.'[3]

A second telegram commanded: 'On NO account will any part of the Eighth Army be allowed to be surrounded in Tobruk and invested there . . .'[4]

But Ritchie disregarded these orders, and omitted to inform the Commander-in-Chief that the divisions from Gazala had already been ordered back to the frontier.

Thus the defeat suffered as a result of Ritchie's miserably ineffective and ill-conceived counter-offensive of the 5th June, had become disaster. 'By the time Auchinleck realized that the Gazala divisions were on their way back to the frontier, he began to receive a series of telegrams from the Prime Minister that Tobruk should be held in any circumstances.'[5]

General Gott, meanwhile, had persuaded Ritchie that Tobruk could hold out, even if isolated. On the 21st June Tobruk, in spite of Auchinleck's directive, was lost, together with a division and two brigade groups, and a wealth of supplies that should not have been there. The fortunes of Britain were at their lowest ebb.

[1] Liddell Hart, *The Tanks*, vol. ii, p. 171. London, Cassell, 1959.
[2] *The Rommel Papers*, p. 217, London, Collins, 1953.
[3] John Connell, *Auchinleck*, p. 566. London, Cassell, 1959.
[4] *Ibid.*, p. 568.
[5] Liddell Hart, *The Tanks;* vol. ii, p. 182.

CHAPTER TWO

Redemption

I

THE news of the loss of Tobruk, underlining the British defeat and reaching Churchill in Washington from the lips of the American President, smote the Prime Minister like a physical blow. It could have been mortal to his dreams, sweeping him off the stage of war. The New York newspaper headlines left him in no doubt that his personal and political fortunes were at their lowest ebb.

ANGER IN ENGLAND. TOBRUK FALL MAY BRING CHANGE OF GOVERNMENT. CHURCHILL TO BE CENSURED.

It is not surprising that the Prime Minister viewed the loss of Tobruk out of all proportion to its military importance. Tobruk itself mattered little, but the loss of a Division, two brigade groups, together with a mass of equipment and stores, was grievous. Moreover, it had been unnecessary. Worst of all it was a blow to British military prestige at the precise moment when Churchill needed military success to underline his arguments for the North African and Mediterranean strategy he conceived as a true 'Second Front', and as the most realistic route into Europe. The American cross-channel assault, proposed for 1942 and code-named 'Sledgehammer', was fast disappearing into the mists of impossibility from which, save in American imagination, it had never emerged.

The President's gift of 300 Sherman tanks and 100 self-propelled guns, to be shipped at once to the Middle East, was in these circumstances more than princely. It was an American vote of confidence in the British ability to hold on in the Middle East, and for Churchill to hold on at home. It was the tonic the Prime Minister needed. His own decisive hour and the decisive hour of the war in the West would strike together.

At the end of June the Prime Minister returned to London to face a highly critical House of Commons. The heavy swing against the Government in the Maldon by-election underlined the reality of national misgivings. This was more than a mere challenge of malcontents.

Thus while Churchill faced his crisis and his critics at home, Auchinleck and the Eighth Army faced military crisis in the Desert, a crisis that could, and very likely would, take Britain to the brink of irrevocable disaster. Churchill seemed to sense that Auchinleck was the only man who could save him, the only commander capable of taking over a defeated army in the field, and turning defeat into victory. He had done it once, and he must do it again. In the great 'Crusader' battle, the arrival of Auchinleck had transformed a dangerous situation, and Rommel had not been slow to realize the quality of the military mind opposed to him.

On the 25th June Auchinleck flew forward with his Deputy Chief of Staff, Dorman Smith, to assume complete responsibility for the battle while shedding none of the immense responsibilities of his vast command. Meanwhile, to be in command in the field acted as a wonderful tonic. 'The British pride themselves on being good losers', he said to Dorman Smith. 'I'm a damn bad loser. I'm going to win.' He at once took the Eighth Army by the scruff of its neck, and tried to shake it free of all its useless appurtenances, stripping it of its caravans, its non-fighting troops, its excess baggage, and watched the long trails of men on their roads back to Cairo. Those who remained felt at once the strong hand of their Commander. Seven months earlier he had reversed General Cunningham's decision to evacuate the Marmarica. Now he reversed General Ritchie's decision to stand at Mersa Matruh. The Eighth Army would stand and fight and defeat the enemy in the Alamein positions. It would beat the enemy at his own game. Meanwhile, it would do something it had never done before. It would fight a series of mobile battles, gaining time for the reserves to strengthen the Alamein defences. It would draw the enemy on beyond the limit of his strength and communications and kill him at the end of his tether.

Few, if any, in high places harboured doubts that they were living in the decisive hours of the war. Defeat in the Desert would have implications far beyond Egypt, and because of this Auchinleck must do two things: he must defeat the German-Italian army decisively, and at the same time 'at all cost', even at the cost of Egypt itself, he must preserve the Eighth Army in being. He could not say to his army at any time: Here you fight to the death. It must, if needs be, survive to fight another day, another battle, another series of battles. The priorities may have been in a kind of unspecified abeyance, but they had not changed.

The knowledge that Auchinleck had taken personal command in the field, even at the eleventh hour, fortified the Prime Minister. 'It seemed that we should reach a climax on the Parliamentary and Desert fronts at the same moment,' he wrote The words look almost jaunty. Auchinleck was Churchill's only trump card, and he would play him. On June 29th he cabled his Commander-in-Chief:[1] 'When I speak in the Vote of Censure debate on Thursday about 4 p.m., I deem it necessary to announce that you have taken command in supersession of Ritchie as from June 25.'

On July 1st Auchinleck's Acting Chief of Staff noted in his diary 'The Battle of Alamein'. On July 4th the German-Italian army knew that its hopes of victory had disappeared for ever. 'Auchinleck had changed over finally to the offensive and the Eighth Army was never again to know the anguish or humiliations of retreat.'[2]

In fact, while Auchinleck's strategy had been necessarily defensive his tactics had been offensive.[3] It remained, if possible, to add the destruction of the enemy to his defeat, and for twenty-one days the weary Eighth Army strove to answer to the drive of their commander. Auchinleck had the German armour 'rushing frantically to and fro' and hopelessly extended in its attempts to save its weaker brethren. In eight days, according to a Panzer Armee report, the Italians lost the equivalent of four divisions, and were on the point of collapse. Two more Italian divisions had been severely mauled. Half of the enemy anti-tank guns had been lost, and much of the field artillery. The Eighth Army had taken 10,000 prisoners and inflicted heavy casualties. It had also suffered severely in the process, but not too much. Offensively the German-Italian army was immobilized. Strategically it was without a future.

[1] *The Hinge of Fate*, vol. iv, R.U. edition, p. 323.
[2] Agar-Hamilton and Turner, *Crisis in the Desert*.
[3] See Foreword by Maj.-Gen. E. Dorman Smith to B. H. Liddell Hart, *Strategy: the Indirect Approach*.

Underlying all the unease and perplexity generated in these months 'was the plain fact that the fabulous Rommel had been stopped' the official historians wrote. A footnote adds: 'The adjective (fabulous) applied to Rommel is no exaggeration. Auchinleck had written a letter to his commanders pointing out that Rommel was not a superman and that to refer to him as such was bad for morale and was to stop.'[1] By mid-July Rommel was also a very sick man. The Desert had taken its toll.

Auchinleck had fulfilled the dictum of General O'Connor when a brother officer had asked him after Beda Fomm what it felt like to be a completely successful commander. 'I would never consider a commander completely successful until he had restored the situation after a serious defeat and a long retreat.' Nevertheless he was unable to add the destruction of his enemy to his defeat.

Three factors contributed to Auchinleck's failure to achieve the total destruction of the enemy the Prime Minister demanded. First, the heterogeneous nature of his command. The commanders of the Commonwealth divisions had the right of appeal to their governments if they disapproved in any way of the demands made upon them. For two crucial days towards the end of the battle Major-General Sir Leslie Morshead, commanding the Australian 9th Division, insisted courteously but firmly on his rights not to commit his forces without the consent of his government. Auchinleck, keeping his temper, used all his powers of persuasion in vain. Moreover, his corps commanders were too utterly weary to react with the speed demanded if the destruction of the enemy was to be accomplished.

The second factor was his own lack 'of enough fresh well-trained troops to keep up the impetus of the attack'.[2] The 50th Division and the 10th Indian Division were refitting. 'And as a bitter subject for meditation may be added,' wrote Sir Compton Mackenzie, 'that if Auchinleck had possessed even a hundred well-armed, well armoured and mechanically reliable tanks, Rommel's forces would not have lived to fight another day.'[3] It was Auchinleck's bitter misfortune, not that he lacked armour, but that in the crucial hours when Rommel's tank strength had

---
[1] Playfair, *The Mediterranean and Middle East*, vol. iii, p. 360.
[2] Auchinleck, *Despatch*, p. 96.
[3] Sir Compton Mackenzie, *Eastern Epic*, p. 319. London, Chatto & Windus, 1951.

been reduced to twenty-eight 'runners', his Corps commanders were unable to reflect the energies of their Commander-in-Chief. By the end of July the enemy, too, had been substantially reinforced and was out of immediate danger.

Reluctantly, for many hours refusing to face the truth of the position, Auchinleck realized that a period of re-training was necessary. He would, he estimated, be ready to mount the final offensive by mid-September. On July 27th the Battle of Alamein, which was also the last battle for Egypt, was at an end. On that day Major-General Dorman Smith produced the 'Appreciation of the situation', covering the whole of the Commander-in-Chief's command, which:

> was to acquire a unique historical importance as the major piece of documentary evidence which was strong enough over a period of eleven years, to supply grounds for challenging the elaborate apparatus of myth, misunderstanding and mischief by which Auchinleck's handling of his command and his removal from it were surrounded.[1]

The Appreciation forms Appendix 21 of Auchinleck's Despatch.

On July 30th, General Auchinleck informed London of his appreciation of the position. It was not acceptable to the Prime Minister.

II

In the political and military crisis of June and July Churchill and Auchinleck, the one as Prime Minister, the other as army commander, faced their challenges with clear success. Between July 1st and 4th both men emerged triumphant from their personal ordeals, and were closely linked. Churchill demolished his critics in Lords and Commons, Auchinleck reduced his opponent in the field to final impotence and saved Egypt. Beyond that the two men in their major roles were not in unison.

The association of Churchill and Auchinleck proceeded from the outset on two distinct levels. To Churchill the roles of Prime Minister and Minister of Defence were one and indivisible. To Auchinleck, the twin roles of Commander-in-Chief of what was

---

[1] Connell, *Auchinleck*, p. 684.

misleadingly known as The Middle East, but which embraced the Mediterranean, Malta, and the Near East, and that of commander of the Eighth Army in the field, were totally incompatible. To do both at once was impossible. Nevertheless Auchinleck's great achievement in the field, first underlined by the German General Rommel, and finally by the Official Historians, is worth emphasizing from a non-military quarter. In his *King George VI*, Sir John Wheeler Bennett wrote:

> The actual turning of the tide in the Second World War may be accurately determined as the first week of July 1942. After Rommel was repulsed at El Alamein on July 2 and turned away in deference to British resistance, the Germans never again mounted a major offensive in North Africa.[1]

Officially, the 'turn of the tide' would be held back for nearly four months. To achieve this it would be necessary to deny the battle of El Alamein, discredit the Commander-in-Chief, and the Eighth Army, and resurrect the myth of the sick and defeated General Rommel as an almost invincible demon figure. It may be that after so long a run of disasters Churchill and the British people were in need of violent catharsis. They had been alone, and magnificent losers. Now, they were no longer alone, nor were they losers. Such a metamorphosis demanded some indelible mark. Perhaps even a heroic Egyptian 'Dunkirk' would have been more simple to understand, and more stimulating, than this breathless last ditch victory of 'the long distance runner'.

It is pertinent to wonder just how aware of the turn of the tide were the British people at that time. So much becomes so clear by hindsight that it is difficult to believe that events of great import were often at the time obscure. But, whatever was or was not known to the British people, the Prime Minister himself was in no doubt. In June the American Admiral Fletcher had inflicted a strategic defeat upon the Japanese and saved Port Moresby at the battle of the Coral Sea. Less than a month later the battle of Midway in the Pacific wrested the strategic initiative from the Japanese. The Battle of the Coral Sea in particular would have a direct bearing on the struggle in the

---

[1] Sir J. Wheeler Bennett, *King George VI*, p. 542. London, Macmillan, 1958.

Western Desert inasmuch as the 44th Division and the 8th Armoured Division, at that time on the water, escaped diversion to hard-pressed areas in the Far East, and would, barring the accidents of war at sea, arrive to reinforce the Middle East.

The tide of war had thus begun to turn decisively in all but two dangerous areas. In the Atlantic the sinkings of Allied shipping had reached a peak up to that time. In Southern Russia the issue remained uncertain. The Russians kept their allies singularly ill-informed, or uninformed. In the Desert, however, until July 1st, the Germans and Italians had little doubt about their victory. All that Rommel had to do was to defeat the 'tattered remnants of the Eighth Army', and march on rapidly to the Suez Canal. Mussolini was ready for his triumphal entry into Alexandria. The German troops were already tasting in anticipation the pleasures of 'The Town'. and 'The Town' was not unready for this eventuality.

To prevent these things happening was Auchinleck's dual role. The Prime Minister's area of vision, and the responsibility of 'Supreme Command' he regarded as his own, was on a far larger scale. On the highest political and military level he was involved in an operation of agonizing magnitude and implication. Meanwhile, 'the flames of adverse war in the Desert licked my feet', as he put it. The strain upon him in those hours when 'all hung in the balance' was very great. It must have warped his true judgement of Auchinleck's victory, for he wrote: 'During this month of July, when I was politically at my weakest and without a gleam of military success, I had to procure from the United States the decision which, for good or ill, dominated the next two years of war.'[1]

It may be that the stakes the Prime Minister played for were so great that 'small' winnings escaped his full attention. Moreover, he knew success with the Americans must mean the end of his 'supreme' direction of the war in the West. All that he might hope to do was to leave his mark indelibly upon the future course of action.

The perils threatening Auchinleck's unwieldy command were not real and urgent to him, for he remarked: 'Auchinleck, once in direct command (of the Eighth Army), seemed a different man from the thoughtful strategist with one eye on the decisive

---

[1] Churchill, *The Hinge of Fate*, R.U. edition, p. 356.

battle and the other on the vague and remote dangers in Syria and Persia.'[1]

Assuredly, Auchinleck, the warrior, was a vastly different man from Auchinleck the Commander-in-Chief; but were those dangers in the North so vague and remote? The enemy were not yet 'at the gates'. Such a threat might not develop before the late autumn. Perhaps it is not surprising that Churchill's vision, widely ranging the world, narrowed down to an unnaturally sharp focus in the Desert.

From June 28th to July 30th the dialogue between Auchinleck and the Prime Minister is comparable to that of men using similar, but different, languages. They are not exactly at cross-purposes, but cross-purposes possibly conveys the situation. Churchill was, in a sense, only able to lend one ear, and to talk out of one side of his mouth, to Auchinleck, to the Minister of State, Middle East, and to the Middle East Defence Committee.

On June 28th Auchinleck addressed a 'most secret and personal' appreciation of the situation to the C.I.G.S. In it he stressed his weakness in armour, but above all he stressed his resolution (and duty) to keep the Eighth Army in being. 'The Commanders-in-Chief Middle East were bound to make provision for the possibility of our resistance at El Alamein giving way.'[2]

In 'the worst possible case' Auchinleck would fight every inch of the way back to Cairo and beyond. Provisional plans were made on a G.H.Q. level. 'These provisional arrangements appear to have given rise to misconception; they led to the belief in some quarters that the "abandonment of Egypt was envisaged".'[3]

Cairo was a despicable sink of calculated rumours charged with venom, 'a stew-pot', Churchill called it. It harboured many failures, many frustrated and disappointed men, and many more who believed that the Eighth Army would be defeated. But, whoever might harbour misconceptions, the Prime Minister was not among them. He approved of the proper anxieties expressed by the Minister of State, Middle East. He applauded Auchinleck's plans, as Commander-in-Chief, not as Commander Eighth Army, to meet such a worst possible case. It inspired

[1] Churchill, *The Hinge of Fate*, R.U. edition, p. 352.
[2] and [3] Butler, *Grand Strategy*, vol. iii, part ii, p. 612.

the Prime Minister to one of his finest signals, to exhort that 'Everybody in uniform must fight exactly as they would if Kent or Sussex were invaded'.

Before the first week in July was over these provisional plans, and all their worst anxieties, had been overtaken by events and rendered obsolete. At once Churchill sent enthusiastic messages to Tedder[1] and to Auchinleck. But the vulnerable northern flank remained, if not in the Prime Minister's mind, very much in the forefront of the minds of those whose duty it was to preserve Persian oil 'at all costs'. In the same hours of Rommel's defeat at Alamein, the fall of Sevastopol was followed by the fall of Voronezh. It was known that the Germans were forming a Southern Army Group whose role was almost certain to be to advance through the Caucasus. German bombers might be expected to be advanced within range of Abadan, and neither the Prime Minister nor anyone else knew what the Russians would do about it, if anything.

The Middle East Defence Committee estimated that an attack might develop through Northern Persia or Syria and Iraq in the autumn. The forces available to meet such an attack were negligible. On July 9th the Defence Committee sought guidance from London:

> A choice between two serious decisions would have to be made: whether to transfer forces from Egypt to the Northern front, thus securing the Persian oilfields but losing Egypt, or to continue to put the defence of Egypt first, thus risking the loss of the Persian oilfields. 'We have not got the forces to do both', the telegram concluded, 'and if we try to do both we may fail to achieve either. We request your guidance and instructions on this issue.'[2]

There were two answers. The Chiefs of Staff stressed again the priorities. Oil first. This was the guidance to the Middle East Defence Committee, and, of course, to Auchinleck, Commander-in-Chief Middle East. At the same time, the Prime Minister sent his guidance to Auchinleck, the Commander of the Eighth Army, to destroy the German-Italian army in the Desert.

Auchinleck replied from the battlefield, clearly conscious of

---

[1] Air-Marshal Sir Arthur Tedder, C. in C. Middle East Air Forces.
[2] Playfair, *Mediterranean and Middle East*, vol. iii, p. 363-4.

his perilous dual role, that he understood that 'The Prime Minister accepted the risk to the Northern front, and hence to Iraq and oil. Whether it was a justifiable risk he himself could not say. He would continue to apply all his available resources to destroying the Germans in the Desert, as soon as possible.'[1]

What orders, one is entitled to wonder, would the Commander-in-Chief, Middle East, have given to the Commander of the Eighth Army, had he not been one and the same person. In the event, he obeyed Churchill to the best of his ability while facing the full problems and responsibilities of his command.

'As soon as possible' turned out to be not soon enough for the Prime Minister, and through all the month of July he harried his commander in the field, as no commander before (not even Wavell) or since, has ever been harried. It was the 'triple task' of commanding the Eighth Army, corresponding with the Prime Minister and providing against the threat to the Northern front, that finally was too much. Nevertheless,

> By his determination and his imperturbability, Auchinleck had once again saved the situation. He was now confidently holding a position from which a further assault from Rommel could be repelled and an Allied offensive resumed when decisive superiority in men and materials had been created.[2]

III

Throughout this month, despite his dialogue with his Commander-in-Chief in the Middle East, Churchill's main preoccupation was with Grand Strategy, and with his determination to achieve an Anglo-American invasion of North Africa. The forces working against him were formidable, including the US joint Chiefs of Staff, and predominantly General George Marshall. Apart from the extreme distaste of the Americans for any 'Mediterranean adventure', or any diversion, was their determination to project their armies into action in the shortest possible time by the shortest possible route. They would not, or could not, consider that the shortest possible route and the shortest possible time might not be compatible. Moreover, they

[1] Playfair, *Mediterranean and Middle East*, vol. iii, p. 363-4.
[2] Butler, *Grand Strategy*, vol. iii, part ii, p. 615.

distrusted British strategic thinking, and were suspicious of British colonialism.

At the beginning of July the future course of the alliance was poised on the finest balance, and so it continued to the end of the month. General Marshall, powerfully supported by Admiral King, continued to urge the President to switch the main United States effort to the Pacific unless the British gave unequivocal support to 'Sledgehammer', the proposed 1942 direct cross-channel assault. It seems inconceivable that well-informed persons could have imagined such an assault possible, but they did.

Fortunately, the President was doing his own thinking, and he was fully aware of the grave dangers looming in the Middle and Near East. Churchill's old friend and crony, Field-Marshal Smuts, greatly feared an American switch, 'There was always the danger that Britain and America might despair and concentrate on the invasion of Europe. That would have been disaster,' wrote his son, J. C. Smuts.[1]

The British chiefs of staff were certainly far less keen on the proposed North African landings, then known as 'Gymnast', than the Prime Minister, and it may be that the fears of Smuts were justified. It must be remembered that each one of the three main protagonists was looking at strategy from different national, political and geographical positions. A great deal depended on the British ability to defend the vital Middle Eastern and Mediterranean positions, and on June 30th President Roosevelt asked Marshall for an evaluation of the situation in the Middle East, and what he thought the United States could do about it. The President enumerated six main points,[2] revealing his line of thought.

Marshall replied that he thought that the British would withdraw to the Upper Nile; that the Eighth Army would be destroyed; that Rommel would occupy Cyprus and Syria, and eventually seize the Mosul and Basra area, and much else besides. In the event of a German victory the British could block the Suez Canal for at least six months.

American Intelligence (Army G-2) thought that Rommel

[1] J. C. Smuts, *Jan Christian Smuts*, p. 418. London, Cassell, 1952.
[2] Robert Sherwood (ed.), *The White House Papers*, vol. ii, p. 598. London Eyre & Spottiswoode, 1948-49.

might reach Cairo in one week. Army Operations gave him two weeks. In the upshot Marshall and his experts thought that the next forty-eight hours would provide decisive answers, and they were right. It is significant, therefore, that on July 2nd they did not feel inclined to change their opinions.

It may have been difficult as early as July 2nd to assess at long range Auchinleck's victory at Alamein, but two days later the Americans were becoming aware that their worst fears—or hopes—would not be realized. July 1942 was without question the critical month of the Second World War. Between the 7th and 14th the enemy sank 400,000 tons of allied shipping in the Atlantic, and if that kind of attrition continued American intervention in great force in the Western hemisphere might be impossible to mount or to sustain.

The 15th of the month was a crucial day in Washington. Marshall and King urged upon the President to switch the main effort to the south-west Pacific, but Roosevelt held to his wider view. That night he told Hopkins that he didn't agree that 'we' should 'turn our faces away from Germany and toward Japan' even if a direct assault on Europe proved impossible in 1942. Nevertheless, he shared some of his Chiefs of Staffs' distrust of British intentions. 'I am somewhat disturbed about this readiness to give up 1942. Will they also give up 1943?'[1] he said to Hopkins. But the ghost of 'Sledgehammer' was almost laid in his mind. He was becoming more concerned with the build-up of US troops in Britain against the day, and decided to seek the opinions of his advisers in London.

On July 16th Roosevelt drew up a masterly directive summarizing the strategic position, and sent Hopkins, Marshall and King to London to consult with Eisenhower, Spaatz and Admiral Stark. This was the visit on which the three US emissaries by-passed the Prime Minister at Chequers on their way to London by train from Scotland, and went into direct and immediate consultation with their London representatives. It is not difficult to understand Churchill's fury, for this was the writing on the wall he feared, and knew to be inevitable. A '1st Lieutenant' he may have become, but he remained Prime Minister of Britain and master in his own house. He 'threw the book' at Hopkins, and began to throw 'books' of a different

[1] *The White House Papers,* vol. ii, p. 60

kind at Auchinleck, waging his battle to destroy the German enemy. Nothing less, it seemed, would purge Churchill's wrath and anxieties.

On July 22nd 'Sledgehammer' was almost dead, but only on the condition that the cross-channel assault in 1943 would be a certainty. Eisenhower said that the day 'Sledgehammer' was abandoned was the blackest day in history. Marshall and King agreed with him.

Churchill, sensing that his plans for North Africa would now be possible, made the masterly suggestion that General Marshall should command the cross-channel assault in 1943, and that Eisenhower should command the proposed North African landings. But as late as July 30th Marshall was still trying to turn the President's face away from the Atlantic, and Admiral Stark was the only US representative firmly sharing the British point of view. As a naval man he knew the importance of the Atlantic battle, and the immense difficulties and dangers involved in ferrying and supporting troops in a cross-channel attack. At that time the British had a small operation ready to go in. It involved two-thirds of a division plus Royal Marine commandos. It would need 252 ships for a one-day job. It was, in fact, the limit of cross-channel capacity in August 1942.[1]

On July 27th Roosevelt supported the North African landings under the code name of 'Torch', and named the date. 'Torch' would go in on October 30th. It would be an assault landing on an unprecedented scale, straining the Allies to the limits of their combined armed services in the Atlantic Theatre. It involved the landing of a quarter of a million men, with all their vehicles, armour, equipment and supplies, together with their reinforcements and maintenance. Moreover, the assembly of this mass of men, ships, landing craft, and air support, must be managed without alerting the enemy. Meanwhile, Auchinleck's defeat of the German-Italian army in the Western Desert had effectively answered United States expectations of a British disaster.

The Appreciation of July 27th of the Middle East situation prepared by Auchinleck's D.C.G.S. forecast mid-September for the final offensive that would sweep the Germans and Italians out of the Desert for good.

At last Churchill had triumphed. He had written his name

[1] *Operation Jubilee: The Dieppe Raid.*

upon the baton before handing it over to the Americans, and his signature would be on the course of the war. It was not enough. He had won 'Torch'. Now he demanded the destruction of 'Rommel' without delay. The victory would be his triumph in his own field. General Alan Brooke, the C.I.G.S., had left for Cairo, and was capable of dealing with all the problems involved. Attempts were made to dissuade the Prime Minister from 'adventure', but in vain. 'The doubts I had about the High Command in the Middle East were fed continually by the reports which I had received from many quarters,'[1] Churchill wrote. He was about to appoint himself 'The man on the spot'. Instead of 'sitting at home waiting for news from the front I could send it myself,' he wrote. 'This was exhilarating.'

On July 31st he cabled General Auchinleck to expect him in the Middle East on August 3rd. He had already made up his mind to get rid of his Commander-in-Chief, Middle East. He was out for blood, and more than blood.

---

[1] Churchill, *The Hinge of Fate*, vol. iv, R.U. edition, p. 371.

CHAPTER THREE

Catharsis

I

It is difficult—it may be impossible—to understand the motives and emotions which drove Churchill to journey to Cairo in the first days of August, 1942. His complete *volte face* in his attitude to the Command in the Middle East and the Eighth Army in the fourteen days between August 5th and 19th must provide an answer. For seven of these fourteen days he was in Moscow.

The Prime Minister had arranged a personal mission to Moscow in mid-August, and Cairo was on the way, he could argue. This was an excuse for his visit to the Middle East, but not a reason. The reason must be sought in his sense of drama, in his feeling of being not only an actor on the stage of war, but also the dramatist and producer. He had played the lead for two years, from the dramatic opening of Dunkirk through a long chain of disaster and the dissolution of the British Empire. Now the 'Safety Curtain' had come down between the two great acts. The great opening theme of heroic survival and resolute endurance had ended. The great closing theme of total victory was about to begin. There could be little doubt about it.

But something was wrong: the 'Safety Curtain' should have come down upon resounding victory, not merely on the turn of the tide, not merely upon the security of Egypt. The thunder of applause that should have marked the finale of the opening theme was no more than a bridge of sighs. The Prime Minister had worked furiously for that 'curtain', raging at his players from the wings. They had failed. They had assuredly not failed Britain. One thing was certain; the curtain should rise on the final phase of the drama with a great set-piece of glory, and upon this wave he, Churchill, would ride out the play to the end, and beyond into history. He had been within a hairsbreadth, as he had clearly realized, of being ushered off the stage as the victim, if not the architect, of a long train of disasters. Such a fate would not be his. He was resolved, as no doubt he deserved, to bask in the sunshine of the victories made possible, in great measure, by his unshakeable resolution. It was clear that a ruthless surgical operation would be necessary to achieve this end, and he alone could be the surgeon. History could not be permitted simply to take its course.

The third volume of *Grand Strategy*, published twenty-two years after these events, has now underlined the suspicions and convictions of all those who have sought to unravel the truths of these fourteen days of August. Churchill's journey was not necessary. 'The C.I.G.S. was quite competent to perceive and recommend the necessary changes in command.'[1]

It has also made it possible to fill in certain passages in Churchill's messages to the War Cabinet excised from his personal account. When Churchill landed in Cairo on August 3rd he could have had no idea of how he would achieve his ends. He was a superb opportunist. A way would open for him, and he would use it to full advantage. He would feel his way. He would find the actors appropriate to his desires. When the curtain went up again he would be seen to be the producer of victory.

The Prime Minister's presence in the Middle East was a great embarrassment to General Brooke, the C.I.G.S., adding greatly to his anxieties. Churchill, Brooke lamented,[2] raged constantly at 'the failure of the tired, punch-drunk army to dislodge Rommel'. He continued to press for an offensive 'before Auchinleck can possibly get ready. I find him almost impossible to argue with on this point.'

Indeed Churchill was impossible to argue with on any point. Moreover he was obsessed with the myth of the 'fabulous' Rommel that Auchinleck had at last laid. Sir Ian Jacob found him pacing his room, growling 'Rommel, Rommel, Rommel'. It was an astonishing performance.

The work to be done in Cairo was of the first importance, and fell easily within the competence and proper sphere of the C.I.G.S. and his advisers on the spot. The whole question of the immensely cumbersome and geographically absurd Middle East command demanded urgent review. The safeguarding of Persian Gulf oil remained paramount, and Auchinleck's victory

---
[1] Butler, *Grand Strategy*, vol. iii, part ii, p. 657.
[2] Sir Arthur Bryant, *The Turn of the Tide*, p. 441. London, Collins, 1956.

at Alamein, assuring at last the security of Egypt, made such a review possible and timely.

It was clear that the Commander-in-Chief must be at the hub of his unwieldy command in Cairo, and that a commander for the Eighth Army must be appointed without delay. In this matter Churchill favoured the experienced General Gott while the C.I.G.S. and Auchinleck favoured Montgomery. But the really vital matter was to reorganize the High Command itself. What had been called the Middle East, facing west, was more truly the Mediterranean command, for its responsibilities included Malta and Cyprus, and its defence of Egypt, its conquest of Cyrenaica, Libya and Tunisia must depend upon control of the Mediterranean, and the denial of reinforcements and supplies to the enemy. There must be two separate commands, interdependent to some extent inevitably, the Northern Command with its responsibilities in Syria and Iraq, perhaps more properly the subsidiary of the command in India. These commitments must overlap, but they must overlap to mutual benefit, and this they had not done. The Northern command had crippled the Middle Eastern command.

To these ends 'all the talents' had been summoned to Cairo. Field-Marshal Smuts, Field-Marshal Wavell, joined the C.I.G.S., the Minister of State, R. G. Casey, and the commanders on the spot, Auchinleck, Admiral Harwood and Tedder. August 4th was filled with urgent personal meetings, all of these men consulting with each other, and finally meeting for a full discussion with the Prime Minister. 'There was a lot of tension' at the meeting, Casey wrote, the Prime Minister resolved to produce instant action out of the complexities. Those present could almost see his mind making its decisions. He had resolved before leaving London to sack Auchinleck for reasons which, if reduced to ultimate simplicity, must be that Auchinleck was too senior to command an army.

Auchinleck, like Wavell, was one of those rare men of stature, of absolute integrity, of a certain simplicity, who, in some strange way, seemed an affront to Churchill himself. They did not fear him. Whatever insults he might heap upon them, their loyalty would remain absolute. They were without malice, and this, according to one of Churchill's closest associates over a period of thirty years, was impossible for Churchill to understand. It seemed to force him to hit men who would not hit back, and roused him to fury.

On August 5th, Churchill flew to Bourg el Arab to be conducted to Auchinleck's headquarters near Alam Halfa. It was an unhappy day. Australian troops from the reserve brigade were strung out along a stretch of the road as the cavalcade drove eastward. Churchill rode alone in Auchinleck's car leaving the Commander-in-Chief, unobtrusive as always, to drive in a jeep behind the lines of men. The Prime Minister dismounted and walked alone in the middle of the road. Here and there an Australian asked for a cigar and got one. The ordinary soldier, wrapped in his own confined and unique world of harsh realities and great simplicities does not take kindly to politicians, and especially is this true of troops who have been compelled to fight with inferior equipment.

The cavalcade, bumping south on a corrugated track to Auchinleck's austere headquarters, decanted the Prime Minister into a situation he loathed, for Auchinleck chose to live with his army. He lay by night wrapped in his blanket under a shelter on the sand. 'We were given breakfast in a wire-netted cube full of flies and important military personages,'[1] wrote Churchill in disgust.

A few days later Montgomery called it a 'meat safe', but because of it, and because of his leadership in the field, Auchinleck had retained the admiration of his army, and held its morale high through all adversity. I do not know if it is out of place here to quote from *The Crown of Wild Olive*, but it seems to me appropriate:

> Now, remember, whatever virtue or goodliness there may be in this game of war, rightly played, there is none when you thus play it with a multitude of small human pawns.
>
> If you, gentlemen of this or any other kingdom, choose to make your pastime of contest, do so, and welcome; but set not up these unhappy peasant-pieces upon the green fielded board. If the wager is to be of death, lay it on your own heads, not theirs. A goodly struggle in the Olympic dust, though it be dust of the grave, the gods will look upon, and be with you in; but they will not be with you, if you sit on the sides of the

---

[1] Churchill, *The Hinge of Fate*, vol. iv, R.U. edition, p. 376.

amphitheatre, whose steps are the mountains of earth, whose arena its valleys, to urge your peasant millions into gladiatorial war.[1]

It is romantic stuff, no doubt, but it is true. Had generals held it in the forefront of their minds between 1914–18 there could not have been so senseless and tragic a slaughter, and as war became more and more mechanical the need for Generals to lead their armies became more urgent. In the First World War Major-General Elles is the only general known to have led his men in the van of battle. If there cannot be a 'chivalry', as Ruskin also said, let there be a 'canonry', no less honourable, a 'tankery'.

Perhaps there never was a better battlefield than the Western Desert, a clear field comparatively free from civilians and habitation, with the goal of Egypt at one end and Tunis at the other. To a great extent it had revived the 'chivalry' of war, and not all the 'ironmongery' to follow on to the end would reduce war to the abominable terms of the 1914–18 slaughter—until the very end, when it was no longer ironmongery.

On August 5, 1942, in Auchinleck's caravan in the desert, Churchill saw and knew that the enemy had been defeated and had been left without real options. His position was without hope, and he recognized it.[2]

The Prime Minister knew the plans. He knew the orders Auchinleck had issued to his Corps Commanders on July 30th. In silence he went with Auchinleck and Dorman Smith, the D.C.G.S., into the operations caravan, and saw the impregnable lay-out of the Eighth Army on the talc over the battle map. He knew the wealth of reinforcements in men, armour and artillery, arriving and about to arrive. He knew of Auchinleck's offensive spirit, of his plans for attack. But he was furious for the total destruction of the enemy, now. The realism and logic of Dorman Smith's Appreciation, which had convinced the Commander-in-Chief of the need to pause until mid-September, roused Churchill to anger and frustration. 'All at once,' wrote Dorman Smith, 'he (Churchill) began to stab his fingers against the talc,

---

[1] John Ruskin, *The Crown of Wild Olive*, p. 85, 'Everyman' edition. London, J. M. Dent, 1908.
[2] See Notes: Kesselring on Alam Halfa.

demanding that the Eighth Army should attack, "here" or "here".'

The C.I.G.S. had left the party to go up the line, and the three men, Auchinleck, Dorman Smith and Churchill, were alone in the caravan. Auchinleck said quiety and firmly, 'No sir, we cannot attack again yet.'

Churchill turned upon Dorman Smith:

'Do you say that too! Why don't you use the 44th Division?' Dorman Smith quietly supported his Chief:
'The 44th Division isn't ready, sir.'

The Prime Minister did not attempt to hide his rage. The 44th Division had arrived, and should be committed immediately to the offensive. Auchinleck explained his reasons for not committing a green division, untrained in the desert, and unacclimatized. The Prime Minister argued. Auchinleck was courteous, but adamant. 'Because these two officers acted as they did that morning, a division was not squandered and many men's lives were saved, but they set the seal on their own professional doom,' wrote John Connell.[1]

The judgement of Lieutenant-General Sir Brian Horrocks is especially valuable in this context:

As we know now (he wrote) the Prime Minister was moving heaven and earth to get the commander of the Eighth Army to launch an immediate offensive. It says much for Auchinleck's moral courage that, at this time, when he was convinced that such an offensive would have little chance of success, and he was under a cloud, he refused to attack until he was satisfied that his troops were trained and reorganized. The 44th (H.C.) Division straight from the United Kingdom without any desert experience would inevitably have been in this attack. They might well erect a monument to Auchinleck who unquestionably saved them heavy casualties.[2]

But there were to be no monuments.

Churchill left the caravan without a word, and stood with his back turned to the two soldiers. He seemed an alien figure, alien to the desert in his pink plumpness, a denizen from another

[1] John Connell, *Auchinleck*, p. 697.
[2] Lieut.-Gen. Sir Brian Horrocks, *A Full Life*. London, Collins, 1960.

world. Dorman Smith wrote in his private notes of his personal thoughts as he watched that hunched and menacing man staring into the sand.

> I wondered (wrote Dorman Smith) if Churchill was thinking himself into Lincoln's shoes when Lincoln dismissed McClellan at Harrison's Landing after the 'seven days' . . . The old man might be thinking of having us both shot . . . He hadn't spoken a kind word since his arrival at Bourg el Arab.[1]

The Prime Minister's personal account of these days tends to obscure rather than to illumine the scene. He had made up his mind on certain drastic courses of action, but could not have been sure where they would lead him, or exactly how they might benefit him. He had demanded the impossible of Auchinleck, and he must have done that wittingly. The shortest route to an early offensive, if that was what he really wanted, would have been to retain Auchinleck in command, and to let the plans mature. Changes in command must surely bring delay. His choice of General Gott for Eighth Army Commander must indicate that Churchill had no quarrel with Auchinleck's plans or his timings, for Gott would have carried them out to the letter. He would not have been persuaded to commit the 44th Division before its time, nor would he have gone off at half cock. It would be Rommel who would go off at half cock at Alam Halfa, and invite disaster for his army at the end of the month.

The Prime Minister's principal needs were at that moment personal and political, rather than military. His presence in the desert was a considerable hindrance to work and plans in progress, and the comings and goings of his entourage would have been quite impossible in any kind of emergency. That day, looming so large and sinister in the memories of the soldiers involved, ironically may have been nothing more than a day out of Cairo to Churchill, a day to avoid meetings and discussions on the highest level, with Smuts, Casey, and 'all the talents'. He must have reached his conclusions, at least tentatively, on the 4th.

Finally Churchill drove off with Gott, brushing aside the remonstrances of Auchinleck and his staff. The Prime Minister wanted to assess Gott's weariness, to discover, if he could, the will

[1] Diary—private papers.

of so experienced a man to command the Eighth Army. The choice, however wrong-headed it may have been, seems clearly to acquit Churchill of any intention at that time to disgrace Auchinleck, his staff and his army. Gott would never have been the tool for that. Two days later Gott was dead, his aircraft shot down on the way to Cairo, and Gott was killed striving to save others from the blazing wreckage.

II

On the afternoon of August 5th General Brooke returned from a visit to the 4th Indian division, and reviewed with Auchinleck the situation on the war maps, and studied the plans. There was no disagreement. Nevertheless the C.I.G.S. was ill at ease. He knew that Auchinleck, together with his principal staff officers, was about to be relieved of his command. He found himself acting out a charade of a singularly unpleasant kind. He discussed proposals and made appointments that he knew would not be kept. He had argued with Churchill as much as he dared. It was his role to stand between his master and the staff officers and subordinate commanders, and protect them from political decisions. He had failed to do so.

Meanwhile the Prime Minister, having lunched with the Royal Air Force and enjoyed all the luxuries Shepheard's cuisine could provide, had shed his cares, and returned to Cairo 'invigorated' after his long day to send a lively signal to the Deputy Prime Minister.

> Troops were very cheerful, and all seem confident and proud of themselves, but bewildered at having been baulked of victory on repeated occasions . . .
>
> Wherever the fault may lie for the serious situation which exists, it is certainly not with the troops, and only to a minor extent with their equipment.[1]

Such messages must be read as indications of Churchill's state of mind, and not as reports on the troops. His praise is as valueless as his blame, for he had no means of knowing personally the morale of the Eighth Army. He knew only what he was told, and used his information as he deemed expedient. It is important

[1] Churchill, *The Hinge of Fate*, vol. iv, R.U. edition, p. 337.

that it seemed to him expedient on August 5th to praise the troops, for on August 21st he was to commit himself to opposite conclusions, and much more besides. It is important also to understand that the situation in the Desert was no longer grave. That was all in the past.

There was to be one more visitor to the Eighth Army Headquarters caravan before the end. Major-General Dorman Smith had spent the night of the 5th alone to await the arrival of General Wavell, whose views meant more to the soldiers than anyone else's. Wavell listened in silence, as 'impassive as Buddah', while Dorman Smith went through the July story. They went through the Appreciation of July 27th together, and 'I stressed the desirability of Rommel attacking prematurely via the 13th Corps southern flank', wrote Dorman Smith, 'and at last Wavell said: 'Eric, you are very strongly posted here; have you considered making a feint withdrawal to entice Rommel into the net?" '

The idea had been considered, and rejected as unnecessary. Rommel would walk into the net at Alam Halfa. It would be a gesture without hope, but the men who had laid the trap for him would not be there to close it, to make a clean and final killing. Instead as Rommel noted, almost too sick and hopeless to care, the offensive-minded Auchinleck had been replaced by a man of extreme caution. Rommel would be 'an unconscionable time a-dying', condemned to linger on for many weary months, followed up, rather than pursued, to the bitter end.

III

On the morning of August 6th the Prime Minister went into action. He had resolved to split the unwieldy command that had itself split General Auchinleck, and to make a clean sweep of his commanders in the desert. The Eighth Army, immensely reinforced, would be almost a new army built upon the nucleus of those who had endured for many months. Let the past be forgotten, and let victory spring immaculate from the desert sands, the stage new set.[1]

[1] In Aug. '42, Auchinleck, as C. in C. undivided M.E., was forming in Egypt a powerful General Reserve, either to reinforce 8th Army, or to reinforce 10th Army. This reserve would become operative in early September. Churchill, ignoring the danger to Persia likely to arise in October, gave all this reserve to Alexander for an offensive in the Desert, so leaving Iraq/Persia empty.

CATHARSIS 61

Egypt, Palestine and Syria would be commanded from Cairo. Persia and Iraq from Basra or Baghdad. General Alexander would be summoned to command in Cairo, 'relieved of all responsibility for the Persia and Iraq front'. Never again would a commander-in-chief of the Middle or Near East be compelled to look in all directions at once. Auchinleck, 'honourably' sacked, would be offered Persia and Iraq, a sop to the ex-Commander-in-Chief, India, ex-Commander-in-Chief from Malta to the Caucasus, and from the Caucasus to the Indian Ocean. General Gott, still alive on the 6th, would command the Eighth Army in succession to General Ritchie. Lieutenant-General Montgomery would succeed General Alexander in 'Torch'.

The War Cabinet in London did not like the idea of splitting the Middle East Command, nor did they approve of the proposed treatment of General Auchinleck. They thought that Churchill's proposal would 'convey the impression that a command was being created in order to let him down lightly.' Auchinleck was far too big a man for that. It seemed that Churchill hesitated to drive the knife home, and to do a clean job. His reaction was to 'take up the cudgels for General Auchinleck', and reveal his thoughts in a long message home-dated August 6th/7th:

> At the head of an army with a single and direct purpose he commands my entire confidence. If he had taken command of the Eighth Army when I urged him to I believe we should have won the Gazala battle. And many people here think the same. He has shown high-minded qualities of character and resolution. He had restored the battle to Sidi Rezegh and only recently has stemmed the retreat at Alamein. There is no officer here or in India who has better credentials.[1]

It was not bad equipment, inferior tanks, inadequate anti-tank guns, low morale that had brought the Eighth Army to the brink of disaster, but the 'obstinacy' of General Auchinleck. That is what it boils down to, and it is difficult not to sympathize with Churchill in his frustration. He has the best Army Commander, possibly in the world, and he is too senior to command

[1] See Notes—reconstructed message. Butler, *Grand Strategy*, vol. iii, part II, p. 654; Playfair, *The Mediterranean and Middle East*, vol. iii, p. 368.

an army! His dislike of the 'chain of command' is fully justified, but it is not his 'pigeon', and he cannot put it right. Yet his instincts in appointing General Alexander over Montgomery to command the Eighth Army seem to me to recognize a weakness in the British Command structure. In effect he has two commanders. It is a problem that exercised the mind of General Fuller between the wars. It is a plea for an 'executive officer', a true second-in-command, an ever-present understudy to the commander. The commander is thereby free to control the battle, in the field when he should be in the field, and not in an 'armchair' miles behind the lines. If he is killed his understudy is there to take his place.

The army commanders of the First World War were not cowards, but the prisoners of a system they had not the imagination to change. Their Chiefs of Staff were in no sense their Seconds in Command, nor their understudies. At long range commanders condemned enormous numbers to unprofitable death in the mud of Flanders. The system persisted. It held Auchinleck in Cairo while weary or inefficient army commanders frittered away their chances. Nevertheless, it was an error of judgement to appoint a Staff Officer, General Ritchie, to the command of the Eighth Army. He should have chosen the senior corps commander. It would not have been ideal, but it would have been much better.

There was a danger that the whole art and purpose of generalship would be lost. In armoured warfare on a brigade and divisional level it had been regained. Brigadiers and Generals shared many of the discomforts and dangers of their men. Their senior battalion (or equivalent) commanders replaced their brigadiers when killed or wounded. Senior brigadiers replaced their major-generals when they were casualties. But these men, perhaps outstanding in their commands, were often failures on a higher level. They were not 'understudies', and understudies at the top were a pressing need of modern warfare. The Americans were to show the way.

That, as I see it, is one of the outstanding lessons of the war in the Desert in 1942. Auchinleck was a victim of an archaism.

On August 7th General Gott was killed, and Auchinleck, unaware of the fate in store for him, at once telegraphed to the C.I.G.S. to send for Montgomery to take command of the

Eighth Army. Meanwhile, Auchinleck appointed Lieutenant-General Ramsden, G.O.C. 30th Corps, as Acting Commander. De Guingand was the newly appointed Brigadier General Staff on the recommendation of Dorman Smith. All had had their orders; all knew their tasks. They were in a sense a 'B' team, but in the unlikely event of an emergency while Auchinleck was in Cairo, they would know how to deal with it. There was no lack of a sense of purpose, no lack of faith, amounting to certainty, that they would finish the job and add the total destruction of the enemy to their victory at Alamein.

On August 8th, Colonel Sir Ian Jacob, 'feeling as if he were just going to murder an unsuspecting friend', delivered the Prime Minister's message of dismissal to General Auchinleck in his Desert headquarters: 'I could not have admired more the way General Auchinleck received me, and his attitude throughout. A great man and a great fighter.' Jacob wrote.

There was no question of accepting the 'grimy sop' Churchill offered, not because it was a 'sop', but because Dorman Smith had demonstrated to him that it was militarily and strategically unsound, and secondly because when he learned that Churchill's 'mind seemed to be veering towards putting Iraq-Persia under India' he suspected 'that the offer was made to him in the certainty that he would refuse it.'[1]

It is impossible to know. But it is certain that had Auchinleck accepted, it would have been impossible to erase the First Battle of Alamein from the records, to denigrate and discredit Auchinleck himself, and to deny the achievements of his Eighth Army prior to October 23rd. No one, however, and least of all Auchinleck, could have foreseen such a turn of events. As for himself, he preferred 'oblivion'. 'He had always determined when his time came, to set his face against any sop.'

The scene was hastening to its end. In Cairo all was bustle as the new men arrived. Auchinleck and his D.C.G.S., Dorman Smith, were alone in the Mena Hotel, remembering their last luncheon together in the Mohamed Ali Club before flying to take over the battered Army in the Desert on June 25th. As soon as he handed over to General Alexander on the 15th of the month Auchinleck would fly to India, as he thought, to retirement. As for Dorman Smith, he had been consigned to oblivion. It

---

[1] Connell, *Auchinleck*, p. 709. See Notes—Auchinleck letter to C.I.G.S.

distressed Auchinleck more than his own fate, for this one alone of all Churchill's dismissals seemed without a shred of justification. Together they had saved Egypt. Dorman Smith was, in fact, the victim of bitter criticism behind the scenes from those who resented his brilliance, and his inability to suffer fools gladly. Moreover the Brigadiers General Staff of the Eighth Army, Whiteley, and the newly appointed de Guingand, disliked his close association in the battle of Alamein with the Commander-in-Chief.

On August 11th, Churchill left Cairo for Moscow. On the 17th he returned to Cairo to meet his new Commanders, to visit the Desert, to be entertained, not in 'a wire-netted cube full of flies', but in the manner to which he was accustomed. Together with General Alexander and the C.I.G.S. he listened to General Montgomery's masterly recitation of the plans he and the C.I.G.S. knew so well.

IV

In Moscow the Prime Minister had managed to assuage Stalin's anger in regard to a Second Front and to interest that potentate in the coming Anglo-American landings in North West Africa. The Prime Minister had 'held out, somewhat imaginatively, a general picture of next year's "big operation" '. It had been an uneasy passage, and upon his return Churchill cabled to his colleagues in London that Stalin now knew the worst. *Grand Strategy*[1] questions the truth of this statement. 'By every statement, short of an absolute promise, Stalin had been given to understand that his western Allies would launch a very great operation in 1943.'

This could only refer to the assault on North-West Europe, longed for as urgently by the Americans as by the Russians. In August 1942 such an assault remained a real hope, but only I believe if the Anglo-American landings in North West Europe could be called off, and the whole effort made the foundation of the greater task. 'Torch' and the assault on North-West Europe in 1943 were unlikely to be possible. The one factor that could influence these momentous possibilities would be the early and total destruction of the German and Italian armies in the

[1] Butler, *Grand Strategy*, vol. iii, part ii, p. 663.

Western Desert. 'Torch', a sound proposition in May or June, was much less sound as time went by and the Eighth Army in the Desert received its immense reinforcements.

It is impossible to know exactly what hopes or fears played in the Prime Minister's mind at this time. Did he really want an assault on North-West Europe—ever; or did he prefer his 'soft underbelly' strategy as a substitute, a better way? An assault on North-West Europe could never be a purely British move, and would only be possible with American power. Strategically the pattern of such an invasion would be dictated by the USA. If so, nothing would have induced him to give up 'Torch', and if he would not give up 'Torch' the urgency of British victory in the Desert became less acute. The great victory Churchill desperately needed and longed for could be carefully calculated to make the most of the landings. It would be running things fine, but not too fine.

I believe that upon his return to Cairo Churchill was still 'playing by ear' and by instinct, vulnerable to the venomous rumours rampant. He had received little or no assurance from the Russians about the Caucasus; but he had managed to put the whole dangerous area out of his mind, leaving it virtually defenceless while he concentrated all the forces available in the Middle East upon his obsession with Rommel. There was no means of knowing that Hitler's insane obsession with Stalingrad would save the British from possible disaster, and relieve them of all embarrassment.

The discussion in Cairo on August 3rd and 4th,[1] dominated by Auchinleck, and in which the Commander-in-Chief had spelled out the priorities, as he had had to do, provide the clues to the Prime Minister's state of mind, and to his actions. An account of these vital conferences is absent from the *Hinge of Fate* record. One thing was clear to him: that if he were to have the victory he craved to restore him in the 'image' of Dunkirk, and crowned with victory, the dangers and demands of the Northern front must be ignored, and Rommel and his army must be seen to be destroyed.

For this reason he had made a clean sweep of the old command, and had appointed Alexander, relieved of all reponsibility save only for the total defeat of Rommel. He knew that

[1] Playfair, *The Mediterranean and Middle East*, vol. iii, p. 365-6.

the outcome was assured; that the July battles had brought the German-Italian army to the very end of its tether. He knew of the heavy sinkings of enemy supply vessels in the Mediterranean, while at the same time he saw the great reinforcements in men, armour and artillery arriving for the Eighth Army.

There was much to do to set the stage for the decisive victory that was an urgent political necessity for Churchill, and for the prestige of Britain, before the Americans took over. The days were numbered. The emergency measures of late June were reactivated, as though 1st Alamein had never been, as though a powerful enemy was at the gates. 'At any moment,' Churchill wrote,[1] 'Rommel might attack with a devastating surge of armour. He could come in by the pyramids with hardly a check . . .'

He even tried to persuade Lady Lampson to send her baby son out of Cairo, but Lady Lampson, as he admits, 'did not take his advice, and none can say she did not judge the military situation rightly'.

On the Prime Minister's instructions every soldier, 'all the office population of Cairo, numbering thousands of staff officers and uniformed clerks' were armed and ordered to action stations. Rifle pits and machine gun posts were manned, bridges mined . . . There they all were, ready 'to arrest an armoured rush along the causeways' while at Alamein the Eighth Army waited in its prepared positions, thirty miles in depth, and with flanks secure, to meet Rommel's 200 serviceable tanks with 700 of their own, 200 more in reserve, a wealth of guns, and an abundance of supplies. Rommel himself was gravely ill, under constant supervision by his doctors, and about to return to Germany to recuperate. His army had barely enough petrol for day-to-day use in a quiet period, and not enough in the final analysis to 'motor' unopposed to Cairo. Not only were his supply ships being sunk, but his long lines of communication were mercilessly bombed.

However, these Cairo preparations sounded stirring, a new call to 'fight on the beaches . . .', the foundation, perhaps, of a new myth of the Prime Minister in the role of 'Generalissimo' intervening on the spot to turn the tide of war. It was unfortunate, perhaps, that the tide had already turned, but he had

[1] Churchill, *The Hinge of Fate*, vol. iv, R.U. edition, p. 423.

made the best of it, and in the end the pen might prove mightier than the sword.

On the 19th Churchill went to visit his new General at Bourg el Arab, accompanied by Alexander and Brooke. General Auchinleck had confirmed his decision to refuse the Iraq-Persia offer, and Sir Henry Maitland Wilson was safely installed without the means to defend his vulnerable and vital command. Churchill, however, had ear-marked him for the role of commanding the Nile defences if that 'avalanche of armour' should find enough petrol to give the Eighth Army the slip. Alexander, presumably, would be on the stricken field with Montgomery, wondering which way to look. The past was almost out of the way. The 44th and 51st divisions had arrived, and were already moving forward, and the new armour made it possible for Montgomery to form what he called, romantically, a *corps de chasse*, and with massive reserves. By this means many of the hard-learned lessons of the Desert fighting were unlearned, and the mobility of divisions, armoured, motorized, and fully equipped as powerful self-contained striking forces, would be discarded in favour of a vast armoured battering ram to smash the Panzer Armee Afrika. Only Freyberg, commanding the New Zealand division, and using his personal friendship with the Prime Minister, managed to make of his division the kind of fighting unit Auchinleck had wanted, and which General McCreery, the cavalry expert, and now the new Chief of Staff to General Alexander, had violently opposed. In fact, the powerful combination of armour, infantry and artillery, soon to be seen in action elsewhere in the form of the American 'Regimental Combat Team' and eventually in the British Brigade Group, had been argued for by Liddell Hart many years earlier. All the signs were that the tactics of 1917–18 were about to be re-enacted on this new stage. Churchill would welcome it when it came. 'We see repeated in Egypt the same kind of trial of strength as was presented at Cambrai at the end of 1917, and in many of the battles of 1918 . . .'[1]

But before that time he would suffer many anxious moments, for battles of attrition, even for the side with overwhelming strength, are agonizing experiences for all concerned both on and off the battlefield.

[1] Churchill, *The Hinge of Fate*, vol. iv, R.U. edition, p. 486.

Certainly the Eighth Army had nothing to fear, except many deaths. They could afford to exchange armour at four or five to one and men at three to one, and emerge still with a powerful force to survey a wilderness of enemy dead, and their own.

Churchill seems to have been excited by all he saw and heard. He lunched with Freyberg, and noted with amusement that Montgomery, arriving late, refused to be the guest of a subordinate commander, as was his wont, and ate his sandwiches alone in his jeep. Napoleon, Cromwell, Marlborough, Churchill mused, had had their eccentricities, 'Monty' should have his. It augured well. The Prime Minister had not omitted to alert the controllers of propaganda to ensure full coverage for his new commander and for his battle, a final triumph for Britain 'alone', and for himself, plain for all to see.

On August 10th, before leaving for Moscow, he had cabled the War Cabinet:

> It would seem desirable that the Minister of Information should explain to the newspaper proprietors and/or editors in confidence beforehand what is intended, and impress upon them the importance of giving the army of the Western Desert the utmost stimulus from these drastic changes in the High Command ... Similar action will be taken here by the Minister of State.[1]

The Headquarters at Bourg el Arab was easily accessible to war correspondents, and the beaches as far as the eye could see were crowded with troops, cleansing their bodies of the weariness of months, the desert sores, the dust and sand, the pestilential flies. These men had no doubts that they had won this benison of beach and sea for themselves, for they had withstood the avalanche of an army hot with victory, the Duce, Mussolini, at their heels, ready to snatch his crown. Not a month had passed since that was over. They knew nothing of the new men come to command them, but something of the new men and armour, and the wealth of equipment, come to reinforce them. They had nothing to fear.

But these men Churchill saw with such pleasure on the rim of the sea were the lucky ones on the Northern Flank, a small proportion of those manning the Alamein position. Thirty-five

---

[1] Churchill, *The Hinge of Fate*, vol. iv, R.U. edition, p. 385.

miles to the South lay the Free French, hungry for some news, the Greeks likewise, the English, Scots and Welsh, still 'inaccessible'. How should any man, exalted or not, come to know the temper of an army in a matter of forty-eight hours or a few days, an army of 100,000 men all living in their private worlds, more private still in the midst of war? A week or two before this last visit Churchill had known some twinges of doubt about the reaction of the old Eighth Army to all these changes, to the loss of their Commander-in-Chief whom all had admired, and whose magnificent presence and bearing had been an inspiration when all seemed lost. 'Might it not be taken as a reproach upon them and all their commanders of every grade if two men were sent from England to supersede all those who had fought in the desert?'[1]

To at least one acute observer it seemed that it would be, and the Prime Minister's impact upon many of the troops he saw, and who saw him, was not very pleasing.

> ... the ridge was thinly lined with phlegmatic soldiers, who seemed to be in two minds about the warmth of the reception they were going to give the Old War Horse.
> ... The over-all direction of the war does not inspire much jollity in men who have been consistently chased by superior numbers with better equipment. Besides, they like Auchinleck, and do not see why he should be kicked out for General Alexander and some new Army Commander from England.[2]

Whether some of this feeling registered with Churchill, and may account in some measure for his savage message of August 21st, his shocking denigration of their morale, their performance, their commanders, and his absolution of their equipment, it is impossible to know. Tens of thousands would read his account of these great events for every one who would study the Auchinleck despatch, the Alexander despatch, and would burrow in many archives, and in many minds, to attempt to discover what happened.

Nevertheless, in spite of a certain prejudice against him, the new Army Commander was making a good impression. He was observed sitting somewhat pensive in his jeep, his thin sharp face

[1] Churchill, *The Hinge of Fate*, vol. iv, R.U. edition, p. 375.
[2] Denis Johnston, *Nine Rivers from Jordan*, p. 43. London, Deutsch, 1953.

seeming even thinner and sharper under his 'Digger' hat. He did not look like a General. He was easily approachable. It was apparent that he knew his own mind, and could express himself simply and clearly, and then he sounded like a general. He had covered a prodigious amount of ground in a week, looking and listening carefully, making himself master of the facts. When Churchill, Alexander and Brooke heard his summary at Bourg el Arab, they were greatly impressed. They had heard it all before, but Montgomery's clear grasp of the situation was none the less impressive.

> The essence of the defensive plan was fluidity and mobility and the maximum use of artillery fire. The defensive zone extended for thirty miles behind our forward positions. If the enemy attempted to pass round towards Bourg el Arab, he was to be delayed by our light armoured troops *in front and struck in flank by our armoured force* and mobile artillery groups.[1]

The passage is from the Auchinleck Despatch. It was the plan for Alam Halfa in the positions designed and executed by Major-General Dorman Smith and Brigadier Kisch. It was accepted by the new commanders.

But there was one shock for the Prime Minister: the main offensive would not take place sooner but later. How much later he would not know for some weeks yet, long after September had passed. Perhaps he had forgotten that he had 'sacked' General Auchinleck because his date for his offensive had been 'mid-September', and Churchill couldn't wait. Now, he had to wait. Montgomery was adamant. He would work and fight in his own time, when he was ready. In his way he was as tough as the Prime Minister himself. Churchill might stay up all night and consume brandy. Montgomery would go to bed early and abstain. He believed also in physical fitness achieved by getting up bright and early and running. Even his brigadiers were not immune from this exercise. 'I am 100 per cent fit,' he once boasted to Churchill, 'with my way of living.' 'And I'm 200 per cent fit with mine.' Churchill retorted.

The night of August 20th was a gala night at the Bourg el Arab headquarters. Major-General de Guingand has told of how an A.D.C. was sent into Alexandria to buy brandy for the

---

[1] The passage in italic was 'edited' by Alexander in 1962.

Prime Minister. A product was found, a local vintage, demanding 'a cast-iron stomach and a very good head'. This firewater was poured into a bottle with a French label. It loosened Churchill's tongue, as it always had done, in the days when anxious observers had speculated whether Churchill or Birkenhead would be the first to drink himself to death. The backers of Birkenhead to survive were very wide of the mark. Thirty years on, and Churchill could 'kill' a bottle even of this Alexandrian potency without, as it seemed, being any the worse. The incident, at any rate, must have deeply impressed de Guingand for he has told it twice, the two instances seventeen years apart.[1]

On the next day, August 21st, the Prime Minister sent his report to the War Cabinet expressing his certainty that 'we were heading for disaster under the former "regime" ' and embodying the *canard:* 'Apparently it was intended in face of heavy attack to retire eastwards to the Delta. Many were looking over their shoulders to make sure of their seat in the lorry, and no plain plan of battle or dominating will-power had reached the units.'[2]

The Official Histories have at last refuted this insult to a brave and victorious army and its commanders, but speculation remains as to the inspiration of this message.[3] Some believe that there may have been some kind of 'conspiracy' on that night of the bad brandy, but I do not think so. Brooke, Alexander, de Guingand were generals and not politicians. But the man I seek to understand in this context of his rich and for many years repudiated inheritance, is General Montgomery. He was the

---

[1] Maj.-Gen. Sir Francis de Guingand, *Operation Victory,* London, Hodder & Stoughton 1947, and *Generals at War,* London, Hodder & Stoughton, 1964.

[2] Churchill, *The Hinge of Fate,* vol. iv, R.U. edition, p. 421.

[3] The message of August 21, 1942, is an accurate report of the top-level 'rumours' circulating in Cairo; spread deliberately by a small group of those who had failed in the June battle. The venomous nature of some of these rumours was well-known to Sir Ian Jacob. The passage quoted from his Diary, August 6th, Connell, *Auchinleck,* pp. 549-50 is revealing: 'Everyone regards General Dorman Smith as a menace of the first order, and responsible for many of the evil theories, etc., etc.' It was no part of Sir Ian Jacob's duties then, nor is it now, to publish his Diary notes. Here he is faithfully recording views of others.

One of these 'evil theories' was his belief in greater flexibility. Liddell Hart writes: 'Several of his (Auchinleck's) chief subordinate commanders were not merely critical, but disloyal.'

But Churchill had been influenced by rumours before leaving London for Cairo. 'The doubts I had about the High Command in the Middle East were fed continually by the reports which I received from many quarters.' (*The Hinge of Fate,* R.U. edition, p. 371).

See Notes: Compare message of 21st with messages of 5th, 6th and 7th August in Churchill, *The Hinge of Fate.*

victim, or beneficiary, of his limitations. Whatever the situation, it was always his own. He had digested the situation at Alamein, and the rest would follow as the night the day. It did not matter that others had prepared the ground in advance. It became his ground, and his alone, when he set foot upon it.

If his masterly exposition at Bourg el Arab had 'dumbfounded' General Brooke, it had assuredly impressed the Prime Minister. He perceived at once that 'Monty was on the make'. Churchill had found his general.

* * *

On the 23rd the Prime Minister left for home well pleased with himself. His catharsis was complete. The result of his intervention had been to set back the offensive by six weeks, and to re-create the myth of Rommel.

PART TWO
THE INHERITORS

CHAPTER FOUR

The General

I

WHEN Lieutenant-General B. L. Montgomery landed at Cairo on the morning of August 12, 1942, he must have felt very strongly that fate had taken a hand in his affairs. Less than a week earlier he had been touring Scotland with General Paget, inspecting the newly-formed British 1st Army preparing for its role in 'Torch', the Anglo-American force for the assault on North-West Africa. General Alexander had been nominated to the British command under General Eisenhower. Suddenly Montgomery found himself appointed to the command following Alexander's transfer to the Middle East. Before he had had time to shave the next morning, or to meet his new Commander-in-Chief, he was ordered at once to take command of the Eighth Army at Alamein. The death of General Gott had catapulted Montgomery into an aircraft, and into a dead man's shoes before the dead man had tried them on.

Montgomery was already notorious in military circles, a 'holy terror' to many, mainly to colonels and brigadiers, a charlatan to some, a remarkable eccentric to those inclined to a more tolerant view of his rigid disciplines, forthright 'hirings and firings'. His simple Biblical and Samuel Smiles slogans and exhortations provided amusement as well as irritation, and his frequent skirmishes with higher authority—a feature of his whole military career—probably endeared him to the private soldier, and ultimately to a wide public. He was a law unto himself. To all he was a martinet, a difficult man to know and to work under, except perhaps in a junior capacity. He was his own judge and jury, and undoubtedly a powerful personality, and a 'character'.

Montgomery had the knack of creating oases of serenity round himself, which made him appear unapproachable. He lived a monastic existence, and few would dare to violate his sanctuary. For an officer of field rank to be posted to his staff was generally regarded as a ghastly turn of fortune to be faced stoically, and in the usually vain hope that somehow one would escape the general's eye. A man's face, any kind of hesitancy, mannerism or idiosyncrasy, might bring instant dismissal. Idiosyncrasies were for the general.

Fortunately, such dismissals did not carry a stigma, but were to be expected. Nevertheless they could rankle.

Equally, junior officers summoned to his command and sometimes to his presence in some trepidation, and fortified with a strong drink, often became his ardent supporters and slaves. They were impressed by the extraordinary tranquillity in which he lived; by his quietness, by the direct but not unfriendly gaze of his very blue eyes. He could create confidence as well as awe. He had the knack of encouraging young men to talk, and to find themselves listened to attentively. He seldom interrupted.

Goronwy Rees was one of those who were captivated by Montgomery's personality. In his book,[1] Rees describes his 'posting' to Montgomery's South-Eastern Command headquarters, and his meeting with the general. His brigadier, apprising him of his fate 'shot me a sympathetic look as if he were sentencing me to immediate execution. . . . "He's a bit of a terror, you know . . . you'd better be on your toes, or he'll have you back here in no time and then there'll be hell to pay." '

Rees had the feeling, he writes, that he had been selected for 'a specially dangerous mission, with the particular objective of protecting G.H.Q. Home Forces from this unknown but mysteriously terrifying general. "Of course," said the brigadier, "there's nothing wrong with Monty really. He's just a bit mad and likes showing off. And he's always causing trouble." '

Rees, who had not heard of Montgomery up to that time, found opinion divided in the Mess. The general was a constant topic of conversation. Some thought him a charlatan. 'Mysterious slogans, menacing even in their absurdity, appeared on notice boards. . . . "Do you wake up full of ZING? If not, why not?" '

Many of Montgomery's staff and formation commanders, 'sometimes wondered, with a mixture of alarm and scepticism, whether they were playing a part in war or *opéra bouffe*.'

[1] Goronwy Rees, *A Bundle of Sensations*, London, Chatto & Windus, 1960.

When Rees was summoned to the 'presence' he saw:

a narrow foxy face, long nosed, sharp and intelligent and tenacious, with very bright and clear blue eyes, and a small, light, spare body. The effect was not at all imposing, except for his eyes and an indefinable look in his face of extreme cleverness and sagacity, like a very alert Parson Jack Russell terrier.

Above all Rees was impressed by the oasis of tranquillity surrounding the general. 'That air of calm and peace which he carried with him was so strong that after a moment my panic and alarm began to die away: it was something which one felt to be almost incongruous in a soldier.'

That, at any rate, is one personal and clearly honest view of a man destined for remarkable fame and fortune, and there are now a few score of men in their fifties, subalterns, captains, of those days of war, who would endorse every word of it.

For more than thirty years Montgomery had worked indefatigably at the business of soldiering, and had forged himself into as good a soldier as it was in him to be. Such as he was, he was. His ideas were firmly rooted in the past, and he was, I think, the slave of his limitations. There was only one view, and it was his view. If anyone held otherwise he would be unlikely to survive long in Montgomery's command. His strengths were also his weaknesses. He avoided contact with his peers, and was incapable of free discussion with those, immediately under him, who might not share his military judgements. Inevitably he surrounded himself with his 'own chaps'; that is to say with 'Yes men', but not in a derogatory sense. To his 'own chaps' Montgomery was infallible. The general could not be wrong.

Montgomery's liking for his own company, and for that of his juniors, did not bode well for future co-operation with his equals and superiors. This was soon to be of great importance.

I think Montgomery always lived in a 'now' of his own. There was, in a sense, no before him and no after him . . . He described his new command as a bit of 'a dog's breakfast', but this was his particular brand of 'insurance', enabling him to work his alchemy if it should turn out well, and say 'I told you so', if it didn't. Pure gold was always base metal until, at his touch, it was found to be pure gold. If he were an heir, it was not in his nature to remark upon it, or even to be aware of it.

Montgomery had been swiftly briefed by General Nye, the V.C.I.G.S., before leaving for the Middle East, and he would find out all about his new job when he arrived. It was a wonderful job, perhaps the ripest plum that could have fallen into anyone's lap at that time. The command of an army did not daunt him. Nothing daunted him, partly because he lacked imagination, but overwhelmingly because in his childhood and boyhood he had been forged in a harsh school. To have been daunted would have meant to have been defeated. Life had never been easy for him, nor had he ever known the affection and happiness in childhood that renders a man at ease with his fellows. He had been severely beaten by his mother to the point where the common ground between them had become a no-man's land, and there was only war. He had been forced into a mould of defensive aggression, and for the most part he suffered in stoic silence, driven into himself, convinced that life was a personal struggle in solitude. If he ever broke down he must serve as his own confessor, with no other shoulder but his own to weep on.

Montgomery's need to feel the hand of authority, which may have been at times urgent, revealed itself throughout his career in a curiously provocative indiscipline, a deliberate 'teasing' of his superiors, it seemed, to excite rebuke. In his first command he had provoked his battalion to near mutiny by his inability to understand the ordinary problems of men, to respect their essential privacy, their dignity and their feelings. It was not so much what he did, but the way that he did it, Moorehead remarks.[1] He behaved like a text book, or a computer, and appeared bleak and uncompromising.

His misdeeds were various and unpredictable. As a battalion commander he had become bored with a brigade manoeuvre in the Desert, and had simply opted out with his battalion. The wrath of Brigadier Pile, his commander, had scourged him, but had failed to arouse any sense of contrition, or even the formality of an apology. He had behaved like an insensitive schoolboy.

In England, a Brigadier himself, he 'had let regimental grounds to a fair promoter, bargaining for a payment' of £1,500 which he had split, giving £500 to the Lord Mayor of Portsmouth, and spending the remainder on garrison welfare. But

[1] Alan Moorehead, *Montgomery*, London, Hamish Hamilton, 1946.

for Wavell's support this gross breach of regulations might have been gravely injurious to his career. In his own words he was 'dicky on the perch' for a while.

Again as a corps commander in Auchinleck's Southern Command, Montgomery contrived to be a source of constant friction, deliberately riling his Commander-in-Chief by acts of petty indiscipline, by grossly disregarding orders, and by crass discourtesies. Auchinleck, in the midst of planning and organizing the defences of Southern England against invasion, regarded as imminent at the time, kept his patience and his temper. It involved him in correspondence with Montgomery and with the Adjutant-General.[1] Montgomery was unashamed. It may be that Auchinleck's patience, courtesy and lack of anger infuriated Montgomery. 'A wigging from Brookie. That was something!' he wrote with evident relish on another occasion. It gave him his bearings in a lonely world thick with 'booby traps', mostly of his own contriving. But Auchinleck had treated him as an adult and a gentleman. No 'wigging'. Perhaps it was this that he could not bear. The wrath of Brigadier Pile, the cold, dangerous anger of the War Office, the milder, but equally unmistakable, anger of General Brooke, were manifestations that he could understand, and relish.

Could it be that Auchinleck was soft?

Montgomery was not without charm. He used it sparingly. He had learned to endure, and to live with himself by shedding most of the virtues and characteristics that render a man vulnerable. His acts of ruthlessness, and even of brutality, were seldom personal, but arose out of a certainty that he dared not be weak. To be weak was to lose. He rode himself on a very tight rein, feeling his way, suspicious of courtesy and kindness, distrusting his equals, and in need of 'masters' and 'pupils'. With these he could be at ease.

Montgomery tells the story frankly, but without a trace of emotion, of the incident in his days as a Cadet at Sandhurst when, as one of a gang of young military hooligans, he had indulged a taste for minor brutalities, and on one occasion had set fire to the shirt tails of a fellow cadet. The young man had been badly burned, but had refused to disclose the names of his tormentors. Nevertheless, retribution had caught up with Montgomery, and

[1] John Connell, *Auchinleck*.

he was demoted ironically from Lance-Corporal to Gentleman-Cadet.

It had been a long haul from those far-off days to Cairo in August, 1942. He was fifty-four years old. Two years earlier he had wondered whether he had begun the war a shade too old and too senior, but it had worked out perfectly. His seniority was exactly right to give him the authority desirable in an Army Commander. Above him were the two men who knew him best, General Alan Brooke, the C.I.G.S., and General Alexander. He had served under Brooke with Alexander in the 2nd Corps in France in 1940, and felt that he knew how to manipulate them both from below. He felt safe. Alexander had enjoyed rapid promotion in the Brigade of Guards while Montgomery had climbed slowly, the hard way, in the Warwickshires. Awareness of their vastly different climbs to the near-top had given Alexander a remarkable feeling of tolerance towards Montgomery.[1] Perhaps he had what used to be called a slight 'inferiority complex' in regard to the junior who, given an equal chance, would certainly have been his senior.

This reunion of the 2nd Corps 'masters' in Cairo gave Montgomery the full assurance he needed. All that remained was to take over his army at the time appointed, and to send for his pupils Horrocks, Leese and Dempsey, all of the old 'Dunkirk' 2nd Corps. With his 'own chaps' under him he would be the complete master in his own house, and with none to question his authority. The death of Gott had left an immediate vacancy of corps commander for Horrocks to fill. Ramsden, acting commander of the Eighth Army, who had commanded the 50th Division with distinction through many months of desert fighting, and had finally commanded the 30th Corps in the Alamein battles of July, had been marked by the Prime Minister for the sack. Nothing would be simpler than to replace him with Leese. Other opportunities would soon present themselves. In such matters Montgomery was ruthless and insensitive. His sacking of General Ramsden was marked by the callous observation: 'You're not exactly on the crest of a wave, Ramsden.'

There had been no warning, and there was no further ex-

---

[1] 'He (Montgomery) wants guiding and watching continually and I do not think Alex is sufficiently strong and rough with him.' Arthur Bryant, *The Turn of the Tide*, (Alan-Brooke Diaries), p. 641.

'All the talents' on the lawn of the British Embassy, Cairo shows: *Back row* (left to right): Air Chief Marshal Sir Arthur Tedder; Sir Alan Brooke; Admiral Sir H. Harwood; The Rt. Hon. R. G. Casey. *Front row* (left to right): Field Marshal Smuts; Mr Winston Churchill; General Sir Claude Auchinleck; General Sir Archibald Wavell. August 1942.

The CIGS, General Sir Alan Brooke, chatting with DCGSME Major-General Dorman Smith (left) at El Alamein during the Prime Minister's visit in August 1942.

Mr Winston Churchill with the DCGS Major-General Dorman Smith during his visit to the Western Desert in August 1942.

Mr Churchill gives the 'V' sign to Australian troops lining the road during his tour of Alamein—August 1942.

planation. As for Lumsden,[1] when his turn came, it was enough that Montgomery had decided that the command of a corps was 'above his ceiling'. Lumsden had shared the anxieties of his divisional commanders in regard to Montgomery's use of his armoured corps at 2nd Alamein. Montgomery would make a clean sweep: 'I would then have three reliable Corps Commanders in Leese, Horrocks and Dempsey; they had all served under me before, and Leese and Dempsey had been students under me at the Staff College. All these moves were agreed by Alexander.'[2]

He did not mention that Alexander had also been a student under him, yet the point is significant. Thus by the end of November, 1942, all the senior commanders of the old Eighth Army that had fought Rommel to a standstill in his hey-day, and at the height of his strength, had been removed without trace. Auchinleck, Corbett, his Chief of Staff, Dorman Smith, his Deputy Chief of Staff, Gott, Ramsden, Lumsden, the Corps Commanders. Now the old Eighth Army could be denied its 'star' and its existence. Its last great battle would not be in the records, nor would its regiments wear the battle honours they had earned upon their standards. Even the name of Alamein would be usurped.

No one has put the matter more succinctly than Sir Compton Mackenzie:

> A legend has grown up that the Eighth Army started its career at the second battle of Alamein, and this legend has been preposterously turned into bad history by those who were responsible for denying to all those who served in it before October 23rd 1942 the numeral 8 on the ribbon of the Africa Star. The only explanation for such a denial is the guilty conscience of those who were fundamentally responsible for there ever being any need for a second battle of Alamein.[3]

Montgomery's account of his first hours in Cairo and of his brief interview with his Commander-in-Chief, General Auchinleck, dumbfounded even his nearest and dearest pupils, and profoundly shocked Auchinleck when he read it in Mont-

---

[1] Lieut.-Gen. Lumsden, commanded 10th Armoured Corps.
[2] *The Memoirs of F.-M. Montgomery*, Collins, 1958, p. 141. (Hereinafter called Montgomery, *Memoirs*).
[3] Mackenzie, *Eastern Epic*, p. 318.

F

gomery's *Memoirs* many years later.[1] It also shocked the historians. 'After five minutes in his (Auchinleck's) company it was difficult not to like him, and quite impossible to ever dislike him,' wrote Brigadier Barclay.[2]

Montgomery found it both simple and natural to dislike Auchinleck. Moreover it was his tendency to disparage anyone or anything that took place before he took charge—as he instinctively sought to show the great changes following his advent. The contrasts in the physical aspects of the two men, especially at that time, may in some measure account for it. Montgomery, 'perky and peaky', a sharp-featured bantam of a man, fresh from England after two years without any strain of battle, confronted the giant who had borne the brunt of battle and the stress of his vast command for months, and who was under notice to go. Even the two or three days of command remaining to Auchinleck seemed a ridiculous and unnecessary formality to Montgomery.

It is certain that Auchinleck told the Commander-designate of the Eighth Army very little, if anything, about the past. The strong position of the Army was evident from the maps. The condition of the enemy was reasonably well known, and his expected attack awaited with confidence in the August full moon period. The plans to deal with this attack were at Montgomery's disposal. Beyond that, Auchinleck courteously invited Montgomery to see for himself. He was welcome to go down to the Desert, and to use the time available to put himself as fully as possible in the picture before taking over command on August 15th.

Montgomery's behaviour, according to his own account, in response to this invitation is virtually incomprehensible in a mature man. Early on the morning of August 13th he travelled by car to the Desert to be met by Brigadier de Guingand, the newly-appointed Brigadier General Staff of Eighth Army and one of Dorman Smith's most bitter critics behind the scenes. Together they drove to Eighth Army headquarters while de Guingand briefed his new Chief on the situation. By the time the two men reached the headquarters Montgomery had decided to retain de Guingand as Chief of Staff. The two men had known

[1] See Notes.
[2] Brigadier C. N. Barclay, *On their Shoulders*, London, Faber, 1964.

each other for years, and de Guingand was fourteen years Montgomery's junior. They were opposites, but with an affinity. Both were to prove themselves masters of showmanship and the techniques of public relations. De Guingand was a good mixer, something of a *bon vivant*. It is true to say, I think, that he aimed to please. Montgomery's austerity and dislike of mixing is well-known.

In searching for an explanation of how Montgomery came to believe that any withdrawal was contemplated by the Eighth Army, General Horrocks believes that de Guingand may have been 'quite unwittingly' responsible. De Guingand was certainly new to his job, but he could not have been in any doubt as to the intention of the Eighth Army. Yet, according to the War Correspondent Alan Moorehead, who knew de Guingand intimately, there can be little doubt that the new Chief of Staff was the source of Montgomery's information and beliefs.[1]

It may well be that Montgomery had no preconceived ideas at all on August 13th about the Army's intentions, but upon reaching headquarters he immediately 'cross-examined' Ramsden, the acting commander of the Eighth Army, about the 'plan for a withdrawal if Rommel attacked; certain orders had been issued about withdrawal but they were indefinite.'[2]

But there were no such orders. In June, following the defeat of Ritchie at Gazala, G.H.Q. Cairo had issued orders to deal with an emergency, but these orders had been obsolete since July 4th. They may have remained on a G.H.Q. file, but nowhere else. They were not, nor had they ever been, a part of Eighth Army orders. Ramsden was fully aware of the orders and intentions of the Eighth Army. He would have been well able to conduct the expected battle and to repel Rommel's attack.

It may be significant that, following this 'cross-examination' Montgomery at once dismissed Ramsden from his acting command, an act for which he had no authority whatever. Ramsden, deeply embarrassed, returned to his corps.

Meanwhile Montgomery expressed his disgust with the conditions at Auchinleck's austere headquarters, and decided to move at once to the amenities of Bourg el Arab. It was a wise decision, but he seemed to have no idea at all of the urgencies of July that

[1] Alan Moorehead, *Montgomery*, p. 118.
[2] Montgomery *Memoirs*, pp. 100-103.

had induced Auchinleck to live rough in close contact with his troops. To Montgomery that kind of behaviour seemed quixotic and quite unnecessary.

That first afternoon, after 'some savage thinking',[1] Montgomery decided to usurp command, and composed a telegram to G.H.Q. Thereupon he immediately put himself out of range of a reply. At the same time he knew that it was useless to consult G.H.Q., for there was no emergency, and had one arisen before August 15th, Auchinleck would have dealt with it. The telegram, one must assume, was a gesture in deplorable taste, a petty attempt to wound the outgoing Commander-in-Chief. It did not reach Auchinleck. Montgomery remained out of range until the night of the 14th.

On the evening of the 13th, having seen very little, and read nothing on his own admission, Montgomery ordered de Guingand to assemble the staff at headquarters, and at once gave them a 'pep' talk. The army would stand firm. There would be no question of withdrawal. Let Rommel do his worst. These 'orders', according to Montgomery, involved a complete change of policy, whereas they involved no change at all. His actions of the day were, it seems clear, *'pour l'histoire'*, and to create a tonic 'new broom' impression. Perhaps he did not know that Rommel was a very sick man, and that his remaining armour had barely enough petrol for day-to-day running, and that his hopes of more were fast disappearing. Churchill, baffled by the immensity of the problems facing the Middle East command, had focused upon Rommel to the exclusion of all else, leaving the whole Northern front virtually defenceless. Alexander, therefore, may have accepted a somewhat Churchillian view of Rommel's capacity. De Guingand was certainly well aware of the true position, but may have thought the time inappropriate to inform his new Chief. He knew instinctively that it was dangerous to inform Montgomery of anything he did not wish to know, or contrary to his fixed ideas.

The Alexander Despatch makes it abundantly clear that both he and Montgomery accepted the Auchinleck plan, and acted upon it, strengthening the Alam Halfa positions—as Auchinleck would have done with the wealth of reinforcements rapidly becoming available.

[1] Montgomery *Memoirs*, pp. 100-103.

The original draft of the Alexander *Despatch* reads as follows:

> The plan was to hold as strongly as possible the area between the sea and the Rweisat ridge and to threaten any enemy advance south of the ridge from a strongly defended and prepared position on Alam Halfa ridge. I adopted this plan of defence in principle and if the enemy should give us enough time, I hoped to be able to improve our positions by strengthening the left or southern flank.

On the plea of Montgomery this statement was amended as follows:

> General Montgomery, now in command of Eighth Army, accepted this plan in principle, to which I agreed, and hoped that if the enemy should give us enough time we would be able to improve our positions by strengthening the left or southern flank.

Montgomery's first definite act was to relax the austere conditions Auchinleck had imposed at the time of the desperate emergency at the end of June, and which had prevailed throughout the fierce fighting of July. Everyone should live in as much comfort as possible. His jaunty confidence, coupled with orders such as these, and the flow of reinforcements, at once induced a real awareness in the army that their worst times were over. On August 15th General Auchinleck handed over his command to General Alexander in Cairo.

Many have pondered Montgomery's statements, and especially his initial statement in regard to the intentions of the Eighth Army at the time of his arrival. General Horrocks,[1] Montgomery's favourite corps commander from Alamein to the Baltic, has striven to understand his chief's remarkable aberration. In his book, *A Full Life,* he goes over the events of July at Eighth Army Headquarters:

> At this time Major-General Dorman Smith was with him (Auchinleck) at Headquarters 8th Army as Chief of Staff, while Lieutenant-General Corbett in Cairo acted as Deputy Commander-in-Chief. On July 27th Dorman Smith prepared

[1] Horrocks also recognizes the importance, and 'existence', of the 1st Battle o Alamein.

an appreciation for his commander in which 'the intention' was that the 8th Army would defeat any attempt of the enemy to pass through or round it. There was no mention in this document of any further withdrawal, but even so Auchinleck at first refused agreement because *it did not contain a sufficiently offensive spirit*. There was nothing defensive about Auchinleck at this period. He wanted to return to the offensive as soon as possible. But after further discussion Dorman Smith convinced him that reorganization and training were required before the 8th Army could launched an offensive with any reasonable prospect of success. So the provisions of this appreciation, which envisaged an offensive defensive by the 8th Army, were followed.

... It seems clear, therefore, that from the middle of July onwards Auchinleck never thought of any further withdrawal. Indeed, on July 25th he issued a stirring Order of the Day in which he congratulated the 8th Army on having wrenched the initiative from Rommel ...

There is no doubt that at this period defeatism was prevalent in the rear and particularly in Cairo.

But this does not explain how Montgomery came to believe that Auchinleck, even as late as August 12th, still envisaged the possibility of further withdrawal.

General de Guingand remains the principal living clue to Montgomery's remarkable misapprehension, and in his most recent book[1] makes some amends, especially to Dorman Smith. It is likely that Montgomery's original statement might have died a very swift death had not an immensely powerful ally arrived upon the scene to underline every word, and to grasp the great opportunity his new General's cast of mind gave to him.

But it is important to understand Montgomery. He was at times incapable of accepting ideas from outside unless an opportunity was arranged for him to present them as his own, and doubtless to believe them his own. General Sir Oliver Leese and de Guingand have gone on record on the need to approach Montgomery with the utmost tact with any plan or idea:[2]

[1] de Guingand, *Generals at War*, pp. 184-7. London, Kimber, 1960.
[2] Quoted by Corelli Barnett, *The Desert Generals*, p. 278.

One of them would go to his caravan in the evening and put their case. Monty would shake his head and say: 'Can't do that, can't do that.'

Then in the morning he might say: 'I've been thinking, and had an idea . . .' He would then explain the idea which would be the one put to him the night before.

Probably General Dempsey achieved the greatest success in discussing plans and putting his point of view to Montgomery. He spoke very plainly, but complete privacy was essential. Montgomery feared to 'lose face'.

Throughout his campaigns Montgomery's words do not match his deeds. They tend to obscure rather than to reveal. They seem to represent rather a desire for perfection and order, than an attainment. Constantly he calls upon his 'God', 'The Lord, Mighty in battle!' Inside a rather puritanical 'roundhead', I feel, is a dashing cavalier trying to get out.

Upon taking command of the Eighth Army a new Montgomery began to develop. He was on the road to a success of which he had not even dared to dream. He began to expand, and his inner zest boiled over into words. Does he really believe what he says? Or is he making some kind of personal noise, as a lion roars, or a hyena screams? Is it a form of 'gamesmanship', cunningly thought out; or is it the spontaneous shout of a 'barker' drawing exaggerated attention to his prowess?

It is probably all of these things. He found it increasingly easy to believe that what happened was what he wanted to happen, and since he could not lose, events could always be fitted into a time framework to reassure him of his infallibility. I do not believe that he consciously repudiated his inheritance in the desert, or intended the terrible insult to the old Eighth Army and its commanders, that his words implied. He was simply unaware. Simply, he came, he saw, he conquered.

From the outset, his professionalism, his dedicated life as a soldier, stood him in good stead. No man had laboured more steadfastly to make himself master of his craft. All that he was capable of learning he had learned. To him the whole complex organization of an army was simple, and he could express it all in simple terms. Technically he knew exactly what an army could do, but whether he knew the imponderables, the lessons that only battle may teach, the at times miraculous resources of the human spirit manifest not only in individuals, but in bodies of men, remained to be discovered. Peace is order; war is confusion. It was Montgomery's ability not only to master, but to understand, confusion that had not been tested. Would he dare?

Meanwhile with skill and diligence he learned the facts of his command.

II

At the time of General Montgomery's arrival in the Western Desert industrial and scientific development, translated into the tools and weapons of war, had begun to overtake military events on the battlefield. For twenty years between the wars military conservatism and amateurism had denied many of the fruits of industrial and technological progress to the soldier, and inhibited experiment and development in the military field. After the middle of 1942 British superiority over the enemy was not only in quantity, but in quality and variety. A growing wealth of new weapons would be used by General Montgomery for the first time in warfare. The factors of time and space would be constantly shifting and demanding the consideration of alert and able minds. Command of the air would multiply the power of ground troops in attack or defence. The problems of supply would increase in complexity, and an army would grow a 'tail' of massive proportions. Nevertheless, certain factors would remain constant, notably the art of war itself. Served by a competent staff, a general commanding an army might detach himself from all technical detail, and keep his mind clear to decide the problems of strategy and tactics by which the arts of war might be preserved. The time had passed when the man at the top, whether of an army, a battleship or a bank, could 'know it all.'

The qualities of generalship demanded by the fluidity of battle between opponents whose strengths and fortunes are in a state of constant change, neither of whom deploys an overwhelming strength in man or weapon power, gave way to the manipulation of a mass of ironmongery by one side against the other. Of such a situation General Fuller wrote: 'Even should technical superiority be so overwhelming that by bludgeoning alone an enemy can be rendered insensible, unless warfare is to become ironmongering the artist is still necessary.'[1]

The examination of the generalship of Montgomery begins at this point. The real challenge he faced was not from the enemy, but in the handling of the powerful weapon he now grasped. Ironmonger or artist, that was the question. The desperate plight of the enemy may even have proved a handicap in meeting this challenge, for there was no need for *finesse*. He commanded a Leviathan capable of flattening the opposition. His powerful artillery, his domination of the air, his overwhelming strength in armour, the command of the seas, increasingly denying supplies to the enemy and ensuring his own, acquitted him of the need to dare or to experiment.

Moreover, while it is simple now to see that this was the opening of a new chapter in war, and not simply in the war, it may not have been simple then. Certainly Montgomery was aware of his great strength, but not perhaps of its implications. His inheritance enabled him to play himself in, to discover how best to use his powerful instrument of warfare. He was neither old nor young, nor was he a devotee of any of the conflicting schools of thought that had been a characteristic of the whole period of his military career. He had not been involved in the bitter controversies about armour that had divided the army into 'cavaliers and roundheads'. He was an infantry man dedicated to training in his own fashion. He had studied the 'book' with the utmost diligence and had even contributed chapters to it. As early as 1920 he had become the protégé of Major Tomes of the Royal Warwickshire Regiment. He had attracted the attention of General Sir Ivor Maxse, and was highly thought of by Brigadier B. D. Fisher.

In those early days Montgomery was a keen student of war, thirsting for knowledge of his business. He worked hard to prepare new training manuals and to put his ideas into practice. No troops were more assiduously trained than those with whom he had to deal. He was open to criticism, but was not always able to assimilate it. He read everything he could lay his hands upon that was relevant to his profession, but some things appear to have been against his nature. Outstanding among these things

[1] Fuller, *The Second World War*, p. 164. London, Eyre & Spottiswoode, 1948.

was his failure to grasp the theory of 'the expanding torrent', expounded by Liddell Hart. His whole essentially tidy mind liked the 'set-piece' attack, and all went well until the breakthrough demanded exploitation. Again and again his senior military friends hammered home the vital necessity for swift exploitation of the break-through. He accepts it, but he cannot *think* it, and he cannot do it.

In 1924 Montgomery was lecturing the officers of the 49th division on tactics, and had written two pamphlets on the subject. The problem of exploiting success was not dealt with, and the omission was pointed out to him. In a long letter to Liddell Hart, dated July 24, 1924, Montgomery expressed his views on training clearly and answered various criticisms, notably the following:

> I have not mentioned exploitation anywhere. Perhaps I should have done so, and if I ever get out a revised edition I will do so. I was anxious not to try and teach too much. The first thing to my mind is to get them to understand the elementary principles of attack and defence. But I think you are probably right, and exploitation should have been brought out.

Later in the same letter there is a phrase that seems to me very revealing: 'To launch companies and platoons into the blue is, I consider, unsound. After each bound is reached, allot further ones . . .'

Seven years later Montgomery was still fighting shy of exploitation and the expanding torrent. His draft for the new Training Manual was sent to Liddell Hart for criticism by Brigadier Fisher, Chief of Staff to General Sir David Campbell, G.O.C.-in-C. Aldershot Command. Again the problems of exploiting success were not dealt with. Liddell Hart sent his detailed comments and Fisher wrote:

> September 7, 1930
>
> I had a long talk to Montgomery, and we went carefully through all your criticisms of the new Infantry Training—with the result that the great majority of them are being incorporated in the final proof. The importance of 'the expanding torrent' is being specially emphasized . . .

Yet when the new Training Manual appeared the problems of

exploitation were neither emphasized nor understood. Indeed by omissions of passages from the old manual and the substitution of new, the tactics of the First World War were preserved.

There were other weaknesses. The importance, for example, of surprise was emphasized, but without instructions as to how surprise might be achieved. The Training Manual revealed Montgomery's limitations, his strengths and his weaknesses. He believed passionately in 'Leadership' and in 'Training', but the end purposes of leadership and training are never clear. 'Teach the teachers what to teach before they teach the Tommies,' Montgomery quotes in an early letter, but he omits to teach the teachers what to teach. His intellectual honesty made it impossible to teach doctrines that he was unable fully to grasp himself, and which he would never carry out. The abstract concept was beyond him, and the narrow confines of his practical mind banished much that was practical into the wilderness of the abstract.

As an instructor at the Staff College he failed also to learn from many of his brilliant pupils. Any deviation from the strictly orthodox and old-fashioned was not tolerated. Thus in a Divisional attack exercise those who laid down a preliminary barrage, and moved their troops forward into a direct assault gained full marks. Those who suggested preliminary reconnaissance to discover the strength and exact whereabouts of the enemy were frowned upon. Details of the enemy were not given. Perhaps the enemy was not there!

Such thoughts must not be permitted. Across the river was enemy country. It must be attacked in a set-piece manner. It must never be forgotten that Montgomery's major experience of battle had been in the First World War. He was already a mature man, a senior subaltern 26 years old at the outset. At the finish he was a senior staff officer of the 'Bantam Division' on the Somme, himself a perky bantam of a man, remarkably self-assured. In the early days at Meteren he had led his platoon with great courage, gaining the D.S.O. and being severely wounded. In the stages from Platoon Commander to Senior Staff Officer of a Division he had seen a great deal, and had been appalled by much of it, not only by the dreadful, and often senseless, slaughter, but by the remoteness of the High Command from the battle, from all contact with the men who fought. No man would ever be able to accuse him, however high he might rise, of remoteness from the troops. He would never forget that he owed his life to one of his platoon whose body had sheltered his from enemy fire as he lay wounded. Yet apart from his leadership of his platoon he had little experience of leadership. He had returned to France as a Brigade Major.

I think it is true that Montgomery was completely formed as a soldier at the end of the First World War. He did not grow after that. He became increasingly efficient, but he did not absorb a new idea. At fifty he was the same man he had been at thirty, developed by unremitting toil, dedicated absolutely to his profession, completely assured. He had polished the hard diamond of himself to the ultimate brilliance it could sustain. He had, as he often said of others, reached his ceiling. In terms, say, of a Regimental Sergeant Major he had made of himself a perfect soldier. But there is no training for generalship. There is no real training for the command of an army, or of armies. Alexander was twenty-five years old at Arbela; Arminius was twenty-seven when he destroyed the Roman Legions under Varus at Teutoburger Wald; Belisarius was thirty-one at Tricameron; Clive was thirty-two at Plassey; Charles XII of Sweden was twenty-six at Holowczyn... The list of young and great commanders is long, which does not mean to suggest that men in their fifties are too old. Marlborough was fifty-four years old at Blenheim and Dumouriez fifty-three at Jemappes.

In 1940 in command of the British 3rd Infantry division at Louvain, and on the retreat to Dunkirk, Montgomery was at his best. His division was immaculate. His rapid movement of his troops by night laterally across the line of communications to fill a vital gap on the British left flank, was masterly. He reacted to such tasks with complete confidence. His orders were clear, and his confidence was felt throughout all ranks. When General Brooke was forced to return to England, handing over the 2nd Corps to Montgomery at a moment's notice, Brooke's tears may well have been of relief as well as sorrow. Montgomery was like a rock.

General Horrocks, serving under Montgomery for the first time, a Lieutenant-Colonel, was full of fears of this strange Major-General. He remarks Montgomery's unorthodoxy and recalls that he was already much talked about, and with the reputation of a 'showman'. But Montgomery as a soldier was a model of orthodoxy, and it would be more true to call him eccentric. His eccentricity lay in his personal behaviour. He was blunt to the point of rudeness, and his dry, metallic voice, and limited word choice allied to an inability to conceive that he might be wrong, did not oil the wheels of his personal relationships. Comparative poverty had forced him to choose a regiment of the line. The Brigade of Guards, and the Cavalry were overwhelmingly the provinces of the rich or the well-to-do. His lack of means had also conditioned much of his behaviour. He could not afford high Mess bills. He did not drink or smoke, and while drinking and smoking may have little or no merit in themselves, they do enable men to relax in each other's company in social intercourse. Especially is this true in the Services. Thus Montgomery embraced hard work, went early to bed, and developed a marked professionalism in a service which at times seemed almost to exalt the amateur. Often he seemed like the lone 'player' in the pavilion.

Although these circumstances certainly limited his friendships, stunted his social graces, and affected markedly the development of his military character, they did not cut him off from his fellows. Major Tomes, five years his senior, and passionately devoted to the Warwickshire regiment, saw Montgomery as a future Colonel of the Regiment, and had a real affection for him. Tomes became godfather to Montgomery's son, while Frank Simpson, afterwards General Sir Frank Simpson, stood patiently by Montgomery's side, indefatigable in his kindness and understanding through a time of great personal tragedy. His kindness was not forgotten. For the rest, Montgomery had a genuine regard for the young, and at the height of his fame was ever ready to respond to children.

In England, between Dunkirk and the Desert, he had commanded a corps, and later become G.O.C.-in-C. South Eastern Command. His insistence on physical fitness to the point where his brigadiers had to run before breakfast, and his officers were deprived of their wives, did not make for popularity. His wholesale weeding out of those he did not like, and their replacement with his nominees was characteristic. His refusal to observe the normal courtesies in these matters may have been due to shyness, and a fear that he would not have his way if he consulted his superiors. Unhappily he tended to dislike those to whom he had been discourteous, especially if they had behaved kindly and courteously when he needed the salt of anger.

It is true to say of Montgomery that he had pondered to the utmost of his ability all those military problems that are ponderable. The imponderable remained. Alan Moorehead, a close observer of Montgomery's methods, wrote of him that he had reduced 'the whole art of war . . . to a pattern of a series of numbers; it was all based on units of man-power and fire-power and so forth'.

It is, I believe, a just assessment. But is it possible to reduce an 'art' to a pattern of a series of numbers? Is it possible to assess the at times extravagant resources of the human spirit in terms of 'units of man-power and fire-power and so forth?' Montgomery's battles may provide an answer. Some factors at least are certain: Montgomery abominated disorder, and feared confusion. Few men are likely to have been more conversant with all arms, and all ancillary services in the make-up of an army. He had done his uttermost to eliminate chance, and inasmuch as warfare is calculable he had done his work well. But war is an exercise in confusion. Moreover, it is not possible to produce its shifts and balances, its deviations and its climaxes, off the battlefield. It is the most challenging of all human activities, and a man, however well-trained, is pitch-forked into it as into a new element. It demands all the physical, mental and spiritual resources of man. No man knows whether he will be a good soldier until he undergoes the ordeal of battle. No man knows whether he is able to command an army in battle until he tries.

The great challenge confronting Montgomery was to maintain the mobility, flexibility and striking power of his fighting head against the immense weight of the body and tail of his army. It could become a strait-jacket and a prison, denying generalship. There were already ten men back for each one in front. Would the ten hold the one man back, or impel him magnificently armed and served into combat?

CHAPTER FIVE

Alam Halfa: *the general and the battle*

I

THE battle of Alam Halfa stands clearly as a tide mark in the midst of war, a rare isolated engagement, clear-cut in itself between two massive encounters, and two kinds of warfare. It unfolded in the manner ably foreseen and prepared for by Auchinleck and his generals, and it underlined the nature of the defeat inflicted upon the enemy in the bitter fighting of July. It was a natural epilogue to the first battle of Alamein, and for the Germans and Italians it held the elements of tragedy. It should not have been fought, and yet it was inevitable that it should be fought. It was a bold and desperate venture inviting total destruction, a brave end to a brave struggle.

In terms of the bull-fight the stricken bull made its last charge, hoping for a miracle or the swift death blow of the 'matador'. There was no miracle, and there was no death blow. The sword had changed hands. All that was destroyed was hope. The epilogue had become a prologue to a new and different story.

General Montgomery awaited the full of the August moon and his first engagement in command of an army without undue anxiety. The arrival of the 44th division had enabled him to strengthen his dispositions on the Alam Halfa ridge. His three armoured brigades, each one almost the equal in strength of the entire enemy armoured force, knew their roles. The 7th armoured division was fully briefed for its swift striking role on the enemy flank. His armoured reserves were powerful and growing, and his anti-tank gunners well equipped. The front from the sea to the southern tip of the Ruweisat Ridge was solid and impregnable, and the gap between the ridge and the Quattara depression was covered by a minefield brilliantly disposed. Mines had become a formidable challenge to armour, and Auchinleck's engineers had planned the mine-fields with great skill. Denis Johnston observed the lay-out from the hill of

Himeimat shortly before the battle, and noted the unusual strength of the obstacle:[1]

> Instead of placing our defences across the path of the German advance, some genius had planned our principal mine-fields and defended areas lengthwise along the slope of the ridge, like a ship with its bows facing the oncoming waves, and with very much the same effect. This left the Barrel Track to Cairo wide open . . .

It was a wonderful lure, for if Rommel dared to enter the gap between the Quattara depression and the Ruweisat Ridge his only possible line of retreat would be dominated by the Eighth Army. Yet he had to dare, to attempt by the surprise of speed—the only surprise open to him—to penetrate so far and so fast as to create alarm. At best it was too forlorn to be a hope. Such a penetration would have tested the nerve and generalship of the new Eighth Army Commander, but it was not to be. Instead, from a terribly exposed position Rommel had to attempt to bring the left flank of the Eighth Army to battle, while all the time his slender line of communications would be vulnerable, exposing whatever force he chose to deploy to disaster.

August 25th, the night of the full moon, passed without incident, and the British armour waited, the gunners with eyes and ears strained to catch the smallest echo from the night. On the sixth night of the waning moon, at the last possible moment, the stricken Rommel moved his army to the attack.

Montgomery had become increasingly edgy and irritable with the delay. So alien was Rommel's expected assault to his own ideas of attack that he found himself imagining the enemy attacking in the North, or crushing the New Zealand division on the Ruweisat Ridge. At the same time he concentrated as much as possible on the set-piece battle he was resolved to project as soon as his strength and the standard of training of his army satisfied him. It was his habit, as Horrocks and Moorehead have pointed out, always to be planning the next battle. He did not seem to consider the possibility that there might not be a next battle, not then, nor at any time until he was east of the Rhine, the very end of the line at Luneberg. 'While Rommel was leading his troops in person against our strongly-held

[1] Denis Johnston, *Nine Rivers from Jordan*,

Lieutenant-General Montgomery pointing out various features while talking with officers of the 22nd Armoured Brigade. On Lieutenant-General Montgomery's left is Lieutenant-General Horrocks. August 1942.

The Army Commander looking at a wrecked German tank with Major-General H. R. Briggs, Lieutenant-General Lumsden and Brigadier Fisher, October 1942.

General Montgomery and the Padre during the service, December 1942.

The Army Commander speaking to junior officers of the 1st Armoured Division, October 1942.

Lieutenant-General Montgomery, Commander of the Eighth Army, talking to war correspondents at his Headquarters in the desert. He announced the complete destruction of the Afrika Corps, November 1942.

ALAM HALFA: THE GENERAL AND THE BATTLE 97

defensive positions on the Alam Halfa ridge, Montgomery was planning the battle of Alamein.'[1]

Horrocks, commanding a corps for the first time, was in no position to criticise his Army Commander, and for him whatever Montgomery did must be right.

Rommel, for his part, lived in the immediate now. His wisest course would have been to withdraw westward, to shorten his line of communications, and to harass the Eighth Army in its pursuit to the uttermost. But Hitler stood between him and common sense, and he had become committed to a last desperate fling even when his promised petrol failed to arrive. He had asked for Guderian to replace him, but when that was refused he strove to keep on his feet. If Montgomery could have been with his enemy on the 24th he would have been greatly relieved. On the 23rd Rommel had been too ill to write, but on the 24th he wrote to his wife as cheerfully as he could, 'I'm now well enough to get up occasionally.' Two days later a full report on Rommel's health was sent to his wife. He was having frequent attacks of faintness, and suffering from chronic stomach ailments, intestinal catarrh, nasal diphtheria and considerable circulation trouble. Professor Horster and General Gause, his doctors, wrote that 'He is not in a condition to command the forthcoming offensive'.

But he did command 'under constant medical attention'. By eight o'clock on the morning of August 31st Rommel knew that his thrust had failed. He had left his sleeping-bag with a very troubled face, his doctor noted. He must have feared the worst even before the news reached him. Instead of his spearheads driving thirty miles east by moonlight to strike north at dawn, his troops had struggled all night in the mine-field under constant bombardment. General Bismarck, commanding the 21st Panzer division, had been killed, and Nehring, the commander of the Afrika Korps, was badly wounded. In the course of the next twenty-four hours the Afrika Korps lost seven more of its staff officers, and Rommel himself bombed six times in two hours, diving for the shelter of slit trenches, was lucky to escape with his life.

The story of the Battle of Alam Halfa has been written many times. Perhaps to give Colonel Bayerlein a chance to command,

[1] Horrocks, *A Full Life*.

G

Rommel let the attack go on. There was no possibility of putting the Eighth Army off balance, but he might deal the left flank a heavy blow before he had to strive to withdraw. In a driving sandstorm the Afrika Korps pressed on to attack the Alam Halfa ridge. It was one o'clock in the afternoon before it was ready to move, and two hours later before the XX corps was ready to move on the left flank. 'As for Rommel's tanks,' wrote Sir Compton Mackenzie,[1] 'they were smashed by the 6-pounders with such ease that an explanation for the time it took to realise the need for such a gun baffles the lay mind.'

Petrol stocks were so short that 'the most we could permit ourselves was a few local, limited objective attacks.'[2]

Thus, before it had properly begun, the enemy offensive had to be called off. The 15th Panzer division strove to press an attack against the Alam Halfa position, but without hope of any real success. It was easily repulsed. On the night of September 1st Rommel knew that his task was to save his army. The shortage of petrol was grave, but the exposed position of his troops in the soft sand of the Ragil Depression banished all else from his mind. He knew the powerful formations assembled, as he believed, for his destruction. Miraculously they remained stationary, and it dawned upon the stricken enemy that they were faced by 'a very cautious man, who was not prepared to take any sort of risk'.

In the end to have withdrawn his army in his own time to overlook the British positions from the hill of Himeimat, six miles inside the original British Line, seemed to the weary Rommel almost like victory. He was resolved to stand where he was, and Montgomery would not quarrel with that. For three days and nights in the soft sand of the Ragil Depression, bombed mortared, and shelled, the German-Italian Army had been at Montgomery's mercy. In all there had been eight days and nights of something like inferno for the Afrika Korps. They had lost 2,900 men, 49 tanks and many vehicles, but in the straight fighting they had inflicted 1,750 casualties on the British and put 67 tanks out of action.

Nevertheless, at the end, Montgomery's superiority on the battlefield in tanks alone had risen to five to one. The British domination of the air multiplied those odds. But for the time

---
[1] Mackenzie, *Eastern Epic*, p. 598.
[2] *The Rommel Papers*, p. 279.

being the Afrika Korps were safe. 'We had to break off the offensive for supply reasons and because of the superiority of the enemy air force—although victory was otherwise ours.' Rommel wrote to his wife.[1]

He had no illusions about the future, and neither had the British—perhaps until that hour it had been just possible to cling to the illusion of a miracle. After Alam Halfa both sides knew exactly how they stood.

II

A battle is many things to many men. To some it is final and total, to others it is a sustained and terrible ordeal leaving them lacerated with grievous wounds. To all it is an immersion in elemental violence testing body, mind and spirit to the limits. Within the vortex of the battle, individuals, by their endurance and courage, and by rare deeds of extraordinary valour, will have contributed to victory, or to survival. Those who have remained steadfast will have helped to maintain the subtle links of morale, contributing to the steadfastness of all. Their names will never be known, and their reward will be that they have discovered resources in themselves of which they might otherwise have remained forever unaware. No man who has endured the ordeal of battle is ever quite the same again. He is usually better equipped to face whatever life may hold for him, including death.

There are many unrecorded battles on a small scale, involving perhaps no more than a company of men, a squadron of armour, in which the experience for those involved is total. A major battle is made up of numerous such encounters. The horizons of the ordinary soldier are not wide.

It follows, I think, that sensibility is one of the essential characteristics of the good general. A deep underlying awareness of these things, that they are going on nearly all the time, unrecorded in the War Diaries and reports above Brigade, or Division, will bestow upon such a man the imagination to grasp victory, to sense the factors that are not 'facts'.

Human progress has been achieved by men doing the impossible. It has been accepted as truth that war and politics are arts of the possible. At their highest they are more truly arts of the

[1] *The Rommel Papers*, p. 252.

impossible. The possible demands calculation, skill and choice. The impossible demands an imaginative faith in the ability of men to rise above all circumstances and difficulties, and to attain the sublime. Battles are won by brave men of great sensibility, and often great simplicity, infecting nameless ordinary men to do things that no training could achieve, and no orders demand. Victory is a jig-saw of actions, and splinters of actions, in which the heroic is an ingredient, and which fitted together produce a clear result. It is a result no computer could predict. Yet in the light of history men of rare quality will achieve greatness on a high level to match and to inspire the anonymous heroism of the ordinary men they lead. This is the crux of the matter.

Auchinleck, who could not conceive of any man being less brave than himself, and whose humility was profound, could achieve greatness, and did. Montgomery, who feared the unpredictable, who relied upon the textbook and training, and an assessment of the factors, denied himself the possibility to rise above competence. The vital factor of the human spirit eluded him. He imposed the strait jacket of his severe limitations upon his army. There is no training for leadership in war except on the battlefield. The great general projects his troops into situations in which the human spirit, which can and does transcend ordinary possibility, may operate. The timing is a matter of instinct. History is strewn with the impossible deeds of ordinary men and women. It is by knowing this, and believing in these things, that great leaders inspire their troops to grasp victory.

III

It must be remembered that in a battle involving armies seldom more than 10 per cent of the total strength is likely to be engaged in actual combat at any one time. In that light casualties should be considered. They may seem small in relation to the strength of the army, but to the units engaged they may be very heavy indeed. The Battle of Alam Halfa was a small battle. The initial assault of the enemy, forced to strike at positions some twenty miles to the west of his planned objectives, barely endured for twenty-four hours, employing in the main one armoured division. 'Rarely has any vital battle been as uneventful as that which is now engraved in history as the "Battle of Alam Halfa",' wrote Liddell Hart.[1]

Scores of greater encounters have failed to be 'engraved' at all. The War Diaries of the regiments involved are 'so flat' that they provide only 'the barest material' for the briefest description. Yet to the men of the 5th Royal Tank Regiment, who withstood direct assaults of the 15th Panzer Division, this may seem a statement to evoke guffaws of bitter scorn. The brunt of the enemy armoured attack fell upon the 22nd Armoured Brigade, and the anti-tank gunners. The 4th County of London Yeomanry were also heavily involved, and so was a raw infantry brigade of the New Zealand division in its abortive attempt to harass the retreating enemy. The 14th Essex Regiment on Ruweisat Ridge had an unpleasant time, and the 44th Division with the Greek and French brigades defending the Alam Halfa ridge were greatly heartened by their experience.

To the 13th Corps, commanded by the newly appointed Lieutenant-General Horrocks it had been a cheerful week. He was as new to the command of a corps as Montgomery was to the command of an army. He chafed somewhat at not being allowed to destroy the enemy. His feelings were widely shared.

> ... from the corps point of view it was an infernal nuisance to have the enemy sitting on this hill (Himeimat) from which he could observe everything that went on in the southern part of my sector. I should like to have driven him off Himeimat, which we could have done quite easily.[2]

But Montgomery easily convinced Horrocks that he was wrong. 'Leave them in possession of Himeimat. That is where I want them to be.'

If Montgomery said so, however odd it might seem, then it must be so.

To the Eighth Army as a whole the battle was extremely heartening. It confirmed them in their new strength, and in the quality of their equipment. The enemy had flung his armour against their left flank and had failed to make a dent.

---

[1] Liddell Hart, *The Tanks,* vol. ii, p. 218.
[2] Horrocks, *A Full Life.*

Again to quote Liddell Hart, perhaps the least controversial and undoubtedly the most scholarly of all students of this campaign: 'The battle was won by sitting tight—and offering no target—in a well chosen position that commanded the enemy's line of thrust, while the air force battered the attacking force—which could neither press an assault nor dare to push deeper.'[1]

It is possible to criticize Montgomery for placing his armoured brigades rather far apart, for the 8th was ten miles to the east of the 22nd, and would have borne the brunt of the enemy attack had he made the hoped for progress by night through the mine-field. As it was, the brunt fell upon the 22nd on the evening of the 31st, and by the morning of September 1st the 8th had arrived in support. The 22nd would have had a very sticky time if the enemy armour had been ready to attack earlier in the day. But on September 1st it became impossible for the enemy to continue, mainly owing to shortage of petrol and without hope of new supplies.

Thus far there had not been a test of Montgomery's generalship. He might say, but I doubt that he would, that since each of his armoured brigades almost equalled in strength the entire enemy armoured force, he could afford to split them rather widely. Major-General Gatehouse, recovered from his wounds, and one of the most experienced armoured commanders of the desert war, commanded the 10th Armoured Division of which the Brigades were a part. Brigadier Roberts, later to command the 11th Armoured Division, fought the 22nd Armoured Brigade with skill and fortitude. The 7th Armoured Division under Major-General Renton harried the enemy ceaselessly both in and out of the mine-fields, and the artillery of the New Zealand Division added greatly to the discomfiture of the enemy throughout the long nights of incessant bombardment from land and air. For three days and nights three divisions of the Afrika Korps with all their transport lay in the soft sand of the Ragil Depression in extreme danger of encirclement and total disaster. The area was a blazing inferno of vehicles. The narrow escape route was dominated by the British.

The test of Montgomery's generalship occurred as soon as it was clear that the enemy attack had failed.

---

[1] Liddell Hart, *The Tanks,* vol. ii, p. 218.

IV

Montgomery's failure to destroy the enemy at Alam Halfa must be a measure of his capacity as a general. Alan Moorehead, writing soon after these events, is as emphatic as Horrocks about Montgomery's intention:

> On one matter the C.-in-C. was especially emphatic. This was to be a static battle. Except in the fluid gap in the south no one was to budge an inch in any direction. It did not matter if the enemy were routed; there was to be no pursuit. Everyone must stand fast. The enemy must be beaten off and then left alone.[1]
>
> The reason for this was that the real conflict with Rommel was going to follow later on when everything was ready.

This, I believe, is a true statement and a remarkable one. Moorehead further comments:

> Even years afterwards it is not possible to extract the complete truth because by then the falsehoods of war have been repeated many times and become entrenched; documents are lost, the men, who together had a special intricate pattern of knowledge at some special place and time become dispersed and memory grows uncertain.[2]

The falsehoods of war certainly become entrenched, but one must not be daunted, and those who attempt to piece events together and discover truth should not give up in despair. Certainly some documents are lost, but many vital documents and personal records are preserved to challenge uncertain memory.

The commander of one of the divisions in the battle, a man of long experience in the Desert war before and after Alam Halfa, commented:

> Monty's reason for not destroying Rommel's armour etc. by counter-attack at Alam Halfa, south of Alamein, is altogether too thin. Who would let an enemy escape decisive defeat in order to guy him up as an Aunt Sally to be hit in a

[1] Alan Moorehead, *Montgomery*.
[2] *Ibid.*

set-piece attack 2 months later? The fact, of course, is that Monty was too static of mind to seize an opportunity. I wonder if he ever did seize an opportunity? My opinion is that this disability was responsible for his failure to exploit at Alamein and Akarit.'[1]

The answer to the first of these rhetorical questions is 'Montgomery', and to the second 'No'.

Montgomery's own reasons for not destroying the Afrika Korps are two:

> First, I was not too happy about the standard of training of the Army and also the equipment situation was unsatisfactory; time was needed to put these right. And secondly, I was not anxious to force Rommel to pull out and withdraw 'in being' back to the Agheila position . . . Thus the Battle of Alam Halfa ended in the way we wanted.[2]

Neither of these reasons is good. The training, while it might have left something to be desired by anyone as dedicated to training as Montgomery, was better than for some time, and certainly good enough. The equipment was excellent. Moreover, as I have pointed out, the odds in his favour when he broke off the battle had risen to five to one on the ground, and the three hundred new Sherman tanks had arrived in Egypt.

The second reason cannot be defended. 'It meant,' in Liddell Hart's assessment, 'forfeiting an extraordinarily good chance of destroying the whole German Afrika Korps before it could escape from the bag, in favour of a subsequent head-on and costly attack against Rommel's mined and fortified front—in which case Rommel would have a much better chance of retreating to Agheila if his front were eventually broken.[3]

Montgomery's failure seems to me implicit in his military career and military thinking from the beginning. He was an organiser and a fine 'manager'. He could not 'loose' his troops upon the enemy in his nature. He knew the theory of 'the expanding torrent' and the exploitation of the break-through, but he could not write it into the Training Manual. And he could not do it in the field.

[1] Private Papers.
[2] Montgomery *Memoirs*, p. 110.
[3] Private Papers of B. H. Liddell Hart. *The Tanks*, vol. ii, p. 225.

'My opinion then was, and still is,' said one of his commanders in the field, 'that Monty was living in 1918 and never left it.'

Nevertheless Montgomery had quickly appreciated the situation at Alam Halfa. In the early afternoon of September 1st he ordered the immediate preparation of a counterstroke and of a pursuit force 'to push through to Daba with all reserves available'. In common with every other order of that kind in his career it hung fire until too little and too late. Not until the night of September 3rd/4th was a limited attack ready to go in using elements of three infantry brigades, one of which was new and untried. The attack was launched against the corridor held by the 90th Light Division and the Italian *Trieste* Motorized Division. 'The attack became badly confused, suffered heavy losses, and was abandoned next day.'[1]

Slowly and steadily the Afrika Korps continued its withdrawal until on September 6th it resolved to stand on the high ground of Himeimat, six miles to the east of its start line.

Montgomery's comment is as follows:

> When I saw that Rommel's forces were in a bad way, I ordered a thrust southwards from the New Zealand Division area to close the gap through which they had entered our positions. The enemy reaction was immediate and violent; they began to pull back quickly to the area of our minefield through which they had originally come. We left them there, and I called off the battle.[2]

This statement covers seven days. It does not explain the delay in the counterattack, nor its weak nature. Moreover the enemy reaction was not immediate and violent, but by gradual stages.[3] It is difficult to avoid the conclusion that Montgomery was determined to stage the Battle of Alamein.

Nevertheless this may not have been Montgomery's decision even though he believes it to be. In considering the military performance of generals the political pressures to which they were subject must not be forgotten, even when such political pressures are not specifically documented, nor even voiced. In short, the military performances of the generals engaged in the

[1] Liddell Hart, *The Tanks*, vol. ii, p. 224.
[2] Montgomery *Memoirs*, p. 109.
[3] Maj.-Gen. Sir Howard Kippenberger, *Infantry Brigadier*, p. 211. London, Oxford University Press, 1949.

Desert should not be judged by purely military considerations. It was, for example, unwise of Rommel to follow up the Eighth Army beyond the Egyptian frontier after Tobruk. 'The air forces which should then have taken part in an attack on Malta had suddenly to join in an improvised pursuit and support the army as best they could. The result was that Malta began to strike again . . .'[1]

The result was a decisive factor in the defeat of Rommel at 1st Alamein, and again at Alam Halfa and 2nd Alamein. Had the enemy mounted powerful air attacks upon Malta and ensured supplies to the Panzer Armee Afrika, there would have been time to attempt the conquest of Egypt before the Eighth Army could be adequately reinforced.

As for Alam Halfa, the Official History describes Rommel's attack as 'wildly optimistic'. Success depended upon the D.A.K. advancing 30 miles by night over mined and unknown ground. Nothing could be more 'wildly optimistic', yet it is a loose form of words to use for an exploit arising out of despair, the last hopeless fling of a very sick man, denied supplies, and with all the forces of war moving inexorably against him. The only wise course would have been for Rommel to retreat to El Agheila, and finally to save his army. His political masters refused to consider his true military position and insisted virtually upon his destruction.

Montgomery's decision to break off the battle, and his 'fear' that Rommel might retreat to El Agheila, may have been dictated equally by political necessities. It was not enough to defeat Rommel, nor even to destroy him: it had to be a properly staged affair, politically and emotionally necessary at that time.

Thus 2nd Alamein has in it the elements of a last act in a tragedy, fore-ordained and inescapable for political reasons. Militarily, it need not have taken place at all.

---

[1] *The Mediterranean and Middle East*, vol. iii, p. 392.

CHAPTER SIX

The 15th September

I

LESS than a month before Rommel lay with three divisions at the mercy of the Eighth Army in the Ragil Depression, and was permitted to withdraw to occupy the commanding position of Himeimat, Churchill had sacked General Auchinleck and his Chiefs of Staff because Auchinleck had been unable to promise to attack and destroy the Panzer Armee Afrika by September 15th.

Before the end of July Churchill had been fully informed about the forthcoming Battle of Alam Halfa, and the assault of the Eighth Army planned for the end of September. He had studied the map of the Alamein position and the Appreciation dated July 27th. He knew of the reinforcements arriving and arrived. It was clear to him that if Rommel attempted to outflank the un-outflankable Alamein position at the time of the August moon, he would be in a trap. No man could doubt then or now—and Churchill did not doubt—that Auchinleck would have seized the opportunity for which he had fought and planned. So almost certainly would have Ramsden. These men had been long involved in this affair.

The break-up of the Middle East and army command had preserved Rommel and the Panzer Armee Afrika in being, and would continue to preserve him at least until the long-delayed battle planned to deliver the *coup de grâce* some time in late October.

It is clear that in the last days of July and the first days of August some particular significance had attached to September 15th in Churchill's mind, and that he felt that he must have a promise of Rommel's destruction by that date. I think it is clear also that the defeatist talk to which he had been exposed in London and Cairo had blinded him to the extent and nature of the defeat suffered by Rommel in July. The German-Italian army had not been merely halted, but pommelled into the ground beyond hope of redemption. The Royal Navy, sinking the enemy supply ships, and the Royal Air Force hammering his long communications, underlined the facts.

It seems certain that neither Alexander nor Montgomery would have dared to permit Rommel and his army to escape annihilation between September 1st and 4th had their jobs depended upon it. The priorities must have changed. It is not enough to examine Alexander's easy-going attitude or Montgomery's deep inhibitions to account for the enemy escape. Problems of this nature cannot be solved on the level of Middle East or Army command. As it was, Alexander endorsed Montgomery's decision to accept Rommel's withdrawal, to break off the battle and to prepare for his huge set-piece assault in his own time. None of this would have been acceptable to Churchill in early August. By the end of August the long delay had become merely irritating to a man of his urgent nature. September 15th had dropped out of mind.

The key to Churchill's behaviour may be found in his long struggle from the Arcadia conference onwards to persuade the Americans to mount the North African landings, known as 'Gymnast', 'Super Gymnast', and finally 'Torch'. Behind this idea lies far more than an attack on North Africa. It is the expression of his hopes and fears over the whole field of future strategy. To achieve his aim Churchill had to out-manoeuvre General Marshall and Admiral King before they were firmly in the saddle of war, and win over President Roosevelt to his view. At the heart of his problem lay the necessity to persuade the Americans that 'Sledgehammer', the proposed cross-channel attack in 1942, was impossible, and that his plan was the only reasonable means of bringing American troops into contact with the enemy in the Atlantic-European theatre.

'Sledgehammer', 1942, was an immediate casualty of Churchill's plan, and the Americans had accepted the loss with grave misgivings. It was then feared, and rightly, that the 1943 cross-channel assault, 'Round-Up', would be in jeopardy, and the distrust of British intentions took a powerful hold in the minds of General Marshall and Admiral King. Churchill assured them of his determination to mount 'Round-Up', and partially allayed their fears.

The following passage occurs in *Command Decisions:*

> The American military chiefs, Marshall and King . . . preferring the occupation of French North Africa with all its shortcomings to a campaign in the Middle East or Norway . . . reluctantly accepted 'Super-Gymnast' ('Torch'). On July 24 a carefully worded agreement, drawn up by Marshall and known as CCS 94, was accepted by the Combined Chiefs of Staff. It contained the important condition that the *CCS would postpone until mid-September final decision on whether or not the North African operations should be undertaken.* (The date September 15 was chosen because it was considered the earliest possible date on which the outcome in Russia could be forecast). *If at that time the Russians clearly faced a collapse that would release so many German troops that a cross-channel attack in the spring of 1943 would be impractical, the North Africa invasion would be launched before December 1.* Meanwhile planning for 'Round-Up' would continue.[1]

Here is September 15th, and clear evidence that Marshall and King, despite Churchill's assurances, feared that 'Round-Up' and 'Torch' could not both take place. Thus, at the end of July following the Whitehall conference the issue remained uncertain. It was still uncertain when Churchill embarked for Cairo to confront Auchinleck with his impossible demand for Rommel's destruction by September 15th, and went on from there to confront Stalin in Moscow with an empty bag—unless he could promise 'Torch', and half promise 'Round-Up'.

On July 30th Churchill telegraphed Stalin in regard to his proposed visit: 'I could then tell you the plans we have made with President Roosevelt for offensive action in 1942.'

Meanwhile he had carefully pressed Roosevelt to commit himself to 'Torch' not later than October 30th, behind the backs of Marshall and King. Roosevelt, he knew, was sympathetic to the idea of a North African landing.

The issue was still in doubt when Churchill reached Cairo, and time was running out fast. Somehow he had to beat the deadline of September 15th, and lever 'Torch' away from dependence on

---

[1] Howe, *Command Decisions*, p. 186. Office of Chief of Military History, Washington, 1960.

the Russian situation. Auchinleck, of course, was unaware of these issues, but the Prime Minister was looking for levers wherever he might find them. On August 6th he cabled the War Cabinet: 'A victory over Rommel in August or September may have a decisive effect upon the attitude of the French in North Africa when 'Torch' begins.'[1]

This is a mere groping for justification. The French would not be influenced one way or the other, but Marshall and King might have been softened by a British victory. In a fury with Auchinleck for not only not playing his game, but for not knowing there was a game, Churchill left for Moscow, and committed himself to Stalin. When he returned home towards the end of August he was still uneasy. On July 31st he had suggested that General Marshall should be the Supreme Commander for the 1943 cross-channel attack, but had failed to convince the US Chief of Staff of his commitment.

On August 26th and 27th the Prime Minister sent long messages to President Roosevelt. They should be read in full. The message of August 26th reads, in part: 'It would be an immense help if you and I were to give Eisenhower a directive something like this: "You will start 'Torch' on October 14 attacking with such troops as are available and at such places as you deem fit." This will alter the whole character of preparations.'[2]

September 15th is still a long way off. CCS 94 is ignored. Indeed it cannot be discovered from Churchill's account that 'Round-Up', the situation on the Russian front, and 'Torch' are in any way connected. But Churchill had persuaded himself that the situation in the Western Desert was highly relevant. The penultimate paragraph of the letter of the 26th reads: 'It is evident that these assumptions would be greatly helped by a battle won in the Western Desert. Either Rommel attacks us by the August moon or we shall attack him by the end of September.'[3]

This was precisely Auchinleck's appreciation, and for which he was sacked. September 15th has disappeared from Churchill's mind as a deadline. Among the assumptions in his letter to the

---

[1] Churchill, *The Hinge of Fate*, vol. iv, R.U. ed., p. 379
[2] *Ibid.*, p. 427.
[3] *Ibid.*, p. 428.

President was the possibility of a 'bold audacious bid for a bloodless victory' in North Africa.

Despite Roosevelt's personal commitment to 'Torch', his Chiefs of Staff were not done with, and on September 4th Churchill wrote anxiously to Hopkins. It was an oblique approach to the President 'off the record', and not to be shown 'to our great friend' if Hopkins judged that it 'would vex him'.

> I am deeply perturbed by the way 'Torch' is being knocked about, and above all the needless delays, which add so much to our joint troubles. It had been a long and slow business getting rid of 'Sledgehammer', but when you left here on July 25 all was set for full steam ahead. and I certainly thought that *Marshall had reconciled himself to the President's final decision* ... until a week ago there was no reason why we should not have made the date October 15 ... I thought there was agreement with Marshall and that King had been paid off with what he needed for his Pacific war. But now it seems there is a bad come-back from the professional circles in the American Army, and I have a deep and growing fear that the whole of *the President's enterprise may be wrecked bit by bit* ... Now the earliest that can be hoped for is the first week of November.[1]

As a side issue of minor importance only Alexander and Montgomery could have been pleased about the delay in mounting 'Torch'. If the North African landings had taken place in mid-October there would not have been much gilt on the gingerbread of Alamein II. It might not have been fought at all.

It is clear that Churchill was finding it far more difficult to get rid of 'Round-Up' than it had been to get rid of 'Sledgehammer'. 'Sledgehammer', in a sense, got rid of itself, but the jettisoning of 'Round-Up' is Churchill's triumph.

Neither Marshall nor King were ever truly reconciled, and it was because of this skullduggery, as he undoubtedly saw it, that King turned his face to the Pacific, and starved the Atlantic theatre of landing craft until the end. The President himself ignored the proviso of CCS 94, and in so doing

> effectively jettisoned 'Round-Up' for 1943 ... although Marshall must have realised the fatal impact of Roosevelt's

---

[1] Churchill, *The Hinge of Fate,* vol. iv, R.U. ed., p. 435-6.

action on 'Round-Up', he was reluctant to view it as one that eliminated the conditions stipulated in CCS 94. At the first meeting of the Combined Chiefs of Staff held after his return to Washington he therefore refrained from accepting the 'decision' as final and pointed out that the mounting of 'Torch' did not mean the abandoning of 'Round-Up' . . . Nor was Admiral King willing to admit that the President had fully decided to abandon 'Round-Up' as well as 'Sledgehammer' in favour of 'Torch'.[1]

The President and the Prime Minister were not playing precisely the same game. They were both playing politics, but the President's politics were based on US power in the Atlantic and the Pacific, and a future seen from the power hub of the Americas. The Prime Minister, on the other hand, had absorbed the complexities of European ambitions in his infancy. He had lived with the fall of the great dynasties, and known almost at first hand of the intrigues of Germany, Russia and Turkey in the last ominous years of the nineteenth century. Railway lines were threatening sea lanes as the keys to power and empires. In 1897 the Deutsche Bank had financed the first leg of the Anatolian line from the Bosphorus that would one day reach Baghdad and the Persian Gulf. Here were potent German dreams involving Russia, Turkey and the Near East. Overland also lay the Far East, and the warm water Pacific port Russia must have. And suddenly, unexpectedly, Japan stood in the way in the Far East, as Turkey had stood in the way in the Near East.

From 1898 the end of the century was filled, in the Far East, by bitter squabbles between the European Powers and fierce scrambles for railway concessions and spheres of influence.[2]

Britain watched from the side-lines while Japan doubled her army and trebled her fleet. These things were indelible patterns in Churchill's mind, fashioning his strategic thinking and his attitudes. Greece, Turkey and the Balkans were key pieces on the board in an intricate struggle, with Germany and Russia the leading protagonists, their antagonism veiled by a surface

[1] Howe, *Command Decisions*, p. 187.
[2] J. L. Garvin, *These Eventful Years*, Enc. Brit. Co.

harmony. When the German Emperor had proclaimed himself the protector of the Moslems at Damascus in 1898, 'it introduced a secret but mortal discord into Russo-German relations'.[1]

As for Churchill, even then as a young man, all this territory, all this intrigue, all the Near and Middle East was in his mind and eyes. Now as an old man in 1942 this was still his battlefield. He had not forgotten, nor would ever forget, the Dardanelles, nor would he ever forget the vast slaughter of a generation of the British people in Western Europe. Can anyone be astonished that he should seek to avoid another blood bath in Western Europe?

The real rift between British and United States strategy was as wide and deep as the Atlantic Ocean. But it was veiled.

It may be profitless to consider the 'ifs' of these fateful days. While many of the old ingredients of conflict remained, neither Britain nor Germany were any longer the main contestants in the great struggle. The autumn of 1942 was the hinge of history. The United States and Russia were the new protagonists. Henceforth there was a new war demanding a new strategy. When the Russian front held in the autumn of 1942 the combined strategy of the United States and Britain should have been a cross-channel attack in 1943, and the devil take diversions.

The conference in London of July 25th when Churchill hoped that 'all was set for full steam ahead' on 'Torch', was the veritable 'Hinge of Fate' for Britain. The United States, with its immense power waxing fast and not yet ready to take full command, and to assert her authority. Britain, with her power rapidly waning, made through the Prime Minister a tremendous bid to impose her will upon the pattern of war. The Mediterranean and the Middle East were Britain's battlefields in a power context that was disappearing fast. Marshall's instincts were sound.

II

In the midsummer and autumn of 1942 Hitler's military decisions involved his armies in catastrophe, yet it is improbable that any course or courses he had pursued, other than personal suicide, would have had a less disastrous result for Germany. At Casablanca in January 1943 the declaration of 'Unconditional

[1] J. L. Garvin, *These Eventful Years*, Enc. Brit. Co.

Surrender' by the President of the United States and the Prime Minister of Great Britain accepted total warfare on Hitler's terms, and underlined the hopelessness of the German position. Moreover it accepted a revolution in the purposes of war and politics. It signalled a new kind of Europe and a new kind of world. Only the USSR could accept this verdict with equanimity, for the total destruction of Germany would preserve her great internal empire, and present her with the buffer states against the West which she had so long, and so sorely needed. Without a strong Germany there would be a power vacuum in the heart of Europe. Thus in the hour of her waning strength Britain was confronted with new and complex problems. It was no longer a question of survival and of the preservation of as much of British world power as might be possible, but of winning the war in a certain way. It must become a race between Britain and the USSR to reach certain key areas, notably the Balkans, Berlin and Vienna. The only hope for Britain was to persuade the United States to these ends, and to convince her of the political purposes of war. It was a forlorn hope. The United States was a newcomer to these old patterns of war and politics. She distrusted them profoundly. Her purpose was victory and the destruction of the enemy militarily in the most direct manner possible.

Hitler, it could be seen, was the catalyst of a disaster on an immense scale. Compromise had become impossible. In his early days in Austria before the First World War Hitler had become a vessel of Germanic myths. He had absorbed the Pan-German propaganda of Georg von Schönerer and Karl Hermann Wolf calling for German expansion, and proclaiming German superiority over Jews and Slavs. In the eighteenth century the Germans conceived the Rhine as peculiarly their river, from its source in the Swiss Alps through all its course of 700 miles to the Netherlands and the North Sea. It not only belonged to Germany, but so also did the Germanic-speaking peoples of the Baltic provinces, the Low countries, Alsace and Switzerland. Stoked by intellectuals from Arndt to the naturalized German-Englishman, Houston Chamberlain, these turgid emotional beliefs grew to embrace Scandinavia, and in 1915 Friedrich Naumann envisaged a German Mittel-Europa from Antwerp to the Persian Gulf.

It was a potent brew, and in 1917 the Treaty of Brest-Litovsk foreshadowed a middle German 'empire' that would have come true but for their defeat by the Western Allies in 1918. Pan-Germanism never died. It was the creed of Hitler from his earliest days, and in the middle of 1942 with all central Europe, the Balkans, Western Russia and the Ukraine, together with France, the Netherlands, Norway and Denmark, in German hands, with Italy and Spain under Fascist dictators, it seemed to Hitler that he had been the instrument of German destiny, and that he could not and must not fail. Southeastward lay the final dream of Empire expounded by Naumann.

Perhaps there was no going back. Perhaps it no longer mattered what course Germany might choose. But it was this dream, far more than the need for oil, that forced Hitler to commit von Paulus and the Sixth Army to the disastrous defence of Stalingrad, and drove von Kleist to the Caucasus. It was madness. It blinded Hitler to the defeat of Rommel by Auchinleck in July, and should have condemned the German-Italian army in North Africa to destruction at Alamein II.

There were, in Hitler's mind, no alternative strategies grand or small. It was all or nothing. There was no compromise. The German armies, still immensely powerful, were too thin on the ground to hold what they had, yet to shorten the lines, to withdraw, even to strike telling blows, and to negotiate for peace, was impossible for Hitler. He confronted, and forced his generals and armies, and all Germans, to confront the meaning of total war. He had denied himself the options hitherto available to conquerors who knew when to stop. He would drive on to the bitter end.

Strategists have seen quite clearly the courses open to the German armies in Russia in that midsummer and autumn of 1942. Militarily it is clear that he could have moved north-east to seize Saratov and outflank Moscow. He could afford to leave the West to look after itself for at least twelve months. Churchill's strategic bombing programme had denied to the British the landing craft and aircraft they needed to operate as a sea and land power, and had exposed Britain to defeat in the Atlantic.

In the event the defeat of the German 6th Army at Stalingrad, von Kleist's abortive advance to the south-east, and the sacrifice of Rommel in North Africa seem fore-ordained. Hitler could not admit the failure of the Afrika Korps even in the last fateful days of Alamein II when he compelled his defeated army to stand and fight, and compromised the retreat to Fuka.

It had been a tragic story from the beginning. It could only end in tragedy. The war was lost and won, but millions of many races were yet to die, and millions more to suffer torments to sear the imagination of mankind. All the doors to sanity were shut.

PART THREE

ANATOMY OF A LEGEND

CHAPTER SEVEN

2nd Alamein

I

IN the twelve days and nights from the night of October 23rd to November 4th, a German-Italian army, heavily outnumbered in men, overwhelmingly inferior in armour, artillery, ammunition and equipment of all kinds, deficient in petrol, and denied manoeuvre or reinforcement, inflicted severe casualties in men and armour on the British army commanded by General Montgomery. Four times the British attacks were fought to a standstill. Moreover, although halted in the midst of successful disengagement and withdrawal, and compelled by order of Adolf Hitler to stand and fight in the Alamein positions, the German commander again succeeded in extricating remnants of his army, to evade his pursuers and to fight successful rearguard actions to the frontiers of Tunisia. The second battle of Alamein was a battle of attrition, a 'Passchendaele with armour', a battle without hope for the enemy, and in which the victors could afford to trade life, arms and armour at more than four to one.

The odds in the British favour are difficult to assess. The superiority in effective tanks was 6 to 1, and with reserves available to bring the odds up to 11 to 1. In men the British had a majority of 8 to 1 over the Germans, and 3 to 1 over the Germans and Italians combined. But the Italian equipment was so poor that the fighting value of the troops was estimated at less than one third of that of the Germans. It is a miracle that the Italians fought so well. But the real odds against the enemy were far greater than these figures suggest. Day and night the enemy was subjected to an immense weight of bombardment from the air and from ground artillery against which he had no effective reply.

In spite of destroying more than three British tanks for each one of his own, the odds against the enemy lengthened steadily. At Tel Aquaquir 90 German tanks fought 700 British tanks to a standstill. At the end the armoured odds in the British favour had reached 20 to 1.

Odds of 5 to 1 are not excessive in favour of an attacker attempting to break through a strong defensive position, but in this instance odds alone do not give a clear picture. The enemy defended a thirty-five mile front, and was thin on the ground for such a coverage. One of his most severe handicaps was the limited movement of his armour due to insufficient petrol. Once he had decided to transfer an armoured division from south to north there was no going back. Thus he was hesitant to do so. Moreover, he was greatly handicapped by the need to conserve ammunition, and was thereby inhibited from shelling the British in their assembly areas. The enemy problem was not to win the battle—which was impossible—but to prevent the British from 'fixing him' and destroying him. He had to save his men and armour from a total involvement from which there would be no escape, and establish and maintain a situation enabling him to disengage and withdraw to a succession of strong defensive positions from Fuka to the Mareth line.

This great and terrible battle, almost certainly the crowning achievement of the Panzer Armee Afrika, even in defeat—a 'Desert Dunkirk'—was also a British victory. It established the reputation of General Montgomery, and became a legend. There was, and is, no mystery about the battle. The troops on both sides fought with dogged courage, and with an endurance that was at times miraculous. It is a humbling experience to study and to contemplate such a battle, and to marvel at the resources of the human spirit.

Whatever the faults on the British side they did not lie with the troops. Major-Generals and Brigadiers led the British armour in the van, and their example was emulated all the way down. The responsibility lies firmly, and peculiarly, upon the army commander, General Montgomery. Whatever there may be of praise or blame is rightly his. His conception of leadership and his management of men make this inescapable.

II

From the beginning Montgomery's freedom from political, or indeed from any kind of interference, was unprecedented. His

Commander-in-Chief, Alexander, in Cairo, himself relaxed and freed from the immense strategic, political and military problems that had burdened Wavell and Auchinleck beyond endurance, nursed his army commander in every possible way, providing all that he desired, and advising so unobtrusively that Montgomery seemed unaware of it. In mid-September Alexander had dealt with Churchill's mild protest that he had been promised the battle of Alamein at the end of the month: 'My understanding with you,' Churchill cabled, 'was the fourth week in September.'[1]

To which Alexander replied: 'I have carefully considered the timing in relation to "Torch", and have come to the conclusion that the best date for us to start would be minus 13 of "Torch".'

The message is nonchalant, almost saucy. So much for Auchinleck, who had never heard of 'Torch', and so much for the necessity to mount Alamein as an important influencing factor in September.

'We are in your hands,' Churchill cabled, and went on gloomily to imagine the enemy taking advantage of the long delay to strengthen his defences beyond all possibility.

The dreaded Field-Marshal Rommel handed over the command of his Army to General von Stumme on September 22nd, and left for home on the following day 'with a heavy heart'. He desperately needed rest and treatment. But for Churchill and Montgomery his presence remained. A photograph of Rommel, his great antagonist, adorned the wall of Montgomery's caravan, together with quotations revealing an inner romanticism entirely lacking from his physical performance. Alongside Drake's prayer on the morning of Cadiz, and Henry V's cry:

O God of battles! steel my soldier's hearts

were the words of James Graham, Marquis of Montrose:

He either fears his fate too much,
Or his deserts are small,
Who dare not put it to the touch,
To win or lose it all.

Very soon Montgomery's own words would sing to the

---

[1] Churchill, *The Hinge of Fate*, vol. iv, R.U. ed., p. 474.

listening world, and few would note that they bore very little relevance to his deeds.

In mid-September it was clear that the dreadful urgencies that had led to the dismissal of the Commander-in-Chief and his Staffs, had disappeared. Montgomery, quite unmoved, even seeming unaware of Churchill's mild reminder to Alexander, was going ahead in his own slow and cautious time. He would launch his offensive when victory was certain, and not before. This was his invariable rule, and it was his astounding fortune that he would be able to stick to it to the war's end. On these terms the attacks of Wavell's generals resulting in the disastrous defeat of the Italian armies would never have been launched; nor would Auchinleck's generals have assaulted the enemy. There had been no certainty in the Desert war until Auchinleck had saved Egypt at Alamein.

These things were swiftly and easily forgotten. A new era of power had dawned. Fortune had eliminated the normal risks of battle, and thereby changed the hitherto imperative attributes of generalship. It was difficult to believe in September that this was the battlefield of July, and of the years before. The army itself was barely recognizable. Of the old senior commanders only Ramsden and Lumsden remained, and they were doomed. New divisions, new and more powerful armour, self-propelled guns and immense reinforcements of artillery, poured in. This was Montgomery's army, and he was tireless in his determination to imprint himself upon it, and to fashion it according to his desires. Incessantly on the move, he swiftly made his presence felt throughout all ranks. Troops were forewarned to 'down tools' and to leap to attention at his approach. 'Impromptu' meetings with isolated units were carefully planned for the benefit of important visitors, and the general soon came to believe that these reactions were spontaneous. He returned salutes with gusto.

Montgomery swiftly established his absolute authority, using his Chief of Staff as a kind of 'Personnel Manager', and confidential 'henchman', while his corps commanders acted as his 'overseers' in the field. Training had always been a fetish. He had expressed himself critically and forcibly on this matter from the first days of his coming, and imposed new and rigid training schedules. In fact there was very little wrong with the state of training of the old Eighth Army, and it would have fought as well in late September as it did in late October. It might have fought better. One of the leading Divisional Commanders, a man long tried and proved in battle, commented:

> When he talks nonsense about training among these troops, one wonders what he expected, or if he referred to the 9th Australian Division who did nearly all the fighting for him at Alamein. To say that he developed his plan to attack in the North because of poor training of his troops is rubbish. If you have ill-trained troops do you throw them at the strongest part of the position as pure cannon fodder? If so, you're a fool.[1]

Montgomery's training methods were in the main old-fashioned, derived from the First World War and painfully orthodox. He did not seem to appreciate that the forward areas are the finest training grounds of all. He had been a peace-time trainer.

> If Monty (wrote a Divisional Commander), instead of making his officers run seven miles a day, had made them turn out and train themselves on the ground, and teach themselves and their men a little battle-skill, they would have got the same physical exercise and learnt to use their brains.[2]

All that Auchinleck had tried to do, and had begun to do to restore the faith of the infantry in the armour, to integrate these two services as fighting implements, was rapidly undone. The new mobile divisions of infantry, armour and artillery, training together, working together, fighting together were isolated again into their old forms, and only the New Zealand Division, which was to bear the brunt throughout Montgomery's campaign in Africa, remained organized in the way Auchinleck had hoped to establish. This was due to General Freyberg's friendship with Churchill.

Auchinleck had sacked General McCreery for his resistance to the new methods proved in the Desert. Alexander at once restored him, nominated him his Chief of Staff, and established the 'Cavalry Club' firmly in the saddle. Montgomery's 'Corps de Chasse', the 10th Corps, was swiftly formed, and armour and

---

[1] and [2] Private letters in the Archives of B. H. Liddell Hart.

infantry divorced at a stroke. The army commander himself was the only man who could then direct the two distinct forces that would have to fight in close co-operation. Corps commanders and divisional commanders could no longer co-ordinate infantry and armour in battle. 'It was like asking an estranged man and his wife to make love,' Correlli Barnett commented.[1] It was a shocking idea, but it meant that Montgomery himself would have full personal control of the coming battle.[2]

Montgomery distrusted all experience save his own. Yet distrust is not the right word: he did not seem able to comprehend that there could be valid experience in which he had not shared. He could not bear to 'inherit' anything, or even to accept that anything good had gone before. He wanted not only his own senior commanders, 'his chaps', but his own divisions, trained by his methods by his men. Divisions that were not in some way his must be inferior, and he could and did keep such divisions out of the line until and unless forced to use them in fighting roles.

The strange streak of extreme meanness that was to deny to the old Eighth Army its 'Star' springs from Montgomery's inability to accept, even thought, from anyone else. Thus there was only one kind of training, his training, one kind of fighting, his fighting, one kind of leadership, his leadership. Those who sought to influence him exercised extreme caution, always careful to ensure that all decisions must seem to be his own, and that at all costs the general's infallibility must be preserved.

III

Immediately after Alam Halfa Montgomery set his staff to the planning of his offensive. There were, of course, numerous plans in embryo. Ramsden had been instructed by Auchinleck in early August to work intensively on a plan 'for a deliberate attack south of the Tel el Eisa salient with a view to making a rapid advance along the coast road.'

It was the nucleus of this plan that Montgomery adopted as his own, announcing that since everyone had previously attacked in the south he would attack in the north. Meanwhile, elaborate

---

[1] Barnett, *The Desert Generals*, p. 265.
[2] This was the heresy Auchinleck had called 'an army within an army'. It delayed our correct use of armour.

deception plans were evolved to induce the enemy to expect the main attack in the south. Activity throughout the whole army was intense. New divisions and new weapons and equipment had to be integrated daily. 1,000 new six-pounder anti-tank guns and more than 1,000 guns of medium artillery, together with vast dumps of ammunition, fortified the British. In addition 100 self-propelled guns of 105 mm. calibre had reached the Eighth Army with 300 of the new and powerful Sherman tanks, for which crews had to be trained. These things demanded brilliant organization.

The confidence of the Eighth Army was superb. Montgomery told them that they could not lose and were certain of victory. They believed him. He had briefed all commanders down to Lieutenant-Colonels. His manner was crisp, bleak, convincing. He reduced the most complex problems to simplicity. He laid down exactly how the coming battle would be fought, and made it clear that he would personally conduct the whole orchestra down to the smallest detail. In effect he imposed a strait-jacket upon himself and his troops. Only very junior commanders were able to retain the freedom and initiative without which an army would become a robot thing.

Montgomery planned to launch his attack at the time of the late October moon. He made no reference to 'Torch', or to Alexander, but it is significant that the October moon coincided with 'Torch' minus 13. In the event 'Torch' was delayed for four days. It was Montgomery's purpose and clear object not merely to defeat the enemy—which was certain—but to destroy him. He gave the impression that he knew exactly how the battle would be fought. There would be no argument, and in a sense no enemy, not, at any rate, to have a say in the outcome. He referred to his 'Master Plan', as though this were some new concept in plans from which all possibility of failure had been eliminated.

An army commander is normally a remote figure to the 'common soldier', and whatever the physical and mental stature of such a man he is of far less importance to the men of a platoon or a troop than their lieutenant. A good battalion commander is the absolute leader of his troops. He is the man known to them, the head of their family, and the arbiter of their fate. His fate is closely involved with their own. Above that the man in the front line rarely looks. He is involved in battles limited to a few square yards, and often these 'battles' occur at times when the 'Army' is unaware of any kind of battle. The news of a violent platoon engagement might not reach Brigade or Division. Patrolling is incessant between armies in contact, and few activities of war are more dangerous or more demanding in nerve and morale.

The Divisional commander, the Corps commander, is a symbol rather than a real person to the troops. Profoundly pessimistic and totally involved in an alien occupation of strange fascination, the private soldier inhabits a small personal world in which survival is paramount. Victory is as dangerous as defeat. His morale depends upon the excellence of his personal weapons, the reliability of his immediate companions in ordeal, the courage and common decency of his commander, and the ability of artillery and aircraft in his support.

General Montgomery became at first a symbol and then a 'mascot' to the new Eighth Army. His arrival coincided not only with victory, but with their immense reinforcement in arms, equipment and men. He was the new man of the new era to lead them on the long march home. But there is an aura of power, a *mystique*, that removes an army commander from kinship with his fellows, even from those of high rank immediately under him. Power confers isolation, and isolation was peculiarly appropriate to General Montgomery. In a sense he had at last risen to the point where he could be simply himself. His behaviour was of a new kind in the British Army. He was the leader, and all others would do as they were told. He was a natural exponent of the 'leadership principle', a method that has become known in the twentieth century as the 'Führer Prinzep'. It is a method generally alien to the British character, but it can be immensely effective. It denies dignity.

The aim of leadership at its best must be to arouse loyalty and confidence, and to inspire men to discover their talents, and to enrich their community in war and peace by their individuality. Their obedience is freely given and never docile. Such is the democratic ideal. Men of the stature of Auchinleck aroused the kind of faith in men that made such leadership possible. Men did not know whether he would win their battles, but they knew that he was with them, totally involved with them, and that whatever happened he would be responsible. General Slim's leadership was of the same quality, and so also on a lower level was General O'Connor's. In the Eighth Army, divisional commanders like Francis Tuker, Gatehouse, Briggs, Ramsden,[1] and Freyberg aroused the best that was in their men. All these leaders retained the loyalty and confidence of their troops in adversity.

Since Montgomery's armies were never to know adversity or to meet the attacks of an enemy on equal terms, it can never be known how his troops would have reacted to his leadership. It is certain that Montgomery excelled in defence, and it is a strange irony that he should have been called to high command in the the hour of victory, and when his role was to move forward in overwhelming strength against an enemy whose only way was the way back.

Montgomery's name became a symbol of victory, but his type of leadership, manifest after the war in his attitudes to dictatorships in various parts of the world, was undoubtedly of an autocratic nature.

The attributes (of the leadership principle) may be listed as follows: that the will and desire of the leader shall dominate the scene without the countenancing of open criticism, objection or resistance; that some illusion of participation or consent among the followers shall be built up; that some 'scapegoat' mechanism is employed through which difficulties and adversities for which the leader is responsible may be blamed upon others; that the leader alleges he is endowed with unique eminence which may result in imputing to him some status akin to deity; that the total cause espoused, however much it may seem to be invested with social concern, is essentially a forwarding of the selfish interest of the leader.[2]

Montgomery would not tolerate criticism. Whatever happened he was always right. In the midst of battle he threatened Lumsden, his Armoured Corps commander, and Gatehouse and Briggs, two of his armoured divisional commanders, with the sack. Virtually he accused two of his most brave and tried generals of cowardice when his offensive came near to disaster. He rarely admitted to any kind of failure, nor did he acknowledge any cause for success outside himself. Yet at his worst he was never a sinister figure. The lonely, ardent,

[1] Commanded 50th Division.
[2] Orward Tead, *Enc. Brit.*, 'The Art of Leadership.'

anxious boy was not deeply buried within the man. In many ways he resembled Baden-Powell, and would certainly have printed postage stamps with his image upon them, given the chance; nor would his leadership have been damaging to boy scouts. In that kind of milieu he might have found himself. He did not fear the young, nor did he bully them.

By the time Montgomery was ready to launch the second battle of Alamein he had become known to an unusually high proportion of the Eighth Army. Certainly the reactions of the veterans of the Desert war would have been very different from those of the new arrivals. To the veterans his newness and extreme cockiness, his implicit rejection of their old commanders, and of their own long struggle, would have provoked dislike. Their past was all that they possessed, and he wrote it off. No doubt he wished all the army to be as new as he was himself, all his 'chaps', and he strove to make it so. His image was not yet fixed either in the public or the military mind. The search for a hat to reveal his thin, sharp-featured face at its best, was pursued urgently. The Australian hat looked awful. The orthodox peaked cap was good, but not good enough. In that he was simply another general, only slightly smaller, sharper, more talkative and dogmatic.

On October 23rd Montgomery called a Press Conference. Throughout the whole army there was the tenseness and potent quiet that precedes battle. The moment all had waited for had at last arrived. Many had seen their last sunset, and some would never see another dawn. Perhaps only the dead might give a true verdict upon a leader. The verdict of the survivors is always coloured by the outstanding fact of survival. Whatever the mistakes, they were successful: they did not die.

IV

The confrontation of General Montgomery and the war correspondents in his tent at Bourg El Arab on the evening of October 23, 1942, was an event of great significance, and all those present sensed that this was so. For all it was a unique experience. There had been many press-conferences, and many addressed by generals, but none like this. The General himself was unlike any other general his audience had encountered in

General Montgomery, Commander of the Eighth Army, in his famous hat with the badges of many units serving with him.

General Montgomery inspecting men of the 5th Brigade, New Zealand Division. October 1942.

Outside Homs, General Montgomery stops for a discussion with some of his officers. He is here seen talking to the BGS Brigadier Erskine. January 1943.

war or peace. He had the manner of an impresario, a kind of military Barnum presenting 'the Greatest Show on Earth', and with himself playing the lead. 'It has always been my policy that we shall not have any more failures,' he announced briskly. He stressed the importance of morale, as though it were a quality he had invented. Failures were due to 'faulty command and bad staff work. The soldiery—use that good old-fashioned word—will never let you down'.[1]

The implications of the General's crisp remarks were not lost on his audience. Perhaps he was unaware of the profound scepticism of the best of these men; unaware of the nature of their experiences, even of their scholarship, their bitter knowledge of the 'fog of war' and their intimacy with such factors as morale, and death. Of course there were shallow and cynical and ignorant men amongst them, and others who had succumbed to the peculiar temptations of their profession. In Cairo and Alexandria there was not only comfort, luxury and vice, but there were also communications without which a correspondent cannot function. The demands of newspapers are insatiable and as constant as hunger. In Cairo news of a sort abounded. One did not need even to seek interviews, or to buttonhole brigadiers in bars. One simply listened. The myrmidons of an enormous General Headquarters Staff abounded, and there was a constant traffic to and from the field.

The exigencies of war, the immense areas to be covered, the fluid nature of the military operations, the total absorption of commanders and men in the struggle had meant that a war correspondent must be dedicated and inspired to observe and evaluate the variegated pieces in the puzzle of war. Only genius might hope to fit such pieces together. Facilities in the forward areas were either non-existent or primitive. It is virtually impossible for a war correspondent to go into battle with leading troops unless he is 'on the strength', provided with transport, and able to fend for himself in unpredictable situations. If he is able to advance with troops to engage the enemy, and not simply to pursue him, the experience may be of little or no use to his newspaper.

Those directly involved in conflict at close quarters have no time or place to talk. Moreover soldiers share with the bulk of

---

[1] Alexander Clifford, *Three against Rommel*. London, Harrap, 1946.

their fellow men a dislike of having their privacy invaded, their thoughts probed, their hopes and fears exposed. To most soldiers, from generals to privates, personal publicity was offensive, and to be avoided.

Above all, the war correspondent returning weary from the battlefield would almost certainly discover a message from his editor demanding to know why 'unnews', and how their trusted representative had contrived to miss the news of a victory. At times the 'victory' was mythical, but it was invariably best to leave things as they were, relying on time to do its work. Echoing Pilate many were to cry, usually in simulated despair, 'What is Truth?' 'All that I have to do is to give the world the facts,' wrote Denis Johnston. 'But the trouble is, there are no facts. Or perhaps more truly, there are too many of them, and none of them strictly true.'[1]

In the field there were the 'Facts' of the front-line soldier, the 'Facts' of Division, Corps and Army, all at variance, and behind the lines in Cairo there were the facts as seen by the Allied Embassies, and their senior Staffs. The shrewd journalist produced his own version of events, probably as sincerely as anyone else.

> A crooked propagandist does not really have to invent a single lie. And overriding all this hangs a great blanket of fog and confusion through which one can dimly perceive that nobody has a very clear picture at all of what is going on. Not the soldiers—not the Generals—least of all, the Military Spokesmen! Nobody is in a position to place a finger unerringly on the points that really matter, and say This is the Truth about the situation.[2]

This basic situation was complicated by the boyish exuberance of General Montgomery. The 'Facts' remained abundant, contradictory and elusive, but Montgomery believed himself to be the one man 'to place a finger unerringly on the points that really matter, and say, This is the Truth about the situation'. He continued to believe this even when announcing contradictory 'Facts' within a matter of hours. The upshot was, at times, hilarious, and acutely embarrassing to Military Spokes-

---

[1] and [2] Johnston, *Nine Rivers from Jordan*, p. 111.

men. The General signalled 'important victories', on one of which Johnston commented: 'George (Haughton) eventually showed me Monty's signal before we went to bed. In it he wrote off an entire Panzer Division and most of the 90th Light—for the second time in a month.'

And there was the case of 'The Mythical Battle of Matratin', which produced a heart cry from the Desert: 'Loud belly laughs resound through the desert when the news is heard giving Cairo talking about Rommel's forces being cut in two. It is just nonsense. Can't someone *tell* them! *It is not true.*'[1]

The only man never in the least put out by these anomalies was the General himself; nor did he modify his words to fit them more soberly to his deeds. With increasing enthusiasm he continued to 'hit the enemy for six' while stonewalling a steady flow of cautious singles. The fact is that on November 4th the enemy visibly, for all to see, began his weary trek home, and a great many men, including war correspondents, joyously mounting General Montgomery's band-waggon, followed him all the way. The pattern of war became clear while the detail remained obscure.

With the coming of Montgomery a new era had dawned for war correspondents. They were the instruments whereby his fame and fortunes would be broadcast to the world. Their task was to tell in glowing terms of Britain's victory in the desert, and of the General who was the symbol of it. At the appropriate hour it had been arranged that the bells would ring out over all England. By order of the Prime Minister to the Minister of Information all the channels of propaganda would be geared to this end.

From the outset General Montgomery revelled in publicity and public popularity and acclaim. It was meat and drink to him. He seemed to expand visibly. He believed not only all that he said about himself, but all that was said about him. Perhaps, for a little while, he had thought that the clock must strike midnight, and he would be his sharp, aggressive, unloved self again. Soon that was forgotten. It was not a dream. It was true. An expert Public Relations Staff expanded, communications improved, transport for correspondents became more of a right than a miracle, and the General's Chief of Staff was readily accessible.

[1] Johnston, *Nine Rivers from Jordan*, p. 113.

The tragedy was that all this new story was to be built upon the lie of British defeat, and the denial of the triumph of the old Eighth Army. Its very existence was due to Auchinleck, as we should learn at last from the enemy: 'If Auchinleck had not been the man he was—and by that I mean the best Allied General in North Africa during the war—Rommel would have finished the Eighth Army off'. A few, at least, of General Montgomery's audience on the eve of 2nd Alamein were aware of Auchinleck's victory, and of the long ordeal in the desert. Montgomery's predecessors 'had collected players and painfully trained them and struggled to get the instruments, and now he (Montgomery) was being privileged to conduct the finished orchestra', wrote Alexander Clifford. 'They had never had the advantages he had started with'.

Those present noted that Montgomery seemed totally unaware of all that had gone before . . . 'There would be no more failures.' Clifford was one of the few who recorded in those days the feel as well as some of the facts of July 1942. He wrote of the 'flap' in Cairo and Alexandria.

> And in the end, of course, it was all for nothing. For up in the desert Egypt had been saved. The mood of assurance and confidence seeped back from the front like a cloud, and blossomed and swelled and grew in the hot-house air of Cairo. The refugees rather ashamedly returned. Those who were conscious of having 'flapped' too much toted round their explanations.[1]

Clifford recorded some of the last notes of the long symphony.

> Through July the Alamein front thickened and hardened and formed a crust, and as it did so the feeling of tension and emergency died . . . We could drive forward along the bare, stony Ruweisat Ridge which was the backbone of the Alamein line. It pierced the front like an arrow set in a bow . . .
>
> Behind the crust of the Alamein line there was, in those choking days of July, a feeling of freshness and renewal and rebirth. It was very perceptibly the end of one period and the beginning of another . . .[2]

---

[1] Clifford, *Three against Rommel*.
[2] *Ibid.*

It does not sound much like the description of Churchill and others.

Clifford, who was too soon to die, is almost the solitary voice of the old Eighth Army, and it is the voice of a poet and not simply of a sensitive war correspondent trying to pierce the fog of war and record some of the elusive 'facts' of elusive 'truth'. The music of victory had been played out in the desert almost unheard, almost unrecorded. Now there would be a world audience, and all should hear the thunder of the guns, and even see recorded the misty running figures in the smoke, the flash of high explosive, the eruption of mines, and all the martial notes of war. But the truth of battles cannot be learned through the eyes and ears, it may only be sensed by the five senses in unison, and its bitter essence expressed by the sixth sense of a poet. The sour sweat of fear, and all the acrid and vile odours of violent death, the nausea, the stifling pungent fumes of exploding chemicals, the dreadful courage of ordinary men, the marionette bewilderment of the lost, and the rare acts of sublime heroism, are not to be merely seen or heard.

No man could know the nature of the 'concerto' of battle General Montgomery was about to conduct, and for which he had written the score.

> The battle which is now about to begin will be one of the decisive battles of history. It will be the turning point of the war. The eyes of the whole world will be on us, watching anxiously which way the battle will swing.
>
> We can give them our answer at once; it will swing our way.
>
> Let us all pray that 'The Lord mighty in battle' will give us victory.[1]

At twenty minutes to ten o'clock on the night of October 23, 1942, the fire of more than 1,000 guns erupted to tear the darkness to tatters, and behind that barrage, by the light of the full moon, men moved against the enemy outposts to clear the mine-fields, men on their feet to make way for the armoured divisions of the 10th Corps. Four infantry divisions would open the way through two narrow corridors between the Tel El Eisa and the Miteiriya ridges, on the right the northern thrust towards the desert

[1] Personal Message from the Army Commander: 23/10/42, Middle East Forces.

feature known from its shape as Kidney Ridge, on the left, over Miteiriya Ridge. Far to the south the 13th Corps would carry out a carefully worked out series of feint attacks intended to deceive the enemy. It was part of the 'Master Plan'. Within twenty-four hours it was clear that the Deception Plan in the south had failed, and twenty-four hours later the 'Master Plan' had ground to a standstill. For twelve days the 'World', and especially Whitehall, held its breath, Churchill and Brooke undergoing their personal agonies after their fashions, until at last it became clear that Montgomery had re-grouped to fight on the First World War model, a battle reminiscent to Churchill of Cambrai, a battle of attrition.

No man knows what fears oppressed General Montgomery at the peak of the crisis, and again when the great clash of armour at Tel el Aqqaquir came to a halt, and gave the enemy the chance to disengage which, but for Hitler, must have succeeded. Montgomery is silent. According to de Guingand, he was imperturbable. Yet it is certain that 'Montgomery felt more anxiety than he showed', as Liddell Hart deduced. But he kept his nerve. It was not easy even towards the end of the morning of November 2nd when the 9th Armoured Brigade lost eighty-seven tanks in its effort to break the enemy anti-tank screen on the Rahman track.

In the early hours of October 25th Montgomery had bared his teeth to snarl at his Commanders, especially at the Commander of the 10th Armoured Division. He had threatened the Commander of his Armoured Corps, and his Divisional Commanders with him, if they failed to press on whatever the odds.

The next two days are a blank in his *Memoirs,* but on the evening of October 26th he had realized the position, deciding to withdraw, re-group and think again. 'The decision was testimony to his realism, and to his capacity to combine determination with flexibility,' Liddell Hart summed up. 'But it was also a palpable admission of failure in his original plan.'[1]

There were many more agonizing hours before the end, before the dawn of November 4th when the 5th Indian Brigade, having forced-marched twelve miles over unreconnoitred tracks, were ordered to march a further five miles by night to spearhead the last breakthrough.

[1] Personal analysis, Private Papers.

At two o'clock on the morning the Brigade advanced behind a barrage of 400 guns on a front of only 800 yards:

> This devastating wedge of steel moved like a shield before the Essex and Rajputana Rifles. It poured down a cataract which cleansed the ground of every deadly device. One officer said that it was so precise that his men could have leaned against it; another, that his only casualties were those who followed the wall too closely and became queasy with the fumes of explosives. Lines of tracer shell marked the borders of the corridor which the guns cut. A few short savage fights occurred as enemies, who had escaped the torrent of metal, sought to sell their lives dearly.[1]

Another account records the final moments:

> At the first streak of light in the east, the infantry came into broken ground. They saw before them the kidney-shaped contour which they had been shown on the map. The guns lifted and were done; there was quiet but for the crackle of small-arms fire. Out in front little figures scuttled madly, seeking holes. A carrier platoon went out to bring them in. Then another noise, thunder out of the east, and more thunder. The roar mounted. The tanks came plunging through—hundreds of tanks, lunging to the west through the gap the Wedge had made, and wheeling north for the kill. The sun rose on the last of Alamein.[2]

There were still 600 British tanks in action on that morning, but their wheeling to the north was too shallow so that in the end with the last remnant of his tanks, twenty-four only, the enemy disengaged and withdrew. Even Hitler's order to stand and fight that had halted Rommel's successful disengagement on November 3rd, and forced him to turn about, delivering himself into the hands of his enemy, had not brought about total disaster. But for Hitler Montgomery's last effort, 'Operation Supercharge', would have fallen upon thin air. As it was, the German retreat was ordered at 3.30 p.m. on the afternoon of the 4th. They were in a trap, but it was not sprung.

No words would have been more appropriate to the end of the

---

[1] *The Tiger Kills*, London, H.M.S.O.
[2] *History of the 4th Indian Division.*

second Battle of Alamein than those addressed by the Duke of Wellington, in a letter, to a friend after Waterloo: '. . . Believe me, nothing except a battle lost, can be half so melancholy as a battle won . . . but to win such a battle as this of Waterloo . . . could only be termed a heavy misfortune but for the result to the public.'[1]

It had been, as the Duke also remarked, '. . . the nearest run thing you ever saw in your life.' His heart bled also for 'my poor soldiers'.

There were no laments after the second Battle of Alamein, only the unheard laments of those who mourned. The results to the public morale were certainly great, and the impact was satisfactory, especially upon the people of the United States. Montgomery's prestige and British prestige soared at the precise moment when United States power was taking effect.

At his Press Conference after the battle the little General was strutting and preening like a bantam turkey cock.

> Monty received us in the morning sunlight (wrote Denis Johnston) wearing a tank beret with two cap badges. This piece of apparel seemed to be bulking in his mind, because his first words were: 'Well, gentlemen, as you see I have got a new hat.' He then went on to give us several unconvincing reasons for the assumption of so odd a head-dress, and not until he had gone fully into this matter did he turn to the subject of the Battle of Alamein.[2]

It had been 'complete and absolute victory', Montgomery stated, warning the correspondents not to imagine that all was over. 'For a moment we imagined that he was about to qualify his boasting. But not a bit of it. He continued: "Now we are going to hit him for six right out of Africa!" '[3]

Many men have many ways of masking their innermost feelings, and it would be foolish and almost certainly wrong to judge Montgomery's true feelings by his words and his manner. He was, as always, a lonely figure, devoid of adult personal relationships and beginning to realize a talent—perhaps a genius—for public relations.

---

[1] Creary, *The Fifteen Decisive Battles of the World*, p. 411. London, Simpkin Marshall.
[2] Johnston, *Nine Rivers from Jordan*, p. 78.
[3] *Ibid.*, p. 79.

CHAPTER EIGHT

2nd Alamein II

I

THE inheritance of General von Stumme, commanding the German-Italian army in the desert, was the reverse of Montgomery's. Reluctantly, sadly, Rommel had handed over to von Stumme on September 22nd. On the 23rd he had flown to Austria to seek to regain his health. His every instinct was to stay with his army to the end. The army faced a battle without hope, but in a sense there was always hope, if not of victory, then of some unpredictable salvation, to be seized, if such a chance should flare suddenly out of the utter darkness of inevitable defeat. The removal of Auchinleck and his staff was the only faint advantage he could discover, for Montgomery's remarkable caution at Alam Halfa had lit in Rommel a small spark of hope.

How tragic, how ironic, how absurd that the two contestants should be removed by one means or another in the last hour of their mutual ordeal, an hour that belonged to them alone. It was as though a matador, having brought the brave bull to the moment of truth, should hand over the poised sword to another to make the final thrust. That final thrust might so easily strike bone, and become butchery, denying the full dignity of death.

Von Stumme was fully aware of his position. He doubted that he would be adequate to the task, for even defeat has its nuances short of absolute finality. Curiously, it was a task for which General Montgomery would have been admirably suited. Defence brought out his virtues and his talents, and he was a master of withdrawal.

It was von Stumme's hope that he might be able to prevent a break-through, and that a moment might occur when he would be able to disengage. The defensive position of his army was very strong. His line could not be turned, and must be broken, yet the British strength was so great that it was impossible to predict the greatest danger points. His greatest strength had to be in the north, but the probability of total defeat lay in the south, for in the south the British armour would have room to manoeuvre, to break through into the open desert. And all would be lost.

Thus von Stumme strung out his formations over his thirty-five miles of front, from the sea to the Quattara Depression, aware that he was too thin on the ground, aware too of the dangerous 'marriage' of his German and Italian troops. Ideally he would have held his armour well back, poised to counter-attack wherever the main British thrust, or thrusts, might develop. But his petrol supplies were painfully inadequate, denying movement. He had to make up his mind once and for all. 'In the event of the attack developing a centre of gravity at any point, the Panzer and motorized divisions situated to the north and south were to close up on the threatened sector.'[1]

When it was done the defence made a chain in which there were many weak links: 'The Italian armament was unfortunately so inefficient that it had to be distributed evenly over the whole front, thus ensuring that German arms were also available in every sector.'[2]

The main strength of the German-Italian position lay in its mine-fields. Half a million mines, including many captured British bombs and shells, had been carefully hoarded and skilfully placed. These must blunt the British attack, and enable the German and Italian infantry to fight in their forward positions. Yet, with all this, the enemy position was little more than a powerful crust, lacking in depth. Worse still, von Stumme was almost defenceless against air attack, and his guns pitifully inadequate, even if sufficient ammunition had been available. There were only twenty-four of the deadly 88's supported by a mixed bag of captured weapons transported from the Russian front. His supplies of ammunition were such that he decided not to attempt to break up British attacks in their assembly areas, saving his shot and shell until his troops saw the whites of British eyes. Even so, there were times in the battle when it was estimated that his gunners could only return one shell for five hundred from the British side.

Moreover von Stumme's every movement and disposition was under constant surveillance and attack from the air, while the transports with his supplies were harried and sunk so that a

---

[1] and [2] The defence plan was settled by Rommel before he went to hospital. *The Rommel Papers*, p. 300.

mere trickle arrived at Tobruk, a trickle still further reduced by air attacks and naval gunfire upon his land line of communications. For von Stumme and his army the battle was constant. There would be an hour in which the British would launch their all-out offensive, but meanwhile the battle before the battle was crippling. He was too weak to be deceived by the elaborate deception plans laid by General Montgomery.

It might be imagined that the morale of the German-Italian army had fallen, owing to the loss of its leader, to the incessant pounding it sustained, to the defeat it had already suffered, even to the rather wretched rations to which it had been reduced. But this was not so. Nor had it been so in the British ranks in their hours of defeat. Bad morale with the Germans, as with the British, was manifest in the rear, the characteristic of the jealous, the failed, the 'armchair' men. The Germans, too, had their 'Cairo'.

But these things, worrying to generals, did not affect the troops, with their simple philosophies of life and death, and making the best of conditions unimaginable in their peacetime lives. At first von Stumme had been grateful for Montgomery's long delay in mounting his offensive, but soon he realized that he could not take advantage of the delay to gain appreciably in strength. The days dragged by.

The avalanche of high explosive that fell upon the German-Italian positions at 9.40 p.m. on October 23rd was of an intensity and volume unknown since the First World War. It virtually destroyed the 62nd Italian Infantry Regiment, and it disabled almost completely the communications net of the army. To this gigantic barrage von Stumme dared not reply. He has been criticized for not directing his artillery against the British assembly areas, but it is difficult to fault him in any other particular. Soon after dawn on the 24th he drove forward refusing an escort, and accompanied only by Colonel Buechting and a driver, Corporal Wolf. Von Stumme felt that he must have some picture of what was going on. His vehicle came under direct fire from anti-tank and machine guns. Buechting was mortally wounded, and as Corporal Wolf swung the car round on its tracks and raced for safety, von Stumme, a man of fifty-nine, leapt from his seat to cling to the side of the vehicle in an attempt to gain some cover from fire. It would have been an athletic and brave performance for man of half his age. At some point von Stumme died of a heart attack. He suffered from high blood pressure. His body was found the next morning. He was killed in action as surely as if a bullet had found brain or heart.

Meanwhile the German infantry, aided by the mine-fields and close artillery support, held up the British attack.

On October 24th Rommel, unable to complete his cure and suffering grave anxiety, set off for the battlefield to resume his command. He found a shocking situation. The 15th Panzer Division had put in counter-attacks to loosen the British toe-hold on kidney ridge, known as Hill 28 to the Germans. The cost was frightful on both sides, and it was a price the Germans could not afford to pay. The odds lengthened, but after forty-eight hours both sides showed signs of extreme fatigue and depression, and men had reached the limits of human endurance. On the evening of the 26th Montgomery decided to withdraw his battered armour into reserve, and to rest as many of his front line troops as possible. His Deception Plan had petered out in the south, and his Master Plan in the north had failed. The enemy, despite the 'crumbling' pressure maintained against them, had gained a respite.

On the night of the 24th, Montgomery had faced a crisis. It was clear that his infantry and armour, unable to co-ordinate their attacks, were in danger of piling up in the two narrow attack corridors through which he was resolved to force them. The enemy mine-fields had not been cleared as quickly as he had planned, and by daylight on the 24th none of the British armour had got through to its objectives. In the northern corridor, Major-General Briggs, urged forward by the army commander, drove the 1st Armoured Division through into the open by dusk to meet the counter-attack of the 15th Panzer Division. This, Montgomery said, was 'exactly what he wanted'.

In the southern of the two corridors the 10th Armoured Division under Major-General Gatehouse, was jammed. Montgomery insisted that the Division must press on, despite the protests of the Armoured commanders, supported by General Lumsden commanding the Armoured Corps. The only answer to their protests was 'a crack of the whip'. As a result the leading armoured regiment of the 10th Division was almost annihilated.

The exchanges between Major-General Gatehouse and the

Army Commander have been variously reported. Montgomery wrote:

> I discovered that in the 10th Armoured Division, one of the armoured regiments was already out in the open and that it was hoped that more would be out by dawn. The divisional commander wanted to withdraw it *all* back behind the minefields and give up the advantages he had gained; his reason was that his situation out in the open would be very unpleasant and his division might suffer heavy casualties. Lumsden agreed with him; he asked if I would personally speak to the divisional commander on the telephone. I did so at once and discovered to my horror that he himself was some 16,000 yards (nearly 10 miles) behind his leading armoured brigades. I spoke to him in no uncertain voice, and ordered him to go forward at once and take charge of his battle; he was to fight his way out, and lead his division from in front and not from behind.[1]

Montgomery then spoke 'very plainly to the Corps Commander'.

This is a remarkable comment upon the courage and abilities of very brave and experienced armoured commanders. Major-General Gatehouse had heard from his Corps Commander in the field that his attack must continue. Fearing that his armour would be destroyed, Gatehouse left his forward position, and went back to telephone to Montgomery on a field telephone line. He began the call by demanding of Montgomery:

'What the hell's going on?'

He then told Montgomery that his division was jammed in the corridor, and could not get its forward regiment out before daylight. On the forward slopes of Miteiriya ridge it would face annihilation by the enemy anti-tank guns.

Liddell Hart wrote: '. . . the commander (Gatehouse) urged that the push should be suspended as there was no hope of a break-out before daylight. But after another crack of the whip by Montgomery, who overrode the protest of the commander, the division pushed on—and the leading regiment was almost wiped out.[2]

[1] Montgomery, *Memoirs*, p. 130.
[2] Liddell Hart, Private Papers.

Gatehouse and Briggs drove their armour forward, and 'By 8.0 a.m. (the 25th)' wrote Montgomery, 'all my armour was out in the open and we were in the position I had hoped to achieve at 8.0 a.m. the day before.'[1]

There is no hint in his *Memoirs* of the anxieties, and doubts, it is difficult to believe that he did not feel. His commanders, he knew, and the troops, which possibly he did not know, 'became bitterly critical about the continued attempt to push a mass of tanks through such a narrow breach under the enemy's concentrated fire.'[2]

On that same morning Montgomery realized that the New Zealand Division, attempting to thrust to the south-westward, 'crumbling' the enemy, was making very slow progress, and it 'would be a very costly operation'. The attack was switched.

The bitter fighting of the next two days is not mentioned in the *Memoirs*. On the 28th, he wrote: 'I began to realize from the casualty figures that I must be careful.'

II

For two days, while Montgomery re-cast his plans, a terrible battle was waged, the British striving to maintain a hold on Kidney Ridge, and the enemy striving equally desperately to force them back. On the 26th Rommel was once again in command of his hard-pressed army, and appalled by the situation: 'Rivers of blood,' he wrote, 'were poured out over miserable strips of land which, in normal times, not even the poorest Arab would have bothered his head about.[3]

Incessant artillery bombardment supplemented by wave after wave of bombers deluged high explosive upon the German-Italian infantry and armour. Their battle was on the ground alone. They were beyond thought, and extreme fatigue had reduced them to points beyond feeling. To all it was a nightmare. The British were not very different. The din of battle was in their ears, and if there was less hot metal shuddering through their ranks, the effect upon a human is marginal. There is only so much to be borne, and beyond that action becomes instinctive.

[1] Montgomery, *Memoirs*, p. 130.
[2] Liddell Hart, Private Papers.
[3] *The Rommel Papers*, p. 306.

On the 26th Rommel ordered the 90th Light Division up from the south. 'The British,' he wrote, 'were continually feeding fresh forces into their attack.' And he had to do what he could without reserves. It had become clear to him that Montgomery aimed to force a breakthrough between El Daba and Sidi Abd el Rahman. There, in that area, the battle would come to its climax. He made the bold decision to bring the 21st Panzer Division north together with the Ariete Division. His southern front was stripped, and these moves once made could not be reversed.

There was little to hearten Rommel, but the 'astonishing hesitancy and caution' displayed by Montgomery gave him the agonizing hope that if he could concentrate his armour he might hold long enough to make withdrawal possible.

On the night of the 26th Montgomery made his new plan for a right-angled thrust to the north to gain the coast road, and to break out from thence westward. The attack was delayed, but went in on the night of the 28th. It failed. Montgomery himself seems to have forgotten this plan and its failure, but on the 29th, learning of Rommel's movement of the 90th Light Division, Alexander and Montgomery together evolved a third plan, code-named 'Supercharge', to begin with a further night attack, and to be followed by a decisive attempt to break-out to the west. It was timed for the 31st. It reached the coast, but failed to trap the German infantry. Montgomery seems to have been under the impression that his main blow struck the Italians, but in fact it came up against the 15th Panzer Division supported by Italian motorized infantry.

Finesse was now totally absent from the battlefield. There were, in a sense, no tactics. It was an unashamed battle of attrition, a 'push and crumble', and as the British front line troops and armour died, or were exhausted, new men and armour took their places. The end could not be long delayed, and on the night of the 29th Rommel decided to attempt to withdraw. The incessant battering his troops suffered from the bombing, the British artillery and the constant heavy assaults, was agonizing, and could not be borne much longer.

> No one can conceive the extent of our anxiety during this period. That night (29th) I hardly slept and by 03.00 hours was pacing up and down turning over in my mind . . . the

decisions I would have to take. It was obvious to me that I dared not await the decisive break-through but would have to pull out to the west before it came . . . So I decided that morning that if British pressure became too strong I would withdraw to the Fuka position before the battle had reached its climax.[1]

It was a difficult decision because the acute shortage of petrol meant that the non-motorized units would have a poor chance to get away, and much of the infantry would be too closely involved to disengage. To succeed would demand perfect timing.

The British attack did not come on that day, but there was much to increase Rommel's anxieties. At mid-morning he had the news that the transport, *Louisiana,* had been sunk, dashing his last slender hopes of supplies. Then, in the midst of planning the withdrawal with Colonel Westphal, a rumour reached him that two British divisions had advanced through the Quattara Depression, and had reached a point sixty miles south of Mersa Matruh. 'We were aghast,' Rommel wrote, 'because we had virtually no defence against such a move.' A week later Rommel would have treated a comparable rumour with scepticism. By that time he knew more of Montgomery's ponderous methods and elaborate precautions, and had sensed his fear of 'loosing' his armour in the open desert. From his earliest days Montgomery had feared the theory of 'the expanding torrent' and the indirect approach. Moreover he feared to get 'off balance', and thus to deliver the swift and devastating counter-stroke. Instead he stuck to the sober routine of passing one unit through another.

The 29th and 30th were comparatively quiet days. While Rommel reconnoitred the Fuka position, Montgomery constructed his final plan for the destruction of the enemy. 'This was the Master Plan and only the master could write it.'[2]

The blow, at first designed to penetrate 4,000 yards on a front of 4,000 yards, would be delivered on the night of the 31st in overwhelming strength, the infantry of 30 Corps opening the way for the armour of 10 Corps. The troops would move behind an almost solid curtain of fire from 500 guns, and a rain of bombs

---
[1] *The Rommel Papers*, p. 312.
[2] Montgomery, *Memoirs*, p. 133.

General Montgomery in conversation with Marshal Messe. In centre, holding maps is General Freyburg. May 1943.

Italy: December 1943. General Montgomery enters his car after his farewell address to the troops in the theatre (Garrison Theatre, Vasto).

Sicily: August 1943. General Eisenhower decorates General Montgomery.

General Montgomery addressing the war correspondents, 1943.

would descend upon the enemy as wave upon wave of bombers attacked their forward positions.

Rommel, expecting the attack, and grouping his forces as best he could to contain it, was grateful for the delay caused by Montgomery's second thoughts. The attack was postponed for twenty-four hours, and the depth of penetration increased to 6,000 yards. Meanwhile, Rommel had begun the disengagement of his forces on the central and southern fronts, and hoped to 'whip out' his infantry under cover of darkness as soon as the British were fully engaged in the north. It would be touch and go, demanding perfect judgement and timing if he was to succeed in saving a nucleus of his army and armour. He was fully aware that Montgomery had only used a small proportion of his available forces, and that an 'army' of men and armour were in reserve. As it was, Rommel had ninety tanks, a handful of guns, and a few dedicated remnants of his infantry to oppose against the British Leviathan. His communications were in total ruin, and it was imperative that the German generals, including himself, were forward with their troops. On his visits forward he had to dive for cover frequently, and was in constant danger.

III

Operation 'Supercharge' was launched on the night of November 1st, and was immediately checked, the forward troops meeting 'rather more opposition than had been expected, having regard to the gruelling artillery and air bombardment to which they had been subjected.'[1]

The opening delay, although slight, was crucial. 'The 9th Armoured Brigade was thus half an hour behind timetable in crossing its start line, and when dawn came found itself on the muzzles of the powerful anti-tank guns on the Rahman track, instead of beyond it as had been planned.'[2]

The 9th Armoured lost 75 per cent of its strength, nevertheless the costs to the enemy were more than he could bear. The losses suffered by the 9th Armoured Brigade alone would have reduced the German armour to nil.

Already Rommel's rear installations were on their way back

---
[1] Alexander, *Despatch*.
[2] Liddell Hart, *The Tanks*, vol. ii, p. 234.

to Fuka, while his remaining armour attacked the flanks of the British penetration in a desperate endeavour to gain time. The great tank battle of Tel el Aqquaquir had begun.

On the evening of November 2nd, it was clear to Rommel 'that our final destruction was upon us'. The Afrika Korps was reduced to a total of 35 serviceable tanks, and this in itself was a miracle.

On November 3rd with his anti-tank screen still unbroken, and the Eighth Army temporarily halted, Rommel began to withdraw. He planned to reach El Daba that night and to be in the Fuka position on the 4th. He had won a respite of at least a day and a night. 'Seeing that the British had so far been following up hesitantly and their operations had always been marked by an extreme, often incomprehensible, caution, I hoped to be able to salvage at least part of the infantry,' he wrote.[1]

The situation looked very different to Montgomery. In his *Memoirs* under the date, Monday, November 2nd, he records: 'At 1.0 a.m. "Supercharge" began and the attack went in on a front of 4,000 yards to a depth of 6,000 yards. It was a success and we were all but out into the open desert. By dusk we had taken 1,500 prisoners.'[2]

Montgomery then prepared a further 'Master Plan' designed to encompass the total defeat and destruction of the enemy. He seemed unaware that by the time it would be ready to go in on the night of November 3rd/4th, the enemy would no longer be there to receive it. A remarkable, and unpredictable, intervention of 'providence' presented Montgomery with a target, and should have given him the total victory to which he was committed. At 1.30 p.m. on the 3rd, with his withdrawal in successful operation, Rommel was ordered by Hitler to stand and fight to the last.

For Rommel this signal from the Führer was a death sentence for his army. He had consistently informed the Führer's headquarters of the true position in unequivocal terms, but Hitler had embarked upon his insane course of condemning his armies, and later his country, to destruction.

Reluctantly, miserably, Rommel turned again to face the enemy and annihilation.

[1] *The Rommel Papers*, p. 319.
[2] Montgomery, *Memoirs*, p. 136.

The enemy's turn-about, and renewed attempt to hang on to the original position, played into Montgomery's hands. When 'Supercharge' was checked on November 2nd, it became evident that this massive concentration for a breakthrough had again been foiled by the enemy's ability to concentrate in meeting it, on such a narrow frontage. So Montgomery decided to switch the thrust-point a little more to the south, in the hope of finding a soft spot and outflanking the enemy's anti-tank screen.'[1]

Again, miraculously, the enemy imposed a severe but temporary check. The 8th Armoured Brigade was halted, and this caused the 23rd Armoured Brigade with the infantry of the 51st Highland Division and the 5th Indian Brigade to run into trouble in an attack with a south-westerly slant. The 8th Royal Tank Regiment lost twenty-two out of its thirty-four tanks. Nevertheless the end was near. That night the last attack went in under its immense barrage, and the dawn of the 4th brought the end of the second Battle of Alamein.

IV

It is difficult to be sure even now of how much or how little General Montgomery knew of these things. He seems to have possessed to a remarkable degree the facility to put all 'complications' out of his mind, whether for better or for worse, reducing all results to the formula 'according to plan'. He planned alone; he lived alone, isolated for the most part from his senior officers. Set-backs were due to failures on the part of his commanders. Very soon he would be rid of Lumsden, the Commander of his Armoured Corps, and Gatehouse, the greatest and most experienced of his armoured divisional commanders. It would not matter any more. Overwhelming superiority in men and materials would enable him not to embark upon any undertaking until his strength was such as to make defeat impossible.

At his Press Conference in the immediate aftermath of Alamein, Montgomery was too relieved, too jubilant, too close to his astounding fortune fully to realize the implications. In a sense his

[1] Liddell Hart, *The Tanks,* vol. ii, p. 235.

obvious delight in his new tank beret, which so astonished his audience, revealed his perception of values. He was already a kind of talisman, and this hat would make his image. It would be the image of victory, and it would never know defeat. It is almost possible to believe that without the beret the 'Monty' the British public was to put alongside Churchill in its gallery of war heroes, might not have been known. An image was urgently needed, and the beret crowned it. Under that hat he became 'Monty', the eccentric, the victor, the success symbol, his sharp, thin visage showed its strengths rather than its weaknesses. It was, in a favourite phrase of his, 'what the doctor ordered', and he clung to it against great opposition. The Royal Tank Corps was furious at his usurpation of their beret, and the Monarch was 'not amused'. Montgomery stood firm.

He told the war correspondents of his victory in the voice of an oracle. His voice was a curious instrument, crisp, almost toneless, and with the suspicion of a drawl. You felt that the tone would not vary whatever he might say, whether he announced victory or disaster, or contradicted himself in successive sentences. It compelled one to listen carefully. No man ever 'stuck his neck out' more often or in a less dramatic fashion, and it made his statements seem more outrageous than they sometimes were. His obvious pleasure in himself was remarkable, and in a curious way infectious, and endearing. His face creased easily into a smile, but his very blue eyes rarely smiled. They were his outstanding feature, and as cold as glass. Montgomery was to many what Arnold Bennett would have called 'a card'. He was certainly a card. He was extraordinarily stimulating. At times he was within a hairsbreadth of being frankly comical, and his coming introduced a lighter note into the grim business of war. He was certainly a gift to war correspondents.

There was no hint of anything having gone wrong in the smallest degree. The battle of Alamein had gone exactly according to plan. His battles always did, and always would. Any divergence from what had seemed to be the plan was always exactly what Montgomery said he had expected, or exactly what he wanted.

Many years later, Major-General Carver summed up the general situation which made this possible, or seem to be possible: 'In the latter half of the war, intricate as the problems of planning might be, there was seldom, if ever, any danger of one's plans being completely disrupted by surprise enemy action. When mistakes were made, their results were less disastrous and far less obvious.'

Because of this the fiction could be maintained that Montgomery said succinctly and clearly exactly what he was going to do, and did it. Victory, in fact, covers a multitude of errors impossible for the individual observer to detect in the stress and confusion of battle.

The capture of General von Thoma, Commander of the Afrika Korps, in the last hours of the battle, seemed to Montgomery a confirmation of his complete victory. Von Thoma had chosen to fight to the last with his picked troops, and to hold the centre, and this he had done until all that was left was the black smoke of burning vehicles and the stench of roasting flesh. Rommel believed that von Thoma had chosen to die with his troops, and in this he had failed. It might have been kinder of Montgomery not to have invited the captured general to his table, and thus to incur the temporary displeasure of many. It seems odd that von Thoma did not tell Montgomery of Hitler's order to Rommel to turn-about, but by so doing he might have prejudiced the last possible chance for Rommel to escape.

Montgomery may have genuinely believed on that morning that his victory was complete. The smoke of battle had not cleared. The pursuit was on. It must have seemed impossible that an enemy so battered could escape. The Royal Air Force deluged bombs over the escape route. How could the enemy, almost without guns or armour—a mere score of tanks!—hope to screen his withdrawal against an enemy so overwhelmingly equipped as the Eighth Army! Montgomery could not foresee or understand the nature of generalship dedicated to mobility, and the acceptance of confusion. Nor could he understand the brilliance of Colonel Bayerlein, whose task it was after the loss of von Thoma, to save the Afrika Korps.

Yet not all the skill and dedication available to the Germans could have saved the nucleus of an army from destruction on that grim November 4th against a general less cautious, less pleased with himself, than was General Montgomery. And because he was entirely lacking in humility, he could not grow.

V

Between November 4th and 6th the Eighth Army, its corps and divisional commanders deprived of initiative, failed to cut off and to destroy the vital nucleus of the Afrika Korps. In his orders Montgomery had directed the armoured divisions of ten corps to drive north-west 'towards Ghazal Station, so as to get in behind the enemy forces in the Sidi Rahman area and cut them off.'

He seems to have had no idea of the speed with which Rommel must withdraw, and in his *Memoirs* refers at once to a pursuit: 'I gave precise instructions to Lumsden (10 Corps) about development of operations for the pursuit to Agheila.'[1]

It may be, therefore, that he did not believe that he would cut off and destroy the beaten enemy. It may be that in his heart he knew his own limitations, and knew that he would not dare to 'loose his armour', and to develop the 'expanding torrent' he had always feared. His weakness was that everything had to be under his own hand, all the time. He wanted to command, not only an army, but all of its parts down to division. He had forbidden his commanders to use their judgement, and had rejected the pleas of Lumsden, Gatehouse and Briggs to load up with petrol and dash for Sollum.

Exhaustive analyses of the battle and its aftermath reveal beyond any doubt that Rommel's remaining forces were at Montgomery's mercy. Had he acted with speed and courage no power on earth could have enabled the Germans to escape, nor would the rain that began to fall on the afternoon of the 6th have availed them. The attempts to cut off the enemy were too shallow and too slow. Fuka, as Liddell Hart pointed out, fifty miles to the west was 'an ideal blocking point astride the enemy's line of retreat'.

On the 5th, the first moves having failed, another short hook was ordered on Daba. But Rommel, having lost a full day and night by Hitler's command, was moving fast. With the immensely powerful forces on his tail there was no possibility of imposing any kind of check, despite the dedicated courage of his rearguards, and the ingenuity of a small delaying group under

---

[1] Montgomery, *Memoirs*, p. 141-2.

Colonel Voss. Gatehouse and Briggs having been denied their petrol could not hope to cut off the enemy. By the time the British armoured pursuit reached Fuka Rommel had already slipped away. Even the 21st Panzer Division—what was left of it—halted for lack of fuel fifteen miles further to the west, rolled itself into a tight hedgehog, was replenished during the night, and was away again before dawn.

On the afternoon of November 6th the rain began to fall and became a deluge.

> The unfortunate intervention of this rainstorm has always been given as the main explanation of, and excuse for, the failure to cuff off Rommel's retreat. But in analysis it becomes clear that the best opportunities had already been forfeited before the rain intervened—by too narrow moves, by too much caution, by too little sense of the time-factor, by unwillingness to push on in the dark, and by concentrating too closely on the battle to keep in mind the essential requirements for its decisive exploitation. If the pursuit had driven deeper through the desert, to reach a more distant blocking point such as the steep escarpment at Sollum, it would have avoided the risk of interception either by resistance or weather—for while rain is a likely risk in the coastal belt it is rare in the desert interior.[1]

None of this is wisdom after the event. The impossible happened. The enemy, growing in strength as he retreated, always gauging Montgomery's moves accurately and acutely, imposed checks by his mere presence at key points, and reached Tunisia to fight the last desperate battles against the Anglo-American armies. 'It was a masterly retreat—a real text-book job,' wrote Alexander Clifford. 'I do not suppose that ever in history has a withdrawal been so genuinely according to plan.'[2]

By the same judgement the Eighth Army's pursuit was 'a dull and measured affair'. Time and again Rommel and Bayerlein marvelled and wondered at Montgomery's caution and slowness. Week after week 'Their command continued to show its customary caution and lack of resolution,' Rommel wrote. It did not occur to the German General that Montgomery could fear

[1] Private papers: Analysis. B. H. Liddell Hart, November 1958.
[2] Clifford, *Three against Rommel*, p. 322.

any kind of counter-attack from the remnant of his battered and exhausted army, its handful of guns and score of tanks.

Rommel's description of his flight from the battle-field of Alamein is agonizing. He did not expect to escape to Mersa Matruh:

> It was a wild helter-skelter drive through another pitch-black night... Finally we halted in a small valley to wait for daylight. At that time (night of 5th/6th) it was still a matter of doubt as to whether we would be able to get even the remnants of the Army away to the west. Our fighting power was very low... The only forces which retained any fighting strength were the remnants of the 90th Light Division, the Afrika Korps' two divisions—now reduced to the strength of small combat groups, the Panzer Grenadier Regiment of Afrika and a few quickly scratched together German units, the remains of the 164th Light Division. Tanks, heavy and light artillery, all had sustained such frightful losses at El Alamein that there was nothing but a few remnants left... At dawn on the 6th November, we tried to reassemble and get some order into Panzer Armee's Staff.[1]

Montgomery made it clear time and time again that he invested this beaten remnant, not only with miraculous powers of recuperation and counter-attack, but with tactical and strategic objects that had long become obsolete. With the Anglo-American landings far in his rear, Rommel's object would become to reach Tunisia and join with the German Army under von Arnim.

On the morning of November 8th—after the rain—Major-General Gatehouse urged Montgomery to let him drive on to Sollum and Tobruk.

> But the Army Commander would not allow this—emphasizing to Gatehouse, as he did to others at this time, that he was intent to refrain from any 'mad rush' forward that might lead his forces to outrun their supplies and expose them to another of Rommel's ripostes. He showed a continued expectation of such a risk and was determined not to be caught like his predecessors. But such a counterstroke was now far

[1] *The Rommel Papers*, p. 339.

beyond the capacity of Rommel's surviving forces. The Afrika Korps had only ten tanks left.[1]

Again and again Montgomery reiterates that his Army will not retreat. 'The doom of the Axis forces in Africa was certain,' he wrote, 'provided we made no more mistakes.' One of his young officers remarked to him: 'We used to go up to Benghazi for Christmas and return to Egypt early in the New Year.' Montgomery comments: 'I was determined to have done with that sort of thing.'

No reader can doubt that Montgomery believed himself faced with an enemy comparable in power and aims with that which faced his predecessors. In a sense he did not believe in his own victory at Alamein. He implies a remarkable ignorance of the long-drawn-out struggle in the Desert, of the massive battles fought between forces relatively evenly matched, but in which the Germans until the middle of 1942 invariably had the edge in the hitting power of their tanks and anti-tank guns. It implies also that he is ignorant of the Anglo-American landings in Tunisia, landings in which he was to have played a major role but for the death of General Gott. In Montgomery's mind it seems that the only element in the Desert War that is different from the past is his own leadership. This was, and still is, the view propagated to the public.

The long slow march of the Eighth Army to Enfidaville underlined this view.

Field-Marshal Rommel's comment on Montgomery's handling of the second Battle of Alamein, and of its aftermath, is scrupulously fair. He observes that:

> The British had such superiority in weapons, both in quality and quantity, that they were able to force through any and every kind of operation ...
>
> For the rest, the British based their planning on the principle of exact calculation, a principle which can only be followed where there is complete material superiority. They actually undertook no *operations* but relied simply and solely on the effect of their *artillery* and air force.[2]

---

[1] Liddell Hart, *The Tanks*, vol. ii, p. 240.
[2] *The Rommel Papers*, p. 329.

By this Rommel means that there was no need for generalship on the British side. Alam Halfa was won merely by sitting tight, and venturing not at all. Alamein was a series of attacks on narrow fronts against the strongest points of the enemy. It was a battle of attrition, 'A hard and bloody killing match', as Montgomery called it. It did not call for generalship. Mobility and the indirect approach frightened Montgomery. He was, wrote Fuller, 'pre-eminently a general of *materiel* . . . It is difficult to imagine him fighting a Sidi Barrani or a Beda Fomm.'[1]

Indeed, it is impossible. At Alamein he did slowly learn to develop leverage when his successive 'Master Plans' had failed. But he had to be firmly rooted before he dared, and even then his moves were ponderous, cautious and very slow. His delay in remounting his attacks provided the enemy with valuable breathing periods, and inasmuch as it was possible to lose—or not to win—the battle, he came very near to doing so. He had taken the whole burden upon his own shoulders, and at the crucial times his nerve held. The estrangement of his armour and infantry cost him very dear. But his failure as an attacking general lies in his inability to grasp the meaning of balance. His balance at best meant being firmly planted, not on 'two feet', but on three. In defence an enemy would not catch him off balance, but with this kind of balance no child would ever walk, no dancer ever dance, no boxer or wrestler risk a counter-punch or throw. These things are done by a mastery of true balance, which is the essential poise of unbalance. This, above all I think, was his invincible handicap in the role fortune had ordained for him.

It must have been Montgomery's 'object' to destroy the German-Italian army, and to finish the war in Africa, if not in one bite, then inescapably in two. He has nothing to say about his failure, and it may never be known why he failed at Alam Halfa, or why he deliberately abstained.

As for the second Battle of Alamein, his generalship has been carefully and exhaustively examined. Liddell Hart, whose scholarly detachment cannot be doubted, wrote:

> With such an immense superiority Montgomery was certain of victory, by sheer process of attrition—unless he used up

[1] Fuller, *The Second World War*, p. 235.

his tanks so disproportionately to the enemy's loss as to leave him bankrupt, or broke the spirit of his troops in the effort to wear down the enemy.

The basic questions about the generalship in such a case is whether the commander's plan and conduct of the battle (a) gained victory as economically as possible; (b) attained victory without losses so heavy as to jeopardise the certainty of success inherent in the initial odds; (c) attained victory without exposing his army to defeat by counterstroke; (d) succeeded in achieving the complete victory that was promised by the overwhelming odds in his favour.

In analysis of the battle, it has become evident that Montgomery fulfilled only one of these four points—the third.[1]

This is a generous judgement, for the enemy lacked the strength to impose defeat by counterstroke.

Rommel's final verdict was:

> We simply did what we could, with our very meagre resources, to come to terms with the unalterable disadvantages under which we suffered. It was a matter of getting the best out of a hopeless situation. Armed with a pitchfork, the finest fighting man can do little against an opponent with a tommy-gun in his hands.
>
> ... I could not of course have foreseen just how great the strength of the British was actually to be.
>
> In these circumstances, there was never any chance of the army achieving success at Alamein.[2]

Had Montgomery succeeded at Alam Halfa there would have been no second Alamein; had he succeeded in destroying the remnants of the German-Italian army after second Alamein, there would have been no triumphal march to Tripoli and on to Enfidaville. It is impossible to escape the conclusion that after second Alamein it was Montgomery's object to destroy the German-Italian army, and to prevent it from joining with the Axis forces in Tunisia. In this he failed.

---

[1] Private papers: B. H. Liddell Hart. November 1958.
[2] *The Rommell Papers*, p. 333.

CHAPTER NINE

The Triumphal March

I

THE triumphal march of the Eighth Army from El Alamein over 1,400 miles of desert to Tripoli, and thence to the mountains of Enfidaville, was a performance demanding management of a high order. The transport of more than 150,000 men with all their varied equipment, their armour, artillery, ammunition, fuel, workshops and services, their supplies from food to boots and socks, involving many hundreds of items, all necessities of life as well as of death, demands energies, imagination and forethought seldom forthcoming in times of peace. An army marches on its stomach. The 'A & Q' staffs of the new Middle East Command and of the Eighth Army had seen to it, magnificently, that the stomach was well filled.

These things had been made possible after two and one half years of trial and error, throughout which the men on the spot had borne the burden and the blame for all the massive shortcomings and crass stupidities of the men at the back. Perhaps the greatest shortcomings of the previous years had not been a lack of adequate armour and of high explosive ammunition for their armament, but the almost non-existence of the transport aircraft that might well have averted many perilous and too often near-disastrous situations. Indeed, in the final analysis, it may be understood that the strategic bombing programme, absorbing an enormous proportion of British industrial capacity, added substantially to the duration of the war. By this alone 'The Great Amphibian' was denied strategic and tactical flexibility, deprived of a great variety of assault and landing craft and of the close support in the air which multiplies the striking power of armies. Moreover, the outcome of the Battle for the Atlantic was dangerously delayed, and the survival of the Island citadel placed in jeopardy.

In the wider context of the Second World War the Western Desert had become a minor detail at the time of the arrival of

General Montgomery. His true task was to 'mop-up' as swiftly and tidily as possible, while the focus of the war in Africa moved to Tunisia. In a very real sense the intensity of the Second Battle of Alamein underlined the true nature of the struggle that had been waged in the Western Desert. It marked the end of an era, and with every mile the army advanced a new legend grew, and was fertilized by glowing 'Orders of the Day', couched in the style of Napoleon, with exhortations and tributes, and bold statements of brave and devastating intentions. The long journey was punctuated by place names that had bitten hard into memory, and were endowed with a new dimension.

Driving the Eighth Army in the field was General Montgomery, a full General after Second Alamein, and behind him was General Alexander providing all his needs, and more than his needs, with a profligacy and devotion never before known in war. In the van of the army, held on a tight rein and champing metaphorically at the bit, were the armoured spearheads of the 7th Armoured Division, with the infantry of the New Zealand Division, and its attached armour, not far behind.

'Only precautions are worthless,' the great Marshal Saxe had said in circumstances such as these, and by his words General Montgomery whole-heartedly supported this judgement. His purpose was to 'crash' through the enemy, and pursue the remnants with remorseless drive and energy. In practice, however, he advanced with an extreme caution and with many pauses, allowing his adversary the respite without which he could not have hoped to survive. The curb on the spearhead troops of the Eighth Army was never relaxed, despite the urgent pleas of their experienced leaders.

It was soon apparent that the failure to cut off and destroy the beaten enemy in the immediate aftermath of his defeat was not to be made good. The 22nd Armoured Brigade and the 4th Light Armoured were just in time to see the last train-load of enemy rocking out of Capuzzo, the coaches holding the rails by a seeming miracle. The brigadiers cursed and sighed and drove on out of Egypt and through Libya. They had not given up hope. Ahead of them there would be, or there should be, further opportunities over terrain they knew well. Perhaps Montgomery would relent. They skirmished with the enemy rear-guards, and suffered frustration and casualties from the booby traps contrived by the ingenuity of General Buelowius and the enemy engineers. The cautious pursuit gave Buelowius time to gain more time for the retreating rump of an army which lacked the fighting strength of a full division.

The men leading the Eighth Army advance in the van knew, even if nobody else did, that the Afrika Korps had dwindled to a mere shadow, and that its seven thousand men and handful of guns and armour could be overwhelmed by speed and daring. They lacked neither speed nor daring, but they were not free. They outnumbered the enemy all the way at seldom less than ten to one, and they knew that the Italian infantry with which Rommel was reinforced were more of a hindrance than a help. The enemy needed armour, guns and fuel, and of these needs fuel was the greatest. The Italians, therefore, added to the enemy's embarrassment.

On the day that the Eighth Army entered Tobruk the advance guards of the retreating enemy reached the Mersa el Brega line. Rommel had gained almost forty-eight hours, and if he could once reach the Agheila position with his entire force he would gain much more. The next two weeks were crucial. With his transport strung out over two or three hundred miles, observed and attacked from the air, and at times halted for lack of petrol, the enemy's vulnerability was extreme. Even General Alexander's *Despatch* seems to reveal a mild exasperation:

> The enemy was withdrawing through the Jebel and it was a great temptation to imitate our previous strategy by pushing a force across the desert to cut him off at or near Agedabia. General Montgomery was determined, however, not to take any chances, especially in view of the difficulties of the maintenance situation, and 10 corps was instructed to despatch only armoured cars by this route. Later, however, when it appeared that the enemy's retreat had actually been brought to a temporary standstill by lack of fuel, 10 corps was ordered to strengthen, if possible, the outflanking force; this proved impracticable in the then existing circumstances.[1]

Even Rommel, with his growing faith in Montgomery, must have doubted his luck.

---

[1] Alexander, *Despatch*.

The British commander had shown himself to be overcautious. He risked nothing in any way doubtful and bold solutions were completely foreign to him. So our motorized forces would have to keep up an appearance of constant activity, in order to induce ever greater caution in the British and make them even slower. I was quite satisfied that Montgomery would never take the risk of following up boldly and overrunning us, as he could have done without any danger to himself. Indeed, such a course would have cost him far fewer losses . . .[1]

By the time Montgomery permitted his frustrated armour to probe cautiously forward, it was too late, and the enemy was back behind the Mersa el Brega bottle-neck covering El Agheila. Rommel's relief was profound. He had gained more precious time, and had lost scarcely a man.

In spite of the natural strength of the El Agheila position Montgomery must have known that 'there could be no question of (Rommel) accepting battle at Mersa el Brega'. Yet again the German general judged his adversary's moves almost to the very hour. His pursuers reached Benghazi on the 20th, and the 22nd Armoured Brigade was at Agedabia two days later, after a four-day drive across the desert. It was all too late. There had been time for the enemy to carry out comprehensive demolitions, and to harass their pursuers with mines. On November 27th Montgomery brought his army to a halt. It was his intention, he said, to 'annihilate the enemy in the Agheila position'. There was never a chance that he would do so. He wrote that

> . . . I sensed a feeling of anxiety in the ranks of the Eighth Army. Many had been there twice already; and twice Rommel had debouched when he was ready and had driven them back. I therefore decided that I must get possession of the Agheila position quickly; morale might decline if we hung about looking at it for too long.[2]

It is clear that Montgomery created in his mind a threat that had long since disappeared. Perhaps he believed that the German-Italian army had been miraculously reinforced, and

[1] *The Rommel Papers*, p. 360.
[2] Montgomery, *Memoirs*, p. 146.

had acquired attacking strength. Yet he could not have believed that Rommel's course lay forward instead of back. If forward elements of the Eighth Army believed otherwise, surely it was the duty of Montgomery to undeceive them. Indeed, if the Eighth Army showed signs of anxiety at that time, it was an anxiety of frustration, of bewilderment that however fast they travelled it was never fast enough, that their toil was great and their danger even greater, and their 'victories' hollow. The spearheads had travelled nearly 1,000 miles from Alamein, and according to their General, a powerful and dangerous enemy still confronted them. It was difficult to believe.

From November 27th to December 12th the Eighth Army 'looked at' the Agheila position, and prepared to attack. The port of Benghazi was being rapidly prepared to handle the vast supplies Montgomery needed, and mountains of ammunition dumped and brought forward for his bombardments. Meanwhile, Montgomery, by 'bluff and manoeuvre' would attempt to 'bustle' Rommel out of his position. Having fixed December 15th as the date for his attack, the General went down to Cairo to taste his remarkable fame. He had become, as he says, a somewhat 'notorious character'. Reading the Lesson in St George's Cathedral he was in his element, creating 'quite a stir'.

Rommel, meanwhile, had flown back to Germany to try to discover the strategic intentions of the High Command. The supplies he had longed for and urgently demanded were now ear-marked for Tunisia to feed the Army of von Arnim. There was nothing more for him. He had been caught in the fag end of Mussolini's rapidly fading dreams of Empire, and the beginning of Hitler's strategic obsessions. Tripolitania, the last of the Italian African Empire, was about to disappear, and the defeat of von Paulus at Stalingrad was ordained and clearly predictable. The decision to pour men and arms into Tunisia was highly dubious, and must prejudice the defence of Southern Europe. So Rommel argued, but in vain. There was no satisfaction for him anywhere, and he returned to his army to go on doing the best he could, buying time that in the end might be of little or no value. 'To keep the army from being destroyed as the result of some crazy order or other would need all our skill.'[1] he wrote.

[1] *The Rommel Papers*, p. 369.

Meanwhile Montgomery would soon begin to stir again in the desert, and the tedious process of withdrawal must begin in good time. On December 6th Rommel began to withdraw his Italians, and by the time Montgomery signalled his attack with his usual heavy barrage on the night of the 11th, the German and Italian non-motorized infantry had got well away to the west. Montgomery had advanced his attack in the hope of taking the enemy by surprise. His idea was to put in the usual frontal assault to hold and deceive the enemy while his outflanking moves got under way. The 51st Division attacked on the right with the 7th Armoured Division on the left. The New Zealand Division was moving wide round the enemy right flank with the task of putting itself astride the enemy escape route. The 7th Armoured Division, following up fast, would then smash the enemy against the New Zealand anvil. The result would be 'the Battle of Matratin', which never actually took place.

According to Montgomery Rommel was 'unnerved' by his preliminary attack, and thus escaped. Unnerved, or warned, the German commander withdrew his hopelessly outnumbered forces, evaded the trap set for him, and retreated to Buerat. He had 'spoilt Montgomery's plan'.[1] The British, Rommel thought, had not noticed his departure, for on December 13th 'they put down a violent barrage on our old positions'.

Montgomery summed up:

> I ordered the New Zealand Division to halt and reorganize at Nofilia, and followed up Rommel's army with light forces, making contact with them in the Buerat position which they were holding strongly.
>
> The battle of Agheila was now over; that position was firmly in our hands.
>
> We had in fact achieved our purpose.[2]

The purpose could not, therefore, have been to annihilate the enemy in his positions; nor to bring him to battle at El Agheila. It was always a case of heads I win, tails you lose. He had expected to catch the enemy, but had once again failed. Rommel had heard the Cairo broadcast announcing that his army was in a bottle which Montgomery was about to cork. Even with the

[1] Liddell Hart, *The Tanks*, vol. ii, p. 242.
[2] Montgomery, *Memoirs*, p. 147.

90th Light Division halted for lack of petrol the German commander escaped from the bottle. Rommel's fear now was that the Anglo-American armies in Tunisia might move to strike him in the rear in the Gabes gap. His main anxiety was to evacuate Tripolitania with all speed, and he had no doubt that if he were forced by his High Command to stand and fight at Buerat he would be destroyed . . . 'It would need a miracle for us to hold on much longer,' he wrote. 'What is to happen now lies in God's hands.'

The Field-Marshal did not seem to realize that 'The Lord, mighty in battle', was in partnership with Montgomery. And then, suddenly and without expectation, Rommel and his army were granted 'yet another reprieve'. Montgomery had halted to re-group and prepare for the Buerat battle and a ten-day 'dash' to Tripoli. Meanwhile the threat to the Gabes position in Tunisia grew in urgency, and on January 13th Rommel ordered the 21st Panzer Division to move west with all speed. The threat of the Eighth Army had become the least of his worries. Montgomery had halted for nearly a month to build up the strength and supplies he regarded as minimal. 'Montgomery,' Rommel wrote in retrospect, 'had an absolute mania for always bringing up adequate reserves behind his back and risking as little as possible.'[1]

The retreating remnant of the Panzer army had lacked all power to counter-attack, and all Rommel had hoped to do was to 'force the enemy into repeated approach marches and deployments and thus gain as much time as possible'. In this he had been successful beyond his hopes. At first he had feared that Montgomery would put his weight behind his outflanking drives, and had he done so there could have been no escape for the Panzer Army in the immediate aftermath of 2nd Alamein, nor at Mersa el Brega or Nofilia. Montgomery had become completely predictable. There would be the build-up, the barrage, the frontal assault on the right (north), the cautious outflanking 'drive'. For the dash to Tripoli it would be the same again, the infantry on Montgomery's right, the 51st (Highland) Division, the armour on the left, a concentration of 450 tanks.

Against this massive strength, supported as always by powerful

---

[1] *The Rommel Papers*, p. 380.

Allied air forces, the enemy could muster thirty-six German and fifty-seven Italian tanks. In artillery and anti-tank guns he was even more seriously outnumbered. Rommel had kept himself closely informed of Montgomery's elaborate preparations, and on January 13th a wireless intercept revealed that the British would attack on the 15th. In fact, the British artillery began to move forward on the night of the 14th, and on the 15th the German armour took the impact of the leading British tanks. 'We had neither the petrol nor the ammunition to guarantee a defence,' Rommel wrote.

That night he began to withdraw, and to prepare as best he might to confront a new enemy. He was very close to disaster. A little less caution on the part of Montgomery, and the Eighth Army entry into Tripoli should have been crowned with victory. But Montgomery was beset by anxieties. The burdens of command were great, and his peculiar loneliness may have seemed like a prison. He had cut himself off from his equals and senior officers, and deprived himself of critical discussion. Behind him there was always Alexander to advise, but Alexander was not the master Montgomery's nature needed. He was too easy-going, riding Montgomery on a loose rein, agreeing virtually to everything. The CIGS could provide the occasional harsh corrective Montgomery needed, but the CIGS was too far away.

Montgomery's final instructions, as always, 'provided for a due measure of caution to be exercised by the outflanking formations, as I wished to avoid heavy casualties to our tanks'.

Alexander's despatch sadly underlined the situation, remarking that the outflanking troops had 'felt with some caution round the enemy's anti-tank screen'.

Alexander was the Commander-in-Chief. The responsibility was his. From the beginning he had acquiesced in Montgomery's defensive and cautious tactics. Alam Halfa had set the pattern, and 2nd Alamein had engraved it deeply.

It is very difficult to discover a rational basis for Montgomery's fears, yet there is no doubt that they were very real. Perhaps somewhere deep in his mind was the feeling that with his immense superiority he ought to have destroyed his enemy, just as he ought, all those years ago, to have expounded the theory of the 'expanding torrent' in his training manuals.

Alan Moorehead, completely under Montgomery's strange

spell, wrote: 'Montgomery admits that this was the moment in the campaign when he almost lost heart'.

And Montgomery's battle cry has the agonized quality of a *cri de coeur:* 'Nothing has stopped us since the battle of Egypt. Nothing will stop us now. On to Tripoli!'

The Eighth Army had built up a full ten days supply forward, and the organization, the 'A & Q' Staffs, all the way back to Cairo, had not only responded to every demand made upon them, but had shown themselves capable of near miracles. The supply difficulties, according to Moorehead, were monumental. 'It was realized that if it failed to get through to Tripoli by January 25th the Army was finished.'

By whom was it realized? Could it conceivably be true? 'Again it was a battle of the left hook followed by the punch along the coast. While half his slender force made an inland wheeling march across fantastically difficult country . . . Montgomery himself took command on the coast.'[1]

The description of Montgomery's overwhelming strength as a 'slender force' is curious. It is an example of the 'myth' in the making. For a hundred days war correspondents, exhilarated at being on the move, being unmistakably on the winning side, had been pouring words of triumph into their newspapers. It was all honest, and in a sense it was all true—as far as it went.

It is possible that Montgomery, with his 'mania' for having everything at his back, was at least as conscious of the immense proportion of his great army he had left behind at Benghazi as he was of the powerful striking force he had at his immediate command. No doubt he would have been happier with his whole army forward, but it could not have made any difference to his physical ability to deal with his task. Very few men, sometimes no more than a 'company' or a 'squadron' spearhead an army as it narrows down to the sharp brave point. The army selects the corps, the corps selects the divisions, the divisions select brigades, the brigades select the battalions, the battalions the companies, the companies the platoons. In the final analysis the outcome may depend upon the drive, initiative, the courage and resolution of a man, a sergeant, a corporal, a private soldier. And that will depend upon the quality of a 2nd lieutenant, depending upon a captain, upon a lieutenant-colonel, all the way back

[1] Moorehead, *Montgomery.*

through the brigadiers and generals to the army commander. This is the long hard shaft of which the striking prong is far away, and the army commander, knowing its temper, hurls it into battle with all his might, with all his knowledge, with all his skill. It is as important that he knows what is a man, as that he knows what is an army.

To an army commander an army must be a living thing, a thing of flesh and blood, of mind and spirit, before and after it is a thing of facts and figures. No computer can give the answer to what an army may achieve, and if a computer is relied upon, an army will achieve its physical and factual capability, but not its human and spiritual capability, for no man knows, nor will ever know, how to feed such abstracts and intangibles into a calculating device. A calculator will be safe; that is all. In terms of the 'computer' all great commanders have achieved the impossible. Moreover, and above all, there is the deed of sublime heroism at the crucial moment of the crucial hour. It does not happen often, yet it happens more often than the records show, and when it does happen it too depends on the temper of the whole weapon of which it is the ultimate expression.

Soon after Montgomery launched the advance that must take him to Tripoli he began to feel that it was not making satisfactory progress. He was edgy and increasingly irritable. 'The advance was becoming sticky,' he wrote, 'and I was experiencing the first real anxiety I had suffered since assuming command of the Eighth Army.'[1]

The anxieties were imagined rather than real, but were manifest in his behaviour. He could not leave the 51st Division to get on with the job it understood so well. On the 20th Montgomery gave its commander what he describes as an 'Imperial rocket', and this had an immediate effect. More than probably its effect, apart from depressing the commander of the division and his staff, and adding to the harassments of his spearhead engineers in their dangerous encounters with mines and booby traps, was to relieve Montgomery himself.

Virtually he took personal command of the 51st Division. To him an army was a bludgeon. He bludgeoned first with his artillery, and with air power, and then he bludgeoned with his armour and infantry, 'cracking the whip'.

[1] Montgomery, *El Alamein to the Sangro*, p. 36. London, Hutchinson, 1951.

Many of those who rode with the Eighth Army on this last lap to Tripoli felt nothing of Montgomery's fears, and expressed their excitement brilliantly. They were first-class reporters, experienced in warfare. 'There was just a hope,' wrote Clifford, 'that Rommel might be brought to battle, but it was a very slender one.'[1]

It was a hope, and not a fear to Clifford, and since he did not feel this hope in a vacuum of his own thoughts, it was a hope coming to him from the troops. 'We expected a frantic double pursuit which would bring us to the gates of Tripoli in about six breathless days.'[2]

Clifford notes that the Highlanders (the 51st) were expected to get away to a slow start, and that it was 'calculated that mines and demolitions on the road would hold them up'. Montgomery evidently did not share this view.

The reporters who travelled with the Highland Division were unaware of 'stickiness'. 'Privately,' Clifford wrote, 'we all believed that there would not be very much to fight against. With the British tanks already round his right wing Rommel would surely be evacuating the Zem-Zem line as fast as he could go.'[3]

And, of course, Rommel was getting away as fast as he could go, and very worried that it might not be fast enough. Montgomery and Moorehead seem alone in their fears.

> There was a mad infectious exhilaration in the air ... The whole Highland Division seemed to be on the move, sprawled across the countryside in what looked like a chaotic race. Men grinned through the dust and shouted from truck to truck as they jolted past. An irresistible madness seemed to have taken hold of everybody, a wild lust for the chase.'[4]

Here is the authentic voice out of those times, and all who shared in these adventures will recognize its truth. If only, if only Montgomery had been able to escape from himself to share the moods of his army, if only he had known what a marvellous weapon he might wield, if only he had been able to hit 'sixes' with that magnificent bat instead of 'singles', to loose his armour

---
[1] Clifford, *Three against Rommel*.
[2] *Ibid.*
[3] *Ibid.*
[4] *Ibid.*

boldly, to arouse all its zest and élan, to overwhelm the enemy. But he could not. The practical side of him was all 'canny Scot',[1] the adventurer and the cavalier lived only in his dreams and in his words.

On January 23, 1943, the 11th Hussars drove into Tripoli, and out again on the other side. The 1st, 3rd, 5th, 40th and 50th RTR were among the first of the spearhead troops to reach the city. Rommel's forces were already back behind the Mareth line, screened by his rearguards while he reorganized his mind and his men to meet an enemy on two fronts. It was a miracle that he was there, that he had survived, and would, within a month, strike a massive blow against the US 1st Armoured Division in the Kasserine Pass. The final end in Africa was very near, and he had no illusions about it.

Meanwhile the long struggle in the Desert was over.

II

For more than two years Tripoli had been the distant and glittering prize beyond the reach, but seldom beyond the hopes and ambitions of the Eighth Army. General O'Connor, with the old Western Desert Force, the matrix from which the old Eighth Army had grown, had brought it almost within reach before he had been turned back, not by the enemy, but by the political decisions of his masters. There were those, having survived those far-off days, who would never forget O'Connor's brave victory at Beda Fomm. They had even reminded General Montgomery, but to no avail, that O'Connor had dared to place his small force across the line of retreat of an army outnumbering it many times. But to Montgomery, these things, all that had happened before he came, came under the heading of 'mistakes of the past'. He would not repeat them. And gradually the spirit that had made such things possible was seeping away. It had been almost a 'guerilla' spirit, an inspiration coming from the Commander which made men ready to break through the barriers of self-preservation, and emerge whole—or dead. It was still manifest in the Long-Range Desert Group. It was still in the 4th Indian Division, whose commander disliked the idea of 'special' troops.

[1] I am aware that he is Northern Irish.

What others could do his men could do, given the chance. And often he had proved it. That, too, was in the past.

Thus Rommel and his army, despite the directive of the Führer, that had forced him to turn-about at Alamein on that fateful November 3rd, had survived. He had been deprived by that insane decision, of a nucleus to make it possible to do more than survive, and even survival had not seemed possible. The Navy and the Air Force had severed the main arteries of his supply lines, and only a faint trickle had got through to keep the heart beating. The Navy and Air Force had harried him constantly, depriving him of the smallest chance to gain strength to counter-attack. They had, many times, delivered him and his weary remnants ripe for the kill. And at last the German rearguards had demolished the harbour and wharves of Tripoli, and blown the dumps, and departed from the desert. It used to be said that the Eighth Army would be pursuing the 90th Light Division to the end of time. The whole business had settled into a pattern.

Nevertheless Tripoli crowned Montgomery's triumph, and the triumph of his Eighth Army, the one with the 'star', the one he had made his own and modelled to his will. His personal message was read out to the troops on January 23rd:

> Today, 23rd January, exactly three months after we began the Battle of Egypt, the Eighth Army has captured Tripoli, and has driven the enemy away to the west towards Tunisia. By skilful withdrawal tactics the enemy has eluded us, though we have taken a heavy toll of his army and air forces.
>
> The defeat of the enemy in battle at Alamein, the pursuit of his beaten army, and the final capture of Tripoli—a distance of some fourteen hundred miles from Alamein—has all been accomplished in three months. This achievement is probably without parallel in history. I congratulate the whole Army, and send my personal thanks to each one of you for the wonderful support you have given me.

It was all true. It had been a magnificent feat of organization and supply, always demanding immense energy and ingenuity, and at times achieving near miracles. General Alexander and his Staff, the 'A & Q' staffs from top to bottom, had provided General Montgomery with the tools of victory in abundance.

His Chief of Staff de Guingand, had proved himself a human dynamo, a 'maid of all work', serving his master. The Royal Navy and the Royal Air Force had given magnificent support all along the line, and had provided air cover for the forward troops. Everyone had known, even before Alam Halfa, that the old days of shortages were over. Men no longer had to make do. There was not much to grumble about—except the war itself. The Army lost its lean and hungry look.

With all this Montgomery had been too timid, too cautious, and in the end too anxious, to put his troops across the enemy line of retreat and destroy him.

The credit for Tripoli belonged more to Alexander than to Montgomery, but the triumph was all, or nearly all, Montgomery's. His new status was confirmed, his legend writ in sand, but scored at least for a generation. At the Prime Minister's request Alexander had sent a victory message home, making it dramatic and colourful:

> General Alexander to Prime Minister. Sir,—The orders you gave me on August 15,[1] 1942, have been fulfilled. His Majesty's enemies together with their impedimenta have been completely eliminated from Egypt, Cyrenaica, Libya and Tripolitania. I now await your further instructions.[2]

Those further instructions, along with much else, had come out of the Casablanca conference at which the new Allied Command structure had taken shape. General Alexander would take command of the new 18th Army Group under General Eisenhower, to drive the enemy out of Tunisia and into the sea. The matter was urgent. General Montgomery would proceed with the Eighth Army to assist these operations, to relieve the severe pressures sustained by the British 1st Army under General Anderson in Tunisia, and on the United States 11 Corps, at first under Major-General Fredendall, and later under Lieutenant-General Patton. The sooner Montgomery reached the Mareth line, and turned it, the better, and then his task was to drive on through the narrow Gabes gap, on to Tunis by way of Sfax and Sousse. If he moved swiftly and boldly it might still be

---

[1] 18th in fact—see Alexander *Memoirs*.
[2] Churchill, *The Hinge of Fate*, vol. iv, R.U. ed., p. 578.

his fortune to administer the *coup de grâce* to his enemy. But there was not much time.

Meanwhile, it was apparent that General Montgomery enjoyed a fame perhaps unique in the story of war. For 100 days the headlines of the newspapers of Britain, the Dominions and all the Commonwealth, and of the United States of America had borne his name. From Alamein to Tripoli the 'English-speaking peoples', and especially the people of Britain, read and heard over their radios, and finally saw, the news they had hungered for through more than three years of 'blood, toil, sweat and tears'. It was irresistible, and Montgomery was its indestructible hero. Every man had played his part well, including the Public Relations staff, the General's personal photographer, and the moving camera teams. The film of *The Desert Victory* would bring the thunder and the flash of guns into the eyes and ears of multitudes, and would enable Montgomery to marvel at himself as he waited to attack the enemy in the Mareth line.

It is ironical, but very natural, that Montgomery's every failure to catch and to destroy the enemy had added to his fame and stature as an army commander. It was a serial story of which every instalment was awaited with excitement, and with the knowledge that the 'hero' would be sure to prevail.

Had this story come to an end after Alamein, or even before Alamein, Montgomery would almost certainly have become just another half-forgotten name of one who had served his country well. Innumerable stories were told about him, as men journeyed to and from their labours, paused over cups of tea or coffee, or drank their pints of weak beer. Even his repeated destruction of the 90th Light Division was a matter, not for criticism, but for affectionate laughter. Old Monty! His every eccentricity was dissected with glee. His ruthlessness, his sackings of senior officers, even his boorishness, had become amusing to a vast public, if not to his brother officers. Sweethearts and wives adored him, the saviour of their men folk, and lonely women admired him affectionately from afar. His 'fan' mail rivalled that of a film star.

Almost every man of the Eighth Army home on leave shared in his commander's glory, and knew himself different from other men. The armies in the Far East fighting desperately in shocking conditions to stem, and turn back, the tide of the Japanese, were almost forgotten. The new British 1st Army already fighting hard in the mountains of Tunisia was barely known, but was rapidly growing a pride of its own. When the time came its units would take steps to ensure that they were not mistaken for the Eighth Army. Jealousy was natural, and rivalry was good for morale. The 78th Division was one of the first to prove it, proudly proclaiming its loyalties.

On February 3rd the Prime Minister and General Sir Alan Brooke, the CIGS, flew out to Tripoli to share in the triumph, and to be the guests of Montgomery in his caravan, as they had been before Alamein. Their protégé and choice had fulfilled their most sanguine hopes, and they were proud of him. The Prime Minister wrote a further 'Chapter' of praise in Montgomery's note-book, and preserved the march of the Eighth Army by the magic of his words in a short address to the Headquarters troops: 'Ever since your victory at Alamein you have nightly pitched your moving tents a day's march nearer home. In days to come when people ask you what you did in the Second World War, it will be enough to say: I marched with the Eighth Army.'

On that day the first ship sailed into the wrecked port of Tripoli, and soon the convoys would be coming in, signalling the end of the Army's supply problems. On the 4th Montgomery stood with his distinguished guests on the reviewing stand to watch the march-past of the 51st Division.

There is no braver sight than that of the Highlanders marching to the strange, eerie, deeply moving music of the bagpipes. It is a sound that acts like a potent drug upon the hearts and guts of men, and not surprisingly there were tears running down Churchill's cheeks. But Montgomery was the hero. His confidence was completely restored, and his anxieties were behind him for ever in the Desert. No man who heard him speak could doubt that he regarded himself as the complete master of the art of war. He said so, underlining his words with a trick of repetition that he was perfecting, and which was most effective with the junior members of his many audiences.

It would have been impossible for any human being to have remained unmoved and unchanged in some degree by the marks and proofs of fame, backed by affection, that now enveloped

General Montgomery. He had become the symbol of victory, the 'mascot' not only of his army, but of a nation. He gloried in it, but was not spoiled by it. He did not question it, nor did it arouse in him any signs of humility. His faults and virtues remained much as they had been, but he became, if anything, kinder. The chip he had always worn on his shoulder had been smoothed away, and while he appeared to be aggressive in speech, his voice had lost some of its metallic coldness. At times it could be almost 'fruity'. He was as sure of himself as perhaps it is possible for a man to be. He had been confirmed in his belief in his infallibility, and would brook no argument. Yet he had begun, almost imperceptibly, to mellow. It was a process that would take a very long time. His dry, withdrawn nature began to respond to the end of the long drought that had been his life, with brief and rare oases, from the beginning.

It is in the nature of men to evade self-knowledge, and it would be difficult with certainty for any of us to make a short list of men of whom we could say: they knew themselves. Certainly such men as Churchill and Montgomery would not be among them. It was the essence of their particular strength that they did not know themselves. Their egocentricity would not admit the thought.

General Montgomery had played his part to the limit of his limitations. His merits as a soldier were great, and his professionalism was rare and valuable in an army[1] that had suffered too much from amateurism. On the retreat to Dunkirk he had shown his mettle, and it was an irony of fate that had cast him in the role of an attacking general. In defence his caution and meticulous attention to detail were assets. In attack these traits condemned him and his troops to 'ironmongery', on an increasing scale. Yet because of his inheritance, and because the tide had turned irrevocably against the enemy, he had fitted his role to perfection. His limitations had produced the long story that Britain needed. The people could savour every mouthful, digesting victory slowly and not at a gulp. Montgomery had preserved for them the villain equally with the hero.

Inevitably now there would be some less glamorous chapters, but Montgomery's star would remain in the ascendant. In Cairo at Easter, reading the Lesson in the Cathedral, he would

---

[1] Army in the wider sense.

enjoy his fame. In London in May, 'incognito' at Claridges, he would know the plaudits of the crowd wherever he went, his beret, his army sweater showing six inches below his battle dress, instantly recognized. This was his 'uniform', and even the Monarch would take him as he was, but not without a smile.

Meanwhile General Alexander, the victor in Africa, the Commander of 18 Army Group was unrecognized and almost unknown. He was as happy in his role as was his subordinate in his.

CHAPTER TEN

On to Tunis!

I

THE need for the Eighth Army to make all speed into Tunisia, and to bring relief to the hard-pressed Anglo-American troops, was great. Yet it was natural, psychologically and administratively, that the Eighth Army, as well as its commander, should show a tendency to pause at Tripoli, to rest for a little while upon its laurels. The momentum that had carried it forward from Egypt could not be maintained. Moreover it had almost sprinted over the last lap of the course to the winning post. There was the need to re-open the port of Tripoli, and to move up the 10th Corps from Benghazi, to set in motion an enormous 'tail', to get a second wind. Quite naturally General Montgomery wanted to draw his army together again; to bring its powerful body into closer contact with its head, ready for the final bound in North Africa.

Moreover the army, and its commander, were well pleased. After the attrition it had suffered at Second Alamein its commander had shielded the army to the uttermost of his ability. Its leading troops had never lacked adequate air cover, and had been magnificently served by their artillery. Montgomery's caution had become their caution, his will their will. Perhaps it had been too easy. Armies, like men, are fashioned and tempered in triumph and in disaster, as well as in the dull, harsh grind of life and death daily toil. The new Eighth Army, after its first 'fright' at Second Alamein, had had nothing to fear. Montgomery had never dared to put his weight and drive behind the outflanking columns that could have given him victory. Conversely, he had tended to drive the engineers who alone could pave the way for his infantry.

Characteristically Montgomery's policy was inhibiting, instilling caution into those to whom caution in war is dangerous. No army and its commander more urgently needed a hard fight against equals, to know the bitter salt of defeat or near defeat, and thus to find its deep inner strengths. Victory alone is not enough. Fortunately, in its heart there still lived the old Eighth Army, the men who had played out that long and terrible game of war from one end of the desert to the other.

Naturally the new Eighth Army's breast swelled with pride. It had been for 100 days in the centre of the stage, the sole point of focus of a nation's hopes, and a nation's dreams, providing the stuff of myth and legend at the precise hour that myth and legend were needed. In their inner consciousness the British people sensed that despite their struggle, the bright star of their supremacy, their Empire, was setting fast; that the might that had sustained them and ruled the seas for more than a century, was almost done. The physical presence of their new great ally in their homeland, and now in North Africa, reminded them of truths they were not yet prepared to face. They had faced much. The long loneliness of nearly three years, with all its near disasters, its triumphs, its hours of hope and fear and glory, was over, and at the eleventh hour the twilight had been illuminated by a blaze of sunshine in the desert. Montgomery and his Eighth Army had become the story all men would tell.

If any man would be able to keep these deeds in the public eye it would be General Montgomery, but inevitably all that lay ahead would be seen in a larger context. They would be an army, no longer fighting a 'private war' of their own, but a great war alongside other armies. Montgomery himself would be in competition with his peers. It would be a new challenge. Nevertheless it was in the hearts of the men of the Eighth Army, and at the edges of their minds, that the great days of glamour were nearing their end. Ever since Second Alamein a British Army had been fighting hard in the mountains of Tunisia against a German Army infinitely better equipped than the army Rommel had commanded in its last struggles. The German Army in Tunisia was at first a match for its adversaries, and at times more than a match. Having come within twelve miles of Tunis in November, the British 1st Army and the US 11 Corps had been thrown back, and had steeled themselves for a bitter struggle in difficult mountainous country threaded with narrow passes. In the south, areas of marsh, and salt lakes added to the hazards.

The Eighth Army had stolen the 1st Army's thunder. Moreover, the British people, deeply aware of their condition, tended to take pride less in the achievements of their army in Tunisia than in the set-backs at first suffered by the inexperienced troops of their mighty ally. It enhanced the performance of their own men, and added a touch of spice to the drama of their swan song. Long before it reached Tripoli the new Eighth Army was developing a personality of its own. Montgomery had set his mark upon it. His rule was absolute, and his will was felt and effective at least down to brigade level, and beyond that, according to the quality of the brigadiers. It was, on the whole, a happy family, but it bore blemishes arising out of its commander's fears and prejudices. The worst of these was his treatment of the 4th Indian Division, never to be forgiven or forgotten by the division or its commander. Montgomery's gratuitous insult to General Auchinleck immediately upon taking over his command, and his inability to acknowledge his inheritance, reflected his dislike of the Indian Army. Its commanders belonged to another 'club', the wrong club. Its troops were not trained by him. Moreover, it seemed to Montgomery that any praise or acknowledgement given to those who had preceded him must detract from his own fame and achievement. His behaviour towards the 4th Indian Division after Second Alamein shows him at his worst. Against his own stated policy he split up Indian divisions, and denied them the roles they believed that they had earned. Thus he insulted not only some of the finest troops under his command, but denied his army their fighting services. 'Many who were present in the Middle East at the outbreak of war will remember the sense of relief which came with the prompt arrival of the 4th Indian Division. This formation shared all the vicissitudes of the early desert battles . . .' wrote a reviewer in *The Times Literary Supplement*.[1]

Montgomery relegated the division to menial second-line duties.

> 'The Army Commander's intention is, I think,' wrote Brigadier H. K. Dimoline, CRA of the Division, 'to employ the Fourth Indian Division in the same manner as the rest of the Indian units in Palestine, Cyprus and Egypt, i.e. as garrison troops, useful fatigue parties for salvage, and as police:

---

[1] September 16, 1965. Review of *A Roll of Honour*, The Story of the Indian Army 1639–1945 by J. E. Elliot.

ON TO TUNIS! 177

namely in the same manner as the Libyan Arab irregulars and the other second line troops employed.'[1]

The Division and its Commander, Major-General Tuker, were outraged, and Tuker wrote at once to his Corps Commander, Lieutenant-General Horrocks. He pointed out that his Division had seen more service in the Desert than any other. 'I do not think that anyone would deny that it is the most experienced division in the Empire.'

It had fought at Sidi Barrani, and in the mountains of Eritrea and in Syria. It had fought from Tobruk to Agedabia, in the Gazala battle and at First Alamein. Its contribution to Second Alamein had been notable.

General Horrocks agreed with every word, and forwarded General Tuker's letter to Montgomery with a covering letter of his own:

> Although this Division has only been under my command for a short time I have had the opportunity of going round a good many units. I concur with the remarks in the attached letter. There is no doubt that this is an experienced Division, more experienced probably than any other Division in the Middle East. It is imbued with a fine fighting spirit and in my opinion it would be a tragedy if this fine Division was not given a further opportunity of representing India alongside United Kingdom and Dominion forces.[2]

Montgomery ignored these messages, and gave no hint that he had given the pleas of his generals, or the merits of the Division, any consideration at all. On the face of it Montgomery's behaviour is boorish in the extreme. It seems to reveal a lack of sensitivity, even of common sense, that is alarming. Moreover, such an attitude would not be conducive to high morale.

Perhaps all that had gone before was truly a closed book to the new general. Perhaps he had eliminated the long struggle in the Desert from his consciousness, relegating its great battles to the status of mere skirmishes, as Alexander would do.[3]

But the 4th Indian Division had many triumphs ahead. It would fight in Tunisia. It would help to storm the heights of

[1] Compton Mackenzie, *Eastern Epic*, p. 603.
[2] Mackenzie, *Eastern Epic*, p. 604.
[3] *The Alexander Memoirs*, ed. John North, p. 16.

Monte Cassino. 'At the beginning of March 1943 Montgomery at last practised with an Indian Division what he preached for British Divisions just over five months earlier. The physician had healed himself' wrote Sir Compton Mackenzie.[1]

Or perhaps the mountains of Tunisia induced Montgomery to remember the abilities of Indian troops in that kind of country. Outwardly General Montgomery seems a simple sort of man, but inside he was a maze of complexes and complexities. He suffered greatly by his inability to mix freely as friend, relaxing in the company of his generals, enjoying discussion. In his limited sphere he heard only the things he wished to hear. No voice would dare to question his authority in the smallest matter, and his generals were compelled to use the greatest tact in approaching him on any serious matter in which their ideas might be in conflict with his own.

There was nothing unique, or unusual in this. It is perhaps one of the great tragedies of the human condition that men of power seldom invite candid comment and free discussion. Yet, in most cases the blame must lie also with their associates. There is a passage in Sir John Kennedy's, *The Business of War*,[2] which illustrates this situation in regard to Churchill. The Prime Minister had 'savaged' Sir John Dill and insulted the army. 'I cannot tell you how angry the Prime Minister has made me. What he said about the Army tonight I can never forgive.'

Kennedy suggested to Dill that 'It would be great fun' to give the Prime Minister a taste of his own medicine. A list of current legitimate criticisms of the Prime Minister's handling of affairs was easily made. 'We both began to laugh,' wrote Kennedy.

But why laugh? Why not say these things to Churchill?

Perhaps the greatest need of many great men is a sense of proportion, a sense of humour. At least Churchill was constantly attended by men of stature, some of whom bravely opposed some of his wild ideas, but Churchill disliked the company of his equals in wit and expression. He would tolerate no man who might become a rival.

Montgomery, a far lesser man, preferred only the company of the young. He had constructed a personal hierarchy in which he had his place, a kind of 'House-Master', subordinate to the

---

[1] Mackenzie, *Eastern Epic*, p. 605.
[2] pp. 63-4.

'High-Master', and of course to the 'Board of Governors' and 'The Lord, Mighty in Battle'. But in his 'House' he was unchallenged. He heard only those things he wished to hear, and it is in the nature of young men to please their seniors of exalted rank. Montgomery's young men were not sycophants, but they were lieutenants and captains sitting at the feet of the commander of an army.

Montgomery had established a Tactical Headquarters in which he chose to live an austere life, served by his chauffeur and batman. Here he could relax in the company of his dedicated young men, very much like a scoutmaster round the camp fire. The young men he had chosen were, I believe, devoted to him. Almost certainly he felt affection for them, and especially for his personal *aide*, John Poston, whose death in 1945 moved him deeply. In his *Memoirs* he wrote:

> Reference has been made to the team of liaison officers which I organized to keep me in touch with events on the battle front. These were young officers of character, initiative and courage; they had seen much fighting and were able to report accurately on battle situations. I selected each one personally, and my standard was high. It was dangerous work and some were wounded, and some killed. They were a gallant band of knights.[1]

In such passages Montgomery reveals his romanticism, and his remarkable simplicity. He reveals also his ideas of leadership and a benevolent paternalism. He inhabited a very narrow world, and dared not adventure beyond its limits. It was the world of a child who sees the deeds he longs to do as deeds already done. Through the accounts of his young men he shared their adventures vicariously. They knew him well; they admired him greatly; they were able to relax, and to laugh in his company. They were his disciples. Yet they shared a cultural wilderness, divorced from the rough and tumble of war, however much their tasks led them into danger. They did not learn to command men and to lead them into battle.

Such a system of 'favourites' could lead to a great deal of trouble. Troops and their commanders would easily believe that they were spied upon. It is a tribute to the young men and to

[1] Montgomery, *Memoirs*, p. 531.

Montgomery that this did not happen. There was indeed considerable criticism of General Montgomery in the Eighth Army, but the troops regarded him with easy, tolerant affection, and his eccentricities delighted them. He was their genuine 'mascot', and he did not dislike the description.

II

The arrival of Field-Marshal Rommel and his battered nucleus of an army in Tunisia had stimulated immediate action. Early in February General von Arnim, commanding the 5th Panzer Army, had launched an offensive against the British 1st Army, forcing limited withdrawals in the north, while Rommel, attacking from Gafsa, inflicted a massive local defeat upon the US 1st Armoured Division in the Kasserine Pass. For a week the situation was serious and confused.

In the midst of these events General Alexander reached General Eisenhower's Allied Headquarters in Tunisia on the 15th of the month, and took over the command of the newly-formed 18th Army Group on the 19th. Four days later Field-Marshal Rommel was appointed to the command of the German and Italian armies in Tunisia. Both generals had inherited difficult situations, but whereas Alexander's problems were largely administrative and tactical, Rommel's were strategic on the highest level, governed by a rapidly deteriorating supply situation. It had been a strategic blunder of the first magnitude to commit German armies to the defence of Tunisia, and would lead to a disaster in Africa not much smaller in degree than the disaster at Stalingrad. It could still be avoided.

General Alexander's new command comprised the British 1st Army in the north under General Sir Kenneth Anderson, the US 11th Corps in the centre, and the British Eighth Army in the south, still extended over 700 or 800 miles, with its advance guards in Tunisia and the 10th Corps in Benghazi. There were also numerous, ill-equipped bodies of French. It was a command demanding not only skill in generalship, but tact and moral courage in Alexander's relations with his Allies. It was necessary and urgent to accustom US troops to the realities of battle without breaking their hearts, or depressing their spirit. It was also urgent to assess the capabilities of commanders. It was early for decisive judgements, but decisive judgements had to be made. Almost at once General Fredendall was replaced in command of the US 11th Corps by General Patton, a soldier whose professionalism and flair for command was often blurred by his flamboyant character and robust eccentricities. From the first General Alexander achieved good relations with the Supreme Commander, General Eisenhower, and his Chiefs of Staff.

Meanwhile on February 15th, while Alexander confronted these urgent and difficult problems in Tunisia, General Montgomery was lecturing to senior officers in Tripoli on 'How to make War'. General Horrocks, whose admiration for Montgomery was unbounded, accompanied General Patton to this performance. The American general was not impressed. His ideas of warfare, based to an important extent on his deep personal study of the campaigns of General Sherman in the American Civil War, were diametrically opposed to those of General Montgomery, and soon he would have many opportunities to demonstrate his methods. No man defied logistics more boldly than General George Patton, nor with more success. Few men were more enslaved by logistics than General Montgomery.

The pressing need of the hour was for the Eighth Army to advance rapidly upon the Mareth positions held by the Italian 1st Army in southern Tunisia, and thus swiftly to relieve the pressures Rommel was able to exert upon the centre. Mareth, a powerful defensive position between the Matmata hills and the sea, and behind the line of the Wadi Zigzaou, would present Montgomery with his next battle, the first since Second Alamein. To this encounter it seemed to the Americans that the Eighth Army advanced 'with the majestic deliberation of a pachyderm.'[1] The phrase reveals more their lack of love for Montgomery, than a fair assessment. It is true that Montgomery ordered the advance of his forces with his accustomed caution and canny calculation, resolved to ensure the overwhelming superiority in every department of war, without which he was unwilling to confront the enemy. To the observer the advance seemed slow, but in fact he made good speed. The armoured spearheads had never paused, and the Long Range Desert Group had crossed the Matmata Hills to make contact with the British 1st Army in early

[1] U.S. Army in World War II: *Mediterranean Theatre of Operations*.

February to provide Montgomery with all the information he could desire.

On February 15th the 8th Armoured Brigade took Ben Gardine unopposed, and two days later the key road centre of Medenine was occupied by the 22nd Armoured Brigade. 'There was no sign of the enemy.'[1]

It was here that the veteran commanders of the armoured units showed their resource and courage. On this level, and at this distance from the army command it was possible for commanders to take risks. Thus by 'a brilliant feat of arms' Lieutenant-Colonel Hutton, a real 'Desert Fox' and master navigator of armour, seized positions on the Tadjera Ridge and secured by a *coup de main* the start line for the assault on the Mareth positions. He did more: he gained vital time, and imposed a check upon the Afrika Korps which would render its assault upon Medenine both late and hopeless.

Rommel, in fact, was forced to face two ways, unable to follow up or to consolidate his early successes against the US 11th Corps, he faced a constant threat to his communications through Gafsa. It was even possible that Patton, given his head, might have burst through to Gabes and the sea. Indeed Patton needed some restraint to keep clear of Montgomery's line of advance from Mareth. At the same time Rommel was engaged in massive command problems and frustrating arguments with the German and Italian High Commands. He was also on the verge of serious illness, and his doctors insisted in early February that he must return to Wiener Neustadt to continue the cure interrupted in November by the Second Battle of Alamein.

Doggedly Rommel hung on, resolved to do all in his power to save his army and the German-Italian armies in Tunisia. His days, he knew well, were numbered.

The German-Italian command was breaking down at the precise moment that the Anglo-American High Command was taking shape in the field, and functioning with a smoothness for which Eisenhower and Alexander deserve great praise. It is evident, I think, that Rommel disagreed with the German decision to attempt to stand in Tunisia, but since the armies had been committed he wanted to defend a perimeter consistent

---

[1] *The Tanks*, vol. ii, p. 247.

with his numbers, the difficult terrain, and the supplies likely to be available. He could not match his enemies in armour, guns, ammunition or equipment generally, and the gap would widen. The Mediterranean had ceased to be an Italian sea, and the hour was approaching when the armies in Tunisia would be cut off from their bases. Their life-line was tenuous.[1]

Meanwhile the German commander found himself committed to defend a line 387 miles long, and in which there were enormous gaps. He demanded to reduce the line to just under 100 miles from Jebel Mansour on his right to Enfidaville on his left, and to maintain a bridge-head until the last moment. Kesselring, alarmed at the number of airfields this would hand over to the allies, disputed Rommel's view.

Specifically in the immediate future Rommel did not wish the 1st Italian Army under Giovanni Messe to fight in the Mareth position. He felt that the army was certain to be enveloped, and that at least two divisions would be needed for the defence of the El Hamma Gap through the Matmata hills, and to defend his line of withdrawal. Moreover, von Arnim in the north would be under pressure from the British 1st Army. The obvious course, as it seemed to Rommel, was to begin the withdrawal, and to prepare to defend the Gabes-Chott El Fedjadj position. On this very narrow front the enemy might be contained while the lines were shortened.

Meanwhile it was vital to gain time, and to attempt to deliver a punch against the advanced elements of the Eighth Army at Medenine before Montgomery had time to prepare. This was the only hope, and the bold stroke of Lieutenant-Colonel Hutton had done much to deprive him of it. 'The decision to make the attack at all was based on the realization that we only had two choices open to us—either to await the British attack in our line and suffer a crushing defeat, or to attempt to gain time by breaking up the enemy's assembly areas.'[2]

Speed, of course, was essential, and with it tactical surprise. Up to March 2nd there might have been a slight chance of limited success before General Leese's 30th Corps had planted itself firmly in position. Montgomery was very much aware of the need for speed, and of Rommel's intentions. 'I would not be

[1] 168 supply ships were sunk between November and May, and eighteen damaged.
[2] *The Rommel Papers*, p. 414.

ready until 4 March,' he wrote, 'and during the period 28 February–3 March the Eighth Army was unbalanced . . . This was my second period of great anxiety since the advance began.'[1]

General Cramer, commanding the German Afrika Korps, had the miserable task of planning and carrying out an operation that was doomed to failure before it could begin. He mustered 160 tanks, 200 guns and 10,000 infantry against an enemy outnumbering him by more than two to one in armour, and with massive superiority in the air, infantry and artillery. A force five times as powerful would have had a very small chance of success.

Fog veiled the Tadjera hills on the morning of the 6th when Cramer sent his armour into battle to be met by concentrated fire from Montgomery's massed guns, and to be repulsed by the infantry of the 51st Division. Without achieving anything at all the enemy left fifty-two tanks destroyed on that brief battlefield. 'For the Army Group to remain longer in Africa was now plain suicide,' Rommel wrote.

On March 7th he installed General Bayerlein with the Italian 1st Army to do his best to look after the Germans. He then took off for Rome to argue, and thence to the Führer's headquarters. His arguments were in vain. Sickness of the spirit as well as of the body were heavy upon him. His personal struggle in Africa was over. He would never return.

If Rommel's advice had been taken, and a holding action fought while steadily withdrawing into Sicily and Italy, a major disaster might have been avoided, and it is unlikely that the Allied assault upon Sicily would have been advanced by a single day. Logistics more than ever before had become the governing factor.

III

In response to an urgent request from General Alexander on February 20th, Montgomery speeded up the advance of the 30th Corps towards Medenine. The Americans were anxious for the Eighth Army to threaten Rommel's rearguard, and to 'afford relief to the US 11th Corps beyond Kasserine.'[2] 'I speeded

---

[1] Montgomery, *El Alamein to the River Sangro*, p. 45.
[2] U.S. Army in World War II. Official History, *N.W. Africa*.

up events,' wrote Montgomery, 'and by the 26th February it was clear that our pressure had caused Rommel to break off his attack against the Americans.'[1]

But the Americans did not agree: 'Rommel did not withdraw in response to the Eighth Army's threat but in his eagerness to win an early, easy victory over only its advanced elements.'[2]

These statements are a part of a whole truth, expressed clearly by General Fuller: 'Rommel, knowing that Montgomery was not yet ready to advance, decided first to fall upon the Americans and next to attack the Eighth Army, not to win a decisive victory, but to gain time and keep the war going in Tunisia as long as possible.'[3]

It was still difficult for General Montgomery to see himself as less than the principal actor in these affairs, and Field-Marshal Rommel as his opponent. He had attacked Rommel at Second Alamein before Rommel was there; now he prepared to attack him in the Mareth positions after he had gone. There is, in fact, a certain confusion as to who was fighting whom.

After Tripoli, Field-Marshal Rommel was opposed for a short time by General Eisenhower and by General Alexander. General Montgomery's opponent was General Messe, commanding the 1st Italian Army.

By February 20th Montgomery was satisfied that the supplies coming into the Port of Tripoli at a rate of 3,500 tons a day would satisfy his immediate needs. He thereupon began to move his army forward. With his usual care he had begun to plan his assault upon the Mareth positions for March 20th, and one has the eerie feeling that he would have gone ahead in much the same way even if the enemy had withdrawn before that date. He had realized that Rommel must try to break up his leading elements before they had time to settle in at Medenine, and knew, after March 3rd, that such an attack would be 'an absolute gift'. 'Rommel attacked me at dawn. It was very foolish of him,' Montgomery wrote to General Brooke. 'I have five hundred 6-pounder anti-tank guns dug in on the ground; I have four hundred tanks, and I have good infantry holding strong pivots, and a great weight of artillery.'[4]

[1] Montgomery, *Memoirs*, 158.
[2] U.S. Army in World War II, *N.W. Africa*.
[3] Fuller, *Second World War*, p. 244.
[4] Bryant, *The Turn of the Tide*, p. 588.

Montgomery could not be surprised, outflanked, or his positions penetrated. He could have withstood an assault by an enemy at least three, and probably five, times as powerful as that which General Cramer was able to throw against him. It is an exaggeration to call Medenine a battle. Part of the problem it raises in my mind is to account for General Montgomery's personal attitude, and perhaps his personal message to his troops on March 6th, before the German attack, is revealing:

1. The enemy is now advancing to attack us. This is because he is caught like a rat in a trap and he is hitting out in every direction trying to gain time to stave off the day of final defeat in North Africa.

2. This is the very opportunity we want. Not only are we well equipped with everything we need, but in addition the soldiers of the Eighth Army have a fighting spirit and a morale which is right on the top line.

3. We will stand and fight the enemy in our present positions. There must be NO WITHDRAWAL anywhere, and of course, NO SURRENDER.[1]

The first two paragraphs are unexceptionable, but the use of the words 'withdrawal' and 'surrender', both in capitals, seems incomprehensible. They echo his first orders upon taking command. They seem to suggest that withdrawal and surrender are possibilities; that they may be in the minds of his troops. In which case Montgomery is insulting his troops, or grossly magnifying the enemy strength in their minds. But why should he do this? Perhaps, from the outset it was a device to magnify his deeds.

At Medenine he had prepared an immensely powerful ambush. It was dug in and ordered to remain so. This was the general's conception of balance. He had feared that the enemy might catch him off balance, by which he meant that the enemy might attack before he was planted as solid as rock.

The enemy ran head on into the immovable rock, and was severely hurt. The 154 Brigade of the 51st (Highland) Division repelled several sharp attacks during the day. Only three squadrons of tanks came briefly into action. The great mass of the British armour did not move. The anti-tank guns did the rest,

---

[1] *Forward to Victory.*

destroying forty-two out of the fifty-two enemy tanks left on the field. On the British side no unit moved either forward or back.

To Montgomery this brief encounter was reminiscent of Alam Halfa. He remarks that he did not pursue the enemy. At Alam Halfa he had the enemy well within his embrace, and refrained, with Alexander's approval, from closing his powerful arms upon them. At Medenine the enemy failed to penetrate the British enclosure, and was not counter-attacked seriously. That mastery of balance that would have enabled Montgomery to poise his forces for reflex counter-attack always eluded him. He never mastered the 'expanding torrent', and in common with all problems he could not understand, he dismissed it from his mind. All things were simple to him because all things he could not do could not be done.

Immediately after Medenine Montgomery moved steadily ahead with his plans and dispositions for his assault upon the Mareth line. He named his operation 'Pugilist Gallop', and explained it to his commanders, down to lieutenant-colonels, as was his custom. While the 'pugilist' smashed a heavy blow to the enemy midriff, the 'gallop', representing a tremendous left hook, would move at full speed on a 150-mile journey through the hills to outflank the enemy, and smash through the El Hamma gap to Gabes.

It was his invariable plan, yet with the important difference that he gave equal emphasis to both blows. It was his most determined attempt to outflank and destroy the enemy. The 30th Corps would assault across the wide, deep and muddy Wadi Zigzaou on the right, while the New Zealand Division, greatly strengthened, made a wide sweep southward through the Matmata hills. It was a magnificent cavalcade comprising 27,000 men and 6,000 vehicles, the tanks of the 8th Armoured Brigade carried on transporters, the Senegalese of General Le Clerc's force that had marched up from Lake Chad to be in at this first 'kill' on their way to Paris, and in the midst of it all, thirsting for a fight, the Greek Sacred Squadron in their thirty jeeps mounted with machine guns.

Preliminary probing attacks began on the night of March 17th followed by the main frontal assault on a front of 1,200 yards on the 20th. This was preceded by a barrage from 300 guns dropping an estimated 36,000 high explosive shells upon the enemy, while more than 600 bombers and fighters added their bombs to the deluge. Behind this the 151st Brigade of the 50th Division, supported by the armour of 50th Royal Tank Regiment, attacked across the Wadi. Tanks equipped with flails to beat mines, and others carrying fascines for bridging, led with the Royal Engineer detachment.

The Wadi Zigzaou was an anti-tank barrier of daunting proportions. A fifty-foot wide stream flowed in a central channel, and the bottom was soft mud, so soft that a tank sank into it up to its turret. The banks were steep, and masked a second anti-tank ditch. Nevertheless, by March 22nd, 151st Brigade supported by 50th RTR was across the Wadi, and held a bridgehead some two miles long by one mile deep. The position was precarious in the extreme, and could not be closely supported. Soon after noon on the 22nd a resolute counter-attack by thirty tanks of the 15th Panzer Division supported by infantry, marked the beginning of the end. It had been I think, hopeless before it began, and could not seriously have deceived the enemy into believing that it represented the main threat.

On the morning of the 24th, 151st Brigade and all that remained of 50th RTR were back across the Wadi, leaving thirty-five tanks, 200 prisoners, and their dead on the enemy bank. At the same time the New Zealanders had suffered a check south of the El Hamma Gap. Montgomery's plan had now failed, but he reacted swiftly. He had held the 10th Corps armour in readiness to exploit his planned break-through on the central front. Now he ordered Horrocks with the 1st Armoured Division to follow in the tracks of the New Zealanders with all possible speed, while the 4th Indian Division set off through the short cut of the Hallouf Pass, wondering why the Army Commander had not thought of that way through much earlier. It had been well reconnoitred.

The whole weight of the attack was now behind the outflanking movement.

Meanwhile General Messe, commanding the Italian 1st Army, was well aware of the situation, but was hampered by the confusion of orders and intentions reaching him piecemeal from two Supreme Commands, only one of which could impose its will. Field-Marshal Rommel had been stating his view in Rome on his way home, and in the Führer's headquarters. The ensuing arguments and periods of indecision made Messe's situation intolerable. While Rommel's views seemed to prevail, the early withdrawal of the Italian 1st Army to the Chott position was partially begun. This was vaguely the position on the 14th of the month, but by the 17th Kesselring, arguing the need to deny airfields to the enemy for as long as possible, reversed what had not been more than a 'half' decision.

With Generals von Arnim and Bayerlein breathing down his neck, and with Bayerlein's authority challenging his own, the Italian general did remarkably well. He had sent the 21st Panzer Division to reinforce the Italian infantry at the El Hamma Gap, while the 15th Panzer division took up a position to the north-west of Mareth, from which it could support El Hamma or the Mareth line. All the reserves were committed, not only against Montgomery, but against the powerful flanking threat of the US 11th Corps.

In throwing his weight behind the outflanking movement as soon as he saw that his 'Master Plan' had failed, Montgomery had acted with more speed and determination than he had shown at any stage of the campaign. When Horrocks caught up with Freyberg, commanding the New Zealand 'Corps', he found the general under constant pressure from the Army Commander. On March 26th at 4 o'clock in the afternoon, and with close support on a massive scale from the Western Desert Air Force, and with the unexpected help of a dust storm, the 8th Armoured Brigade charged flat out and breached the gap.

A heavy barrage had preceded the attack, and twenty-two squadrons of fighters, fighter-bombers and tank-busters, blasted everything that moved. 'This blitz attack was the most complete example of the close integration of land and air power up to that time.' Montgomery wrote.[1]

Nevertheless, the intention to 'pour through' to Gabes, to cut the escape route of the Italian 1st Army, and thence onward to Sfax, was thwarted by the fight put up by the 21st and 15th Panzer Divisions. On the 24th von Arnim had ordered Messe to pull out from the Mareth position, and by the night of the 27th the last of the Italian non-motorized infantry reached the Chott position in 'a single bound'. On the 29th El Hamma and Gabes

[1] Montgomery, *Memoirs*, p. 163.

were in Montgomery's hands, but once again he had failed to trap the enemy, and was faced with the need to fight a 'set-piece' battle to force the narrow bottleneck of the Chott position across the Wadi Akarit. He had moved farther and faster than ever before, but not quite fast enough. He now moved with surprising speed.

On March 31st Montgomery re-grouped, and on the moonless night of April 6th he attacked across the Wadi with three infantry divisions, the 50th, 51st and 4th Indian from right to left, covered by a concentrated fire from 450 guns.

For the enemy the situation was hopeless. Patton's US 11th Corps had tied down the 10th Panzer Division at El Guettar throughout the Mareth battle. No conceivable help was at hand. In the early evening of the first day General Messe's commanders reported that they could not hold out for another day. The 15th Panzer Division had counter-attacked strongly in the afternoon, and did well until it ran out of ammunition, and was forced to withdraw. At eight o'clock that night Messe began to withdraw with all possible speed to Enfidaville, and the cover of the mountains. The German-Italian command, long at loggerheads, had broken down. Bayerlein alone controlled the Germans, and the Italians, having nothing left to fight with, surrendered in droves.

Nevertheless General Messe's Italian 1st Army was not destroyed, and the chase was over.

IV

Enfidaville was the end of the road for General Montgomery and the Eighth Army. The final victory and the crown of Tunis eluded them, and it may be said of Montgomery that because he never risked a defeat, he never risked a victory. Hitler had delivered the German-Italian Army into his hands in the final phase of the Second Battle of El Alamein, and caution had deprived him of the total victory that should have been his.

Since the Eighth Army had moved out of Tripolitania Montgomery had shown a greater liveliness and flexibility. He had thrown off his anxieties. He was no longer operating alone, but as a part of an Army Group already threatening and harrying the enemy in the rear. He approached Mareth in the certainty of victory, and was prepared to take some risks to cut off and to destroy the enemy. It was his last chance, and he missed it by a narrow margin. It must have seemed miraculous then, as it does now, that the 15th and 21st Panzer Divisions could stem the victorious tide, even for an hour. But they had held on, and the rearguards of the 15th Panzer Division and the 90th Light Division held open the escape route to Enfidaville to the bitter end.

At the Wadi Akarit Montgomery knew that his time had almost run out, and he had ordered the 10th Corps to smash its way through, and to overwhelm the enemy before he could escape. 'By immense endeavours, however, the enemy prevented me from breaking into the open before dark.'[1] Montgomery wrote.

He still believed that he was fighting Rommel, and seemed unaware, even many years later, that Rommel had been absent for more than a month.

The Eighth Army had swept on through Sfax and Sousse, making contact with the US 11th Corps on the Gafsa-Gabes road on the 7th and with the British 9th Corps moving fast eastward out of Fondouk, compelling the enemy to throw out screens to cover the last of the road. On April 13th the leading armour of the 10th Corps confronted the anti-tank ditch guarding the narrow coastal passage between the mountains and the sea. Hammamet at the southern base of the Cape Bon peninsula became Montgomery's objective.

For a day or two Montgomery half hoped that he might be able to 'bounce' the enemy out of his strong positions, but the hope soon died. On the night of the 19th/20th he staged a full-scale attack, backed by the 'great weight of artillery' that had become the prologue to his every move. Small gains were made at heavy cost, but the enemy held. On the 29th he tried again, hurling four infantry divisions against the barrier in vain, and it was clear that he had very little idea of how to tackle mountain warfare.

> ... the more I examined the problem now confronting the Eighth Army the more convinced I became that our opera-

[1] Montgomery, *El Alamein to the River Sangro*, p. 58.

tions would be extremely costly and had little chance of achieving decisive success with the resources available. The enemy was located in ideal defensive country . . .[1]

As to his resources, they were as great as he could deploy in every department of warfare, and both General Bayerlein and von Arnim thought the Enfidaville position too weak to hold. They left the 90th Light Division to do a rear-guard job.

The US Official History comments:

> This attack got off to an unsatisfactory start. General Montgomery, faced with possible failure, obtained General Alexander's authorization to abandon his attempt to reach Hammamet, and to convert the Eighth Army's role to that of holding the enemy by purely local offensive measures, in conjunction with the north-easterly drive of the French XIX Corps.

The end in Africa was 'not without a certain poignancy' for Montgomery and the Eighth Army, as Alexander noted. There is poignancy, too in Montgomery's recollections of these days, and of his exchanges with the Army Group Commander. He had to adjust himself to new circumstances, and it was difficult. In his *Memoirs* he appears to usurp the role of his Army Group Commander, and gives the impression that the suggestion for the 1st Army to take the initiative in the assault on Tunis was his.

Alexander visited his army commander on the 30th, finding him in bed with tonsillitis and influenza. Montgomery describes the visit:

> . . . so I asked Alexander if he would come and see me at my headquarters near Sousse. He arrived on the 30th April. I said it was essential to re-group the two armies, First and Eighth, so that the attack on Tunis could be made with the maximum strength in the most suitable area. I suggested that I should send First Army the 7th Armoured Division, 4th Indian Division, 201st Guards Brigade, and some extra artillery, together with a very experienced corps commander to handle the attack: I meant Horrocks.[2]

---

[1] Montgomery, *El Alamein to the River Sangro*, p. 61.
[2] Montgomery, *Memoirs*, p. 165.

General Alexander corrects Montgomery's aberration with the mild comment: 'But, of course, Montgomery had nothing to do with the attack on Tunis.'[1]

General Alexander had decided on the transfer of troops from the Eighth Army, and had chosen Horrocks to command the 9th Corps when its commander was wounded. On April 18th the 1st Armoured Division had been transferred to the 1st Army, and Montgomery had fallen in with all the transfers with a good grace. It was hoped that the enemy might continue to expect the main attack to come from the Eighth Army, but they were undeceived by radio intercepts warning them of the regrouping. But the expectations of the enemy could not save them from total defeat. On May 6th the 7th Armoured Division led the advance into Tunis while the US 11th Corps and its French units took Bizerta. On May 12th more than a quarter of a million men laid down their arms. Germany had denied to Italy the last chance of a 'Dunkirk', and had isolated her armies completely. As late as May 1st the Italian High Command had made a last desperate attempt to persuade the Germans to let them throw in the Italian fleet, but 'could not get a hearing in Berlin'.

A new pattern is discernible in these last days. It is a pattern that will be repeated in clearer definition in the battles involving armies and army groups from Sicily to the end. Into this pattern General Montgomery's methods fitted well. He could hold a flank with an army, or even with two armies, unleash his enormous barrages, and push and crumble as well as any man. Others would supply the 'expanding torrent'.

---

[1] Earl Alexander of Tunis, *Memoirs*, Ed. John North, p. 38. London, Cassell, 1962.

PART FOUR
UNDER TWO FLAGS

CHAPTER ELEVEN

The Allied Command

I

THE problems of Allied command had become of paramount political and military importance from the moment it had become clear that British and American troops must fight side by side in the Atlantic theatre of war.

Somewhere, at some time, the reconquest of the Continent must begin with the first British or American soldier wading ashore out of the sea; and while experience in North Africa had shown that such a venture could succeed, it had shown equally vividly, and in less critical conditions, the obstacles to success.[1]

The Allied experience in North Africa had put an end to the arguments and recriminations about the timing of the cross-channel attack. The Americans had realized that the long abandoned 'Sledgehammer' had been impossible, and that an assault in 1943 would have been unlikely to succeed.

Even if the Allies had succeeded in establishing a bridgehead in Normandy in 1943, their experience in Tunisia demonstrated that they would have been unprepared for breaking out of this bridgehead and thrusting far toward the heart of Nazi Germany.[2]

Nevertheless the results of the Tunisian campaign were satisfactory. The Americans still regarded the British Mediterranean 'soft underbelly' strategy with suspicion, but they were prepared to invade Sicily, and possibly Southern Italy. That was broadly the position when Roosevelt, Churchill, and their generals met at Casablanca in January, 1943, and announced the policy of Unconditional Surrender, which was to inhibit planning, and obscure the valid object of war to the end, and beyond the end.

[1] John Ehrman, *Grand Strategy*, vol. v. London, H.M.S.O., 1956.
[2] U.S. Army in World War II, *North West Africa*, Seizing the Initiative in the West. Washington, Office of Chief of Military History.

'Henceforth,' wrote General Fuller,[1] 'these two words were to hang like a putrifying albatross around the necks of America and Britain.' They would also hang around the neck of the Supreme Commander, at that moment emerging from comparative obscurity. No scrutiny of the Army Lists of Britain and America in 1940 or 1941 would have provided a clue to his identity. Once it had been recognized, reluctantly by the British, that the Supreme Commander would be an American, General Marshall, the US Chief of Staff, had seemed the obvious choice. This continued to be accepted until December 5, 1943, when President Roosevelt suddenly decided that he would not sleep soundly with General Marshall out of the country.

The British, therefore, were deeply concerned with their own senior commander in the field, the man who would command their armies in the final chapters of the war. Whatever the talents of such a man, it would be important that he should be able to co-operate to the full with the Americans. He must be also a strong man, capable of sustaining British influence in the field, a man of tactical skill and strategic vision, a man of patience, tact, and unswerving resolution. General Alan Brooke, the British Chief of Staff, General Alexander, and General Paget, commanding British Home Forces, seemed the first in line. Few, apart from General Montgomery himself, would have fancied his chances for the job.

Combined planning staffs in London and Washington were learning to work together, and from these embryos the nucleus of a Supreme Headquarters Staff was taking shape. Soon, and with growing urgency, they would await the names of the senior commanders to give their labours relevance.

At the top of the whole command structure stood President Roosevelt and the British Prime Minister and Minister of Defence, Winston Churchill. Beneath them the Combined Chiefs of Staff, the US Joint Chiefs of Staff, and the British Chiefs of Staff. Beneath them the Commanders-in-Chief in the various theatres of war, and the Commanders-in-Chief of Navies and Air Forces. Beneath them were the Commanders of Army Groups and armies. It was a chain that could not afford weak links. It was forged at all levels of two distinct peoples, whose singleness of purpose was not as the blade of a sword.

[1] Fuller, *The Second World War*, p. 258.

The appointment of General Eisenhower as Allied Commander-in-Chief, North African Theatre of Operations, in January, 1943, was an event of far greater significance than it seemed. It was also an inspired choice. He had commanded the Allied invasion of North Africa with quiet distinction and courage. He had won the respect and co-operation of his three senior commanders, all of them British, Air Chief Marshal Sir Arthur Tedder, Admiral Sir Andrew Cunningham, and General Sir Harold Alexander. In close co-operation with the British he had wrestled with the insoluble problems and tangled loyalties of three kinds of Frenchman, Darlan, Giraud and de Gaulle, and had achieved a working arrangement with disparate forces. It was a matter, moreover, on which the Americans and the British did not see eye to eye.

General Eisenhower was destined to the Supreme Command of the Allied forces in north-west Europe. Perhaps no comparable task had ever confronted a military-statesman. The two races providing in the main the substance of his forces were allied in a rivalry of many confused and confusing undercurrents, compounded of envies, grudging admirations, and painful susceptibilities, charged with powerful emotions. The similarity of their languages enhanced, rather than reduced, subtle patterns of behaviour and misunderstanding. The British regarded themselves as profoundly experienced and versed in all the arts of war, and the Americans as brash newcomers, not only to war, but to the manifold problems of an alien continent.

Moreover, these two peoples were in the immediate process of exchanging roles on the world stage. Under General Eisenhower's command British power must decline while American power waxed mightily. This fact, as well as the facts of background and geography, injected a particular urgency into British thinking that was not often reflected in American attitudes. In their strategic aims and concepts the Allies were opposed, often bitterly. American urgencies and priorities were of a different order.

In this unique situation Eisenhower was destined to hold a balance in the field with great skill, forthright honesty, and distinction. He was a man of infinite patience, exquisite tact, an attractive modesty and great personal charm. Outwardly amenable, his quiet unassuming manner concealed a tough spirit. He was a man slow to anger, but capable of swift and ruthless action. With none was he more ruthless than with those, whether generals or corporals, who might threaten the smooth working of the alliance. You could call a man a bastard or a 'sonofabitch', but not with a national label attached. Genuine differences, irritations and angers, were inevitable and permissible, but a line had to be drawn. The forms of patronage and condescension peculiar to both peoples were instantly taboo.

An elaborate command structure was steadily evolving in which American and British were becoming integrated, but not without casualties. In all the team Eisenhower would drive no man would prove more awkward, more difficult, than General Montgomery. His eccentricities, the pedantry of his military dogmatism, his deliberate isolation, and his inability to enter into the problems of others, rendered him peculiarly unsuitable for any co-operative role. Already early in 1943 he was the despair of his mentor, and protector, the British CIGS, General Alan Brooke. 'He requires a lot of educating to make him see the whole situation and the war as a whole outside the Eighth Army orbit,' Brooke wrote in his diary. '. . . It is most distressing that the Americans do not like him, and it will always be a difficult matter to have him fighting in close proximity to them.'[1]

Nevertheless, and virtually unavoidably, Montgomery was about to fight in close proximity to the Americans, and to fight as a member of a team in double harness with the most notable American eccentric of the day, General George S. Patton.

In the spring of 1943, as the Tunisian campaign drew to an end, and the final plans for the invasion of Sicily became of growing urgency, anxieties about General Montgomery were not confined to the British camp. Undoubtedly they exercised the mind of General Eisenhower as he prepared to meet the British general at Gabes at the end of March. Immediately after his victory at Mareth, Montgomery could be expected to be particularly extravagant in his immensely high opinion of himself. His immodesty had become sublime. He seemed to see himself in the role of a Moses, leading his children out of the desert, and clearly the chosen of 'The Lord, mighty in battle'. Soon he would mention God in despatches, to the sour amusement of generals less divinely chaperoned.

[1] Bryant, *The Turn of the Tide*, p. 641.

Eisenhower was a mere fledgling in his job when he confronted the man with 'the thin, bony, ascetic face that stared from an unmilitary turtle-neck sweater.'[1] The contrast between the two men was remarkable. Neither man seemed to fill the popular idea of a leader, yet both achieved extraordinary popularity, especially with troops.

The meeting went off quietly. Eisenhower stayed the night, remembering a first unofficial meeting when Montgomery had commanded in South East England. This meeting escaped the attention of Montgomery's Chief of Staff, de Guingand, but was recorded by General Mark Clark.[2]

> The dapper and hard driving little General had delivered a 'crisp lecture'. In the midst of it Montgomery sniffed the air without looking round, and in a loud voice asked, 'Who's smoking?'
>
> Eisenhower had at once owned up.
>
> 'I don't,' Montgomery said sternly, 'permit smoking in my office.'

The incident had amused Eisenhower, but it was the kind of boorish triviality that could act as a rasp over a raw and sensitive spot in other circumstances, and might easily provoke a man of the nature of General Patton to blow up.

Neither of the generals referred to the incident at Gabes, but it was not forgotten. The Supreme Commander's first official meeting with his new general must have been a considerable ordeal. At the time when Montgomery had been briefly appointed to the command of the 1st Army for the North African landings, he had been recommended to Eisenhower by the VCIGS, General Nye, as not only an able soldier, but a first class co-operator. General Eisenhower could only pray that the last half of the statement would prove true. The re-grouping of the 18th Army Group was imminent, and Montgomery and his army would have to work and fight in close co-operation with others. Fortunately the task of bringing this about belonged to the Supreme Commander's deputy, the commander of the 18th Army Group, General Alexander, and there was no need for

---
[1] Omar P. Bradley, *A Soldier's Story*, London, Eyre & Spottiswoode, 1952.
[2] Mark Clark, *Calculated Risk*, London, Harrap, 1951.

Eisenhower to do more at Gabes than to refer to the prospect with tact.

But there was much more to worry about. The Americans were vulnerable and acutely aware of the criticisms of the performance of their troops in their first encounters with the enemy. The defeat inflicted upon the 1st Armoured Division in the Kasserine Pass was written on Eisenhower's heart, and he was very much aware of his own inexperience, and that of his generals. Moreover American troops were greatly outnumbered, as well as outclassed, by their allies in the field. It would not last, but it was an awkward time. Montgomery was just the man, speaking from his lofty eminence, to remind General Eisenhower of these things. Fortunately Montgomery was too absorbed in his own performance to consider the triumphs or failures of others. His prestige was immense.

Major-General Walter Bedell Smith, the Supreme Commander's Chief of Staff, had just returned from leave with the news that Montgomery was a 'National Hero' in the United States, as well as in his own country. Eisenhower was a good listener. It was clear that Montgomery regarded himself as the ordained liberator of Tunis, a 'lone wolf' commanding a private army in what had been until now almost a private war. He had not yet faced the process of adjustment the immediate future would demand; neither had his very individual and heterogenous army. There were already minor frictions, not so much with the Americans as with the British 1st Army, whose members resented the arrogance and assumption of superiority of Montgomery's troops. They had fought almost as long, and almost certainly harder than the Eighth Army.

> Anglo-American co-operation had survived some hard tests during the preceding months. If the coalition, with the disappointments, frustrations, and recriminations inherent in such a union, could survive the initial and struggling phases, it seemed certain to remain effective . . .[1]

The initial and struggling phases had not yet passed, and the nature of Montgomery's contribution to the easy working of the alliance was a matter of concern to the British as well as to Eisenhower. General Alan Brooke was lamenting that 'Mont-

[1] U.S. Army in World War II. *North West Africa*.

gomery wants guiding and watching continually. I do not think Alex is sufficiently strong and rough with him.'[1]

Soon the British CIGS would erupt in more forceful terms. Meanwhile all was well.

'We were all greatly impressed by our Supreme Commander,' wrote de Guingand of Eisenhower's visit. 'Montgomery who was rather gauging people's merits by the number of battles they had fought—and won, rated him 'a very decent chap?'[2]

It was, perhaps, as high an accolade as Eisenhower could expect on this occasion from the man who was to be the most insubordinate of his subordinates for a long time to come.

According to Montgomery's own reckoning he had fought and won nine major battles with the Eighth Army, giving him a score of nine to nil over his Supreme Commander. Less biased observers might find it difficult to discover a 'major battle' between Second Alamein and the Mareth Line, but to assess Eisenhower's abilities or his role in war by his experience on the battlefield is to misunderstand his function. His ability to command an army is irrelevant. His task was to command the commanders of armies and army groups, and to keep them working as a team, and not one of those who commanded armies in the field, however brilliantly, may easily be imagined filling his role. Moreover he was in direct contact with the Heads of Governments, and his work involved the security of the territories under his command.

Montgomery's Chief of Staff, Major-General de Guingand, was invaluable at the first meeting of his master with the Supreme Commander. He was a good mixer and had all the social talents Montgomery lacked. 'Fortunately,' as General Bradley observed, 'whenever Monty ruffled Americans de Guingand sorted it out.' It was at times a formidable task, and without de Guingand, travelling constantly to smooth out the difficulties created by his commander, Montgomery might not have survived as the leader of the British forces in North-West Europe.

Writing of Montgomery when all was done, Eisenhower commented:

> He deliberately pursued certain eccentricities of behaviour, one of which was to separate himself habitually from his staff.

[1] Bryant, *The Turn of the Tide*, p. 641.
[2] de Guingand, *Operation Victory*, p. 264-6.

He lived in a trailer surrounded by a few aides. This created difficulties in the staff work that must be performed in timely and effective fashion if any battle is to result in victory. He consistently refused to deal with a staff officer from any headquarters other than his own . . .[1]

Both men had embarked upon a difficult journey on that day at Gabes. The first of many crises was at hand.

II

On April 10th, ten days after General Eisenhower's visit to Montgomery at Gabes, the Eighth Army entered the seaport town of Sfax, the objective of the Mareth battle. Montgomery was ahead of the rather generous time-table he had set himself, thanks in very large measure to the work of the Navy, the port engineers, and the first class administrative and supply organization that had filled the 'stomach' of his army abundantly and swiftly at every halt. It is important to understand that no power the enemy might bring to bear could halt or seriously hinder the Eighth Army on its road to Sfax, and thence to Sousse and Enfidaville. The US Official Historians commented upon his 'overwhelming strength' on this occasion. He had 400 tanks, more than 2,000 guns, and a great host of men. Moreover the 9th Corps had entered Kairouan, and would have been easily capable of cutting the road through to Sousse. It was, however, ear-marked for Montgomery.[2]

The capture of Sfax provided the spark for a curious incident which might have had serious repercussions, especially bearing upon the future of General Montgomery. It roused General Eisenhower to anger, and provoked General Alan Brooke to recall Montgomery from home leave nearly two months later.

According to de Guingand, who also reported the background to the incident, Montgomery sent a personal signal to Headquarters, North African Command, as follows: 'Personal. Montgomery to Eisenhower. Entered Sfax 0830 this morning Please send Fortress.'

---

[1] Dwight D. Eisenhower, *Crusade in Europe*, p. 313-4. London, Heinemann, 1948.
[2] Butcher, *Three Years with Eisenhower*, p. 244. London, Heinemann, 1946.

The Fortress arrived complete with its crew of eight United States airmen, and 'Montgomery was delighted'.[1]

Outwardly it seems a gesture of remarkable generosity from one potentate to another. It was not, however, as simple as that.

Major-General Walter Bedell Smith, Eisenhower's Chief of Staff, had visited General Montgomery at Tripoli in February. Discussing the campaign at dinner, and the future co-operation of his forces with the British 1st Army, and the US 11th Corps in Tunisia, Montgomery said: 'Will General Eisenhower give me a Fortress for my own personal use if I capture Sfax by April 15th?'

Eisenhower's poor Chief of Staff, thus cornered, said 'he was sure he would'.[2]

This was not a 'bet', for it was a Fortress to nothing, nor does it seem a fitting subject for a 'bet' or for a reward. Bedell Smith was clearly embarrassed, but it is improbable that he took Montgomery's request seriously. To do so would have been insulting. Certainly he was not in a position to barter his country's Flying Fortresses and their crews in exchange for an Army Commander's natural progress in a campaign.

The incident was not mentioned to Eisenhower, nor was it referred to by Montgomery at Gabes. This seems curious, for if Montgomery regarded his request as serious or amusing surely it would have been reasonable to mention it, especially when he knew himself to be within a few days of claiming his 'winnings'?

Nearly two months later on a visit to Algiers with Churchill to meet General Marshall and Eisenhower for strategic discussions, the CIGS, General Alan Brooke found the Supreme Commander 'boiling over internally with anger over Monty's insistence in extracting a Fortress aircraft out of him for Monty's personal service.'[3]

The extravagance of the demand also infuriated Brooke. It could only have been a joke. According to Eisenhower and his Chief of Staff, Montgomery had signalled his demand to Bedell Smith, and not to Eisenhower. This would have been more natural. Bedell Smith had 'tried to laugh it off in his reply', but Montgomery had been adamant in his demand. The unfortunate Bedell Smith had been 'forced to take the matter to

[1] and [2] de Guingand, *Operation Victory*, p. 235.
[3] Bryant, *The Turn of the Tide*, p. 642.

Eisenhower, who was infuriated that he should be bounced in this way by Monty.'[1]

General Alan Brooke had done his best to 'smooth over the harm that had been done', but without, he thought, much success. He had then recalled Montgomery from leave in England 'to haul him over the coals for the trouble he was creating.'

Brooke's admonitions do not seem greatly to have impressed his difficult protégé. 'He was as usual most grateful for having his failings pointed out to him,' Brooke wrote, but Montgomery was sure that Eisenhower had taken the transaction as a joke.

But the sources of Eisenhower's anger with Montgomery ran deeper. Throughout most of April and May the British Army Commander had constantly bedevilled the final planning of 'Husky', the invasion of Sicily. Moreover he had failed to attend important conferences in person, a foretaste of the behaviour that would add to planning difficulties to the war's end.

'I have caused a most frightful tornado and it is clear to me that I am regarded as a most unpleasant person,' Montgomery wrote to Brooke on April 30th.

In the American view the essence of Montgomery's objections 'was that his part in "Husky" had to be so strong his risk of defeat would be *nil*.'[2] This seems a fair comment. Montgomery wished also to ensure that the capture of Messina should fall to him, and the Americans were not sure that he was going the right way about it. Finally the British Army Commander had most of his way. His opposite number, General Patton, had little to say. He would reserve his comments for the field of battle.

III

While the Eighth Army was grinding to a disappointing halt at Enfidaville, and the North African Command was deeply involved, not only in the final defeat of the enemy in Tunisia, but in the urgent re-grouping and training of forces for the invasion of Sicily, General Montgomery was buzzing about like a bee in a cullender. His personal Flying Fortress enabled him to commute easily at his own will between Algiers, Cairo and

---

[1] Bryant, *The Turn of the Tide*, p. 642.
[2] Butcher, *My Three Years with Eisenhower*, p. 248.

London, and to drop in at his headquarters in Tunis or Tripoli. April, May and June were for him months of varied activity, and rare pleasure. In Cairo and London he was able to confront and to taste his great fame, and to find it very good. Fame has no face or feeling of itself alone, and at last Montgomery was able to feel the impact of the headlines and the broadcasts that had hailed his march from Alam Halfa to Tunisia.

General Kennedy met Montgomery at Northolt on May 17th, and described him stepping down from his Flying Fortress, chatting for a few moments with his American crew and posing for some photographs[1] by his personal photographer. He told Kennedy that he had won the Fortress 'as the result of a bet he had made with Eisenhower... He was quite sure the Americans would never try to make a bargain like that with him again'.

General Brooke's anger over this transaction was still two weeks in the future, but Montgomery, in his account of the incident to Kennedy was fully aware of Eisenhower's reaction. He was, therefore, less than straightforward in his confrontation with Brooke, and his pretence that Eisenhower regarded the matter as a joke does not ring true. It may be that Montgomery was less insensitive to other people's feelings than he liked to appear. To Brooke he was always the gauche, but innocent 'schoolboy' needing correction, and grateful for it. To some extent, at least, it must have been a Montgomery pose. He was finally to thank Eisenhower for 'keeping him on the rails'. It is an odd pose for a grown man; it is an even odder reality.

In London he was fully groomed for his part, dressed in his 'Desert' uniform, battle dress, beret, and sweater showing nearly a foot below his jacket. This was part of his 'image', and in this dress, after a check by the Military Secretary, he would meet the King. He was officially 'incognito' in London, staying at Claridges in the name of 'Colonel Lennox', but it was impossible to keep him hidden. While Alexander walked quietly in the park or strolled the streets, Montgomery had only to show his famous face to be greeted joyously by swiftly gathering crowds. His popularity was enormous, and perhaps unique for a soldier. Old Lord Roberts had enjoyed an affectionate admiration. Kitchener was known to millions from the famous posters of the First World War, but the reaction of the people of England to

[1] Kennedy, *The Business of War*, p. 291.

Montgomery had an especial flavour. There was, as Moorehead observed, no one quite like him. He was as narrow in his views as a Puritan, and as solitary in his ways as a stylite. He had none of the social graces. His glamour was negative, yet potent. He was not so much a hero as a symbol of victory. Few doubted that he was difficult, if not impossible, to get on with, even in his own words 'a bit of a cad'. He might coldly rebuke generals for smoking, sack brigadiers, browbeat and bully as he wished, ban coughing, smoking, and women, and gain thereby in his extraordinary popularity. His remarkable cockiness and pleasure in himself delighted a vast audience. Every 'horrible' story about him was 'funny'. Moorehead wrote[1] that he 'was "placed" in the public mind as a martinet, an eccentric and something of a braggart in the manner of Cyrano de Bergerac.'

Yet with people en masse, whether troops or civilians, he had the common touch. Incapable of relaxed and easy personal relationships with his equals, he could and did respond with simple and obvious delight to ordinary people. Perhaps he expressed some of the longings of the anonymous little man. Unmannered, an obvious 'outsider', he had yet succeeded mightily. He could not only 'live with' the greatest in the land, but he dared to tell them 'where they got off'. For Montgomery all this public acclaim, and genuine affection, filled an aching hollow in his life.

In London he was at first upset that he had not been invited to attend a special service in St Paul's Cathedral, but when he was told that it was because it was necessary for him to remain 'incognito', he was pleased. Yet it was impossible for him to remain 'incognito' or anonymous. He had only to show his thin, sharp-featured face, crowned with the beret and crowds would gather to cheer, and shout their greetings. He had lost one of the most precious freedoms of ordinary men, a condition that had almost driven the famous Garbo to distraction; yet Montgomery was only conscious of gain. Perhaps he was no ordinary man, or he was an ordinary man 'writ large'.

When Montgomery returned to North Africa to face the furious General Alan Brooke, and reveal his contrite heart, most of the troubles he had set in train before his departure for London had been resolved. He had timed his absence well,

[1] Moorehead, *Montgomery*.

leaving de Guingand, confirmed in his new rank of Major-General and Chief of Staff to the Eighth Army, to act for him. De Guingand had been sent down to Cairo early in April to examine the plans for 'Husky', the Sicilian invasion, and Montgomery had at once been critical. On April 18th he had signalled to Alexander that the planning for 'Husky' was becoming acute. He appeared to be unaware that Alexander, the commander of the new 15th Army Group for the assault on Sicily, was far more deeply involved.

On April 19th Montgomery had flown to Algiers to give his seniors a foretaste of his views, and to leave them in no doubt that now that he was on the job they could expect all the weak points in the 'Husky' plan to be ruthlessly exposed. One thing was certain, he would demand more strength and more security.

A minute of the Prime Minister's addressed to General Ismay, for C.O.S. Committee, on March 3rd, would not have deterred him:

> ... 'Husky' is being run on the basis of altogether excessive demands.
>
> Commanders should be made to feel that they have to make some personal contribution to victory if they are to get any honour out of it. Everywhere the British and Americans are overloading their operational plans with so many factors of safety that they are ceasing to be capable of making any form of aggressive war. For six or eight months to come Great Britain and the United States will be playing about with half a dozen German divisions ...[1]

The warning might have been circulated and underlined to General Montgomery as a principal offender. In fact the memorandum expresses the frustration and furious anxiety of the Prime Minister to come to grips with the enemy. He was aware through every minute of his days that the Russians were engaging 185 divisions of the enemy in deadly combat, and he could not speak to them on equal terms. The enormous drain on men and materials demanded by an operation of the size of 'Husky' alarmed him.[2] Three thousand ships and landing craft

---
[1] Churchill, *The Hinge of Fate*, Appendix C, pp. 743-4.
[2] Churchill, *Closing the Ring*, Chapter II, pp. 37-8.

would be needed to carry 160,000 men, 14,000 vehicles, 600 tanks, and 1,800 guns, to the shores of Sicily to assault a mere four to six enemy divisions! Moreover 146 US and 113½ British squadrons totalling 4,900 aircraft would be used in support. There would be two airborne divisions. The islands of Lampedusa and Pantelleria would be reduced by saturation bombing as a preliminary. It seemed a fantastic commitment for the assault upon an island in the Mediterranean, and no one will ever know for certain how much of all this was really necessary. There was always a danger that the whole business of war would get out of hand, that the more that became available the more would be demanded. 'Overlord', the Cross-Channel assault barely twelve months ahead, was already demanding enormous varieties and quantities of material, much of it 'unheard of', the products of ingenious minds.

Yet in the end all would be resolved by men on their feet, the spearheads, the small 'fists' of armies with this gigantic weight behind them. Was it giving them strength? Or was it holding them back? Was there a point at which a great leader should cry—stop! Enough! It took months, even years, to plan and to mount a major assault, and every hour and day seemed to breed more hours and days. In the field, it was clear, war demanded men of action. The days of Dunkirk, of Wavell and O'Connor, of Auchinleck, already in mid-1943 seemed almost as remote as Omdurman.

By the middle of 1943 the Germans had lost more than a million men in twelve months. The battle of the Atlantic, which had reached its ominous peak in March, and could have brought the Allied effort crashing down in ruins, was at last won or being won beyond a doubt. In May there had been only one American division in Britain. Henceforth they would pour across the Atlantic in a steady stream, 15,000 at a time crammed into the great 'Queens' of the Western Ocean.

It is against such a background that the activities of a Montgomery must be seen. Two armies would assault Sicily backed by immense air and naval strength. He would command one of these armies to confront at most four divisions of the enemy. He had left a formidable document with General Alexander, stressing key dates in the final planning: 'I myself, and my Army HQ staff, know very little about the operation as a whole, and nothing whatever about the detailed planning that is going on.¹

In a typical clause in his provisional summing up, he stated: (para. 2–e)

> There is no responsible senior commander thoroughly versed in what happens in a battle who is devoting *his sole attention* to the 'Husky' operation.
>
> If we go on in this way much longer we may have a disaster.²

On his way down to Cairo for Easter to see how his staff were getting on with their planning, Montgomery realized that the old days were over, 'Alexander had let me run this private war in my own way ... Anyhow the more I thought about it the more I realized that the freedom we had enjoyed in the desert was over.'³

Nevertheless he was resolved to remain the *prima donna*, and the public confirmed him in his role. He attended the Easter service in the Cathedral, and the Americans observed drily that his visit was 'widely publicized'. His absence in Cairo at this time had delayed an important conference Eisenhower had wished to hold to debate the 'Husky' plans. The conference, had it been held, would almost certainly have proved abortive, for Montgomery was busily devising what he called his 'Easter Plan', or Plan 9, which implies that the 'nincompoops' working since January to mount the invasion of Sicily had made eight plans, all useless, and that as soon as he gave it his attention the errors were corrected.

On April 24th Montgomery telegraphed his views to Alexander. Like Oliver Twist, he asked for more. 'We have now reached the stage when we can say quite definitely that we require *two more* divisions, assault loaded and to be landed on D-Day in the Gulf of Gela, if the invasion of Sicily is to be a success.'⁴

His objections would mean changes in the plans of the US 7th Army under Patton. He knew he was 'being tiresome', but

---
¹ Montgomery, *Memoirs*, p. 170.
² *Ibid.*, p. 171.
³ *Ibid.*, p. 173.
⁴ *Ibid*, p. 181.

everyone would have to put up with it. Moorehead puts it very well in regard to his later entry into Italy. It was always the same:

> From the beginning Montgomery was opposed to both the general plan and his own part in it. Quite apart from his temperamental dislike of carrying out an operation which he had not designed himself, and in which he did not have a leading part, he believed his own forces were too small for what they were being asked to do.

Montgomery's remarkable illusions about his plans were to remain impregnable. Throughout the war he was involved in and bore a share of responsibility for only one major plan, 'The Dieppe Raid'. It was a typical Montgomery plan, worked out to the last detail. In the main it was a frontal assault. It lacked all flexibility, and left the unfortunate commander of the operation a helpless spectator of a disaster he could do nothing to prevent.

Nevertheless Montgomery's 'temperament' forced him to believe that from Alam Halfa to the Elbe the plans were his, including 'Husky' and 'Overlord'.

On April 26th Montgomery returned to his headquarters, and took to his bed with 'flu and tonsillitis. On the 29th he was unable to attend an important conference in Algiers, and ordered de Guingand to attend for him. When de Guingand's aircraft had a minor crash on the way, Oliver Leese was detailed for the job. It was the beginning of a pattern Eisenhower was to know too well.

On May 2nd another full conference was summoned, and this time Alexander's aircraft was held up. Montgomery wanted to hold the conference without his chief, unaware until his Air Force and Naval colleagues reminded him, that this would be insulting to Alexander. Montgomery at once hunted down Eisenhower's Chief of Staff, Bedell Smith, and finding him in the lavatory, insisted on discussing his plans there and then. 'So we discussed the problem then and there ... He was very upset ...'

On that day and the next the Americans were left in little doubt of the nature of the man with whom they had to deal. By the end of May 3rd Montgomery had forced his demands through. The two armies in the assault must fight in contact: 'Each would be dependent on the other for direct support in the battle ...' The Americans, in effect, must play second fiddle to the Master. It followed, according to Montgomery, that he must be 'Ground Force Commander'—the term was not then used, but would be Montgomery's gambit later in Normandy. General Eisenhower did not agree, and General Patton did not record his views.

The object was clear: the enemy must be prevented from escaping to Italy across the Messina straits. Montgomery would reach Messina as swiftly as possible, while the US Seventh Army formed 'a defensive flank . . . facing west'.

Tentatively the Americans suggested that Montgomery might strike trouble in the Catania plain, but they didn't like to press their views. General Patton, no doubt, would take care of himself, and he might have some ideas of his own.

It does not seem surprising that General Alan Brooke should have found Eisenhower boiling with rage in the aftermath of these exchanges, even excluding the Flying Fortress. On June 2nd General Montgomery assured the Prime Minister of the ability of the forces involved to carry out the successful invasion of Sicily. 'This was only natural, since it was my plan! I also emphasized the need for a master plan which would ensure that, once ashore, the operations would be developed in the right way.'[1]

The final outline plan had been approved on May 13th by the Combined Chiefs of Staff. It called for eight simultaneous seaborne assaults on 100 miles of coast from Syracuse on the east to Palma-Licata on the south west.

It remained to carry it out.

On June 19th King George VI, the guest of Montgomery in his headquarters in Tripoli, bestowed the accolade of Knighthood upon his general.

---

[1] Montgomery, *Memoirs*, p. 183.

CHAPTER TWELVE

'Husky'

I

On July 10th, a little before three o'clock in the morning, British and American troops after a queasy and uncomfortable passage, began to land on the southern shores of Sicily. It had been a stormy night following a stormy day, and it was a wild morning of high seas to make landing difficult on exposed beaches. The bad weather had lulled the defenders into a false sense of security. They were taken by surprise, the Italians having little stomach for a fight. Soon after first light the Allies had solid footholds on the island from Pachino in the south east to Licata in the south west. A fierce German counter-attack by an armoured 'battle group' was repulsed by the Americans at Gela by engineers, infantry and groups of all services, every man fighting with whatever weapons came to hand. It was a revealing action, for it showed the adaptability and individuality of the Americans at their best. Caught on the wrong foot, as it were, they changed feet rapidly. The Germans had already noted in Tunisia how quick their new enemy was to learn.

Thirty-eight days later the spearheads of General Patton's army stormed into Messina, a few hours ahead of the leading troops of the Eighth Army, and looked across the narrow straits to the foot of Italy. The populace applauded, welcoming their conquerors with fruit and flowers. It was the first piece of enemy territory—of enemy homeland—to be won by the Allies.

The conquest of Sicily sounds curiously tame, its small noise lost in the rising crescendo of victory; but it was not tame. It was immeasurably the largest amphibious operation in the history of war up to that time, preceded and accompanied by bombing of appalling violence. It was a foretaste of 'Overlord', and it set a new pattern of warfare.

The importance of the conquest of Sicily is easily underestimated. It brought about the collapse of Italy. It finally opened the Mediterranean, and converted an Italian lake into an

Allied sea. The ordeal of Malta was at an end, and the 'soft underbelly' of the Axis powers was fully exposed. Moreover the attack upon Sicily reflected the inner conflicts in the councils of the Western Allies. It was a compromise without a clear 'Object'.

Had the conquest of Italy been the 'Object' of assault, Sardinia and Corsica, as Eisenhower and others believed, would have been the right target, laying open Italy's long western flank to sea-borne attack. The Germans shared this view, and because the allied target remained in doubt until the moment of impact, the enemy forces were dispersed, not only in Sardinia and Corsica, but in the South of France. Moreover, Italian fears of domination by their dangerous ally limited German reinforcements for Sicily to the reformed 15th Panzer Division and the Hermann Goering Division, with 160 tanks between them.

There were 350,000 enemy troops in Sicily, 275,000 of them Italians, organized in four field divisions, and five coastal divisions. The field divisions had 100 light French tanks. The Germans organized their 75,000 men in five battle groups, parcelling out their tanks between them. They had been refused permission to form a Corps by the Italian Command.

Sicily is a mountainous island, unsuitable in the main for the use of armour in mobile roles. It was, however, naturally adapted for the use of armour in ambush in scores of narrow mountain passes. With the great massif of Etna astride the south-eastern approaches to Messina like a gigantic fortress of rock two miles high, dominating the Catanian plain, the only plain in Sicily, the conquest of the island from the south-east would be a formidable task against the resolute opposition to be expected from the German battle groups. The temptation to 'encircle' the island must have been very strong, even though totally unacceptable to the cautious and inflexible General Montgomery. Eisenhower, not given to 'if' history, ruminated that, 'If we had correctly evaluated the low combat value of the huge Italian garrison we would have stuck to the "encircling" plan and so overrun the island in ten to fifteen days rather than in the thirty-eight eventually required.'[1]

Whatever the method, Etna must be outflanked. It would be profitless to batter an army against that vast bastion, and unreal

---

[1] Eisenhower, *Crusade in Europe*, p. 181.

to believe in 'bouncing' a way through on the steep and narrow coastal road and railway track between Catania and Taormina. Yet it was typical of Montgomery to choose to do this. He was already firmly set in the direct approach preceded by immense bombardment.

There is constantly a sense of frustration in the mind as one seeks to examine these phases of the war in the west, a niggling suspicion that never was there more a time for boldness, nor ever was caution less justified. A sense of unease is discernible in the writing of experienced observers and serious students of war of the calibre of Christopher Buckley.[1] It had grown throughout the slow pursuit in the desert, and in Sicily it found anxious expression. The tide of war that had turned decisively in the autumn of 1942 was never taken at the flood. Ironmongery, as General Fuller observed, threatened generalship and reduced the art of war to brute force bludgeoning. Montgomery was the High Priest of the new technique, the old technique of World War One magnified by the enormous proliferation of weapons. Enormous bomber forces had been created, and must be used—because they were there. Reconnaissance and transport aircraft were invariably in short supply, and the chronic shortage of landing craft jeopardized planning and combined operations to the war's end. Moreover, as time went by a variety of 'experts' took an even greater hand in the preliminaries to action, and complicated planning. Samples of sand and soil were obtained, often by great daring, and minutely examined. One feels that it was only by an oversight that samples of enemy blood and urine were omitted. Analysts analysed *ad nauseam*, and the total plan for an operation like 'Husky' included indigestible masses of useless information. It was negligible in comparison with the plan for 'Overlord', and small even in comparison with the exhaustive studies preceding Montgomery's final crossing of the Rhine.

Did all this really matter? Could not men make landings on hostile shores, or cross rivers, without all this? And if they could not, why then even think of a cross-channel assault in 1942, or in 1943, or indeed one hour earlier than the final date—for up to the very end the detail was pouring in, and being carefully embodied into the intricate pattern.

[1] War correspondent of *The Daily Telegraph*. Later a serious student of war and writer. *The Road to Rome*. Killed in Korea, 1950.

The Western Allies were rapidly becoming slaves of the enormous variety of equipment available. No single bomb or shell or bullet was used if ten or twenty would do—not better, but worse. And while the tails and torsos of armies grew, the 'heads' remained unchanged. In mountainous country the effective spearhead of a division might be, and often was, a single platoon of men. In Italy the leading company of a battalion, itself the leading battalion of a brigade, the leading brigade of a division, the leading division of a corps, battled on for two weeks virtually alone to enable a corps to advance.

Ammunition was becoming complex, and to serve the 'colossal cracks' which were a feature of General Montgomery's attacks from the beginning, it was not only necessary to dump tens of thousands of shells, but tens of thousands of shells in an ever growing variety of calibres and purposes, so that lesser dumps and supply lines proliferated on the routes from the main dumps to the guns. All this reflected a Britain reaching the peak of industrial production for war. It demanded miracles of organization from the factories to the front lines, and armies of skilled men. It multiplied demands on railways, shipping space, road transport.

A vital and important question must be: could a commander in the field cut loose from this enormous burden? Did any commander try to do so? General Patton proved that it could be done. While others, notably General Montgomery, waited and organized, Patton moved. He revealed his capacity to do this for the first time in Sicily. His experience in the battle of Troina, where he found the way blocked by rubble to such an extent that it took bulldozers twenty-four hours to clear a way for single line traffic, urged him to call off bombings and blastings. Meanwhile General Montgomery poured more high explosive into areas deserted by enemy, and destroyed more villages empty of enemy than any general in the history of war. It was not only wasteful, it was monotonous and deeply distressing. It began to reduce soldiers to the role of scavengers.

These things became increasingly oppressive and disturbing as the war wore on. At the same time the means of defence available to the enemy became increasingly meagre and simple. Perhaps, one wonders, this accounts in part for the persistence of his long defensive struggle against enormous odds, for the flexibility and speed of movement manifest to the last, for the resilience that could not, and did not, wait upon the cautious planning, the re-groupings and meticulous timings of General Montgomery.

A sledgehammer is not the ideal weapon with which to crack a nut, especially a highly mobile nut. Yet this, predominantly, was the Allied method. From Sicily to the Baltic and the Elbe it strewed vast mounds of rubble in the paths of the advancing armies, it converted great forests to matchwood, it even blasted mountains and monasteries. It killed very few enemy, for the enemy swiftly learned to move out of the way. Civilians were the principal victims.

Did the Allies realize the German condition in that midsummer of 1943 when great fleets of ships moved majestically out of scores of ports upon their rendezvous area off Malta for the assault upon Sicily? The Germans were defending a shrinking perimeter from the Arctic Ocean to the Caucasus in the east, from Cap Higuer to the North Cape facing west, while from the south new attacks developed, and from the north new attacks must be expected. They had failed also under the seas, and the skies released a sickening and incessant deluge of high explosive upon them.

Hitler believed that had he not defended Tunisia to the last the Allies would have been permitted by the Italians to march to the Brenner unopposed. There were moments of lucidity in that feverish demonic mind, tormented with illusions and delusions. Would it not have been true, Tunisia or not, had we made it true? By boldness, by speed, by behaving like victors? Instead of haggling with Badoglio about the meaning of 'Unconditional Surrender' while time ran out, and the Germans resolved to contest the mountainous way to the north, to fight a desperate rearguard action from ridge to ridge, month after month. Perhaps we could not make up our minds because there were two minds.

There is no answer to these questions, but to ask them is perhaps to encourage a more critical examination of Allied strategy and tactics, and of the purposes of war.

Time, even in the midsummer of 1943, was not on the side of Britain. Unknown 'things' were brewing, not merely rockets, but something else which would finally arouse the horror and awaken the guilt of all mankind. Just as the U-boats might have stalemated the Western Allies, and nearly did, so also might these dreadful 'things', these 'secret weapons', write a sudden finish to all endeavour.

There were threats less speculative than these to the British position. The balance of forces in the field was moving steadily in favour of the Americans. In men and munitions we should soon reach the peak. Only dynamic leadership in the field could maintain British prestige in the Allied Councils, and give full weight to British ideas and ideals. The year 1944 must see the end.

Yet against an enemy fighting a rearguard action the British were 'muscle-bound' by their overwhelming strength, and by their fears. Safety first and speed were in irreconcilable conflict. In June in Algiers General Alan Brooke revealed his fears of cross-channel attack to Eisenhower. These fears were shared by Churchill, General Smuts and the Monarch. The dreadful slaughter of the First World War must not occur again, and perhaps this is excuse enough for the misguided and abortive horror of the strategic bombing offensive. It sought to avoid the dreaded battlefield, the confrontation of men.

These are the larger fears of war. Meanwhile in June 1943 there was the island of Sicily, a stepping stone to the Italian mainland, ninety miles from Cap Bon across the Sicilian Channel, the last obstacle to Allied domination of the Mediterranean, and a new advance base from which Allied aircraft could strike more deeply into South-Eastern Europe.

Yet it was a compromise, a reflection of strategic conflict between the Allies which would bring the Americans to the Quebec Conference in August in what they described as a 'fish or cut bait' mood.

II

The saturation bombing of the island of Pantelleria, and to a lesser extent of Lampedusa, as a preliminary to the assault on Sicily, aroused the unease of many observers. In the three weeks ending on June 11th nearly 7,000 tons of bombs were dropped upon the forty-five square miles of volcanic rock comprising Pantelleria. This massive assault, demanding the incessant use of many squadrons of aircraft, was described by Air Marshal

Coningham as 'a test tube experiment of the effect of intense and prolonged bombing'.[1]

The Italians had developed the island into a subterranean fortress, a minor 'Gibraltar', housing shore batteries and aircraft, an airfield, and a garrison of 11,000 second-line troops. The Achilles heel of the island as a fortress was its total lack of fresh water.

On June 11th, having been without water for three days, the island surrendered in the face of a 'formidable armada' which had waited uncomfortably offshore for some days. It was found that 200 men had been killed, two out of fifty-four shore batteries put out of action, and that the aircraft in the underground hangars were almost intact. It is also possible—even probable—that the two shore batteries had been put out of action by naval gun fire.

While possession of the island was useful in providing a small base for aircraft acting in close support of the seaborne assault on Sicily, it had been effectively neutralized by the air and sea domination of the Allies, and had lost its usefulness to the Axis powers.

It is perhaps absurd to regard the vast expenditures of war in economic terms, but it must be clear that the saturation bombing of Pantelleria was a gross waste of aircraft, high explosive, and effort. Morally it has a more profound significance:

> ... But in these cases
> We still have judgement here; that we but teach
> Bloody instruction, which, being taught, return
> To plague th' inventor ...[2]

Pantelleria lies almost midway between Tunisia and Sicily. It stands alone, more than 100 miles to the north of Lampedusa, and the tiny islands of Lampione and Linosa, comprising the group. Between them they provided a small supplement to the overwhelming superiority of air power deployed by the Allies over the area.

On the night of July 9th two airborne assaults were flown by glider-borne and paratroops to seize key points, and to open the

---

[1] Christopher Buckley, *The Road to Rome*, p. 13. London, Hodder & Stoughton 1945.
[2] *Macbeth*.

way for ground troops assaulting over the beaches of southern Sicily. The results were disturbing. Transport aircraft suitable for the job were scarce, and American Dakotas with inexperienced pilots made up the bulk of both forces. Only twelve gliders out of 133 of the British Airborne landing came down in the planned dropping zone. Of the remainder, forty-seven came down in the sea. Nevertheless eight officers and sixty-five men reached their objective, the canal bridge south of Syracuse, and held it for the advanced patrols of ground troops. Other airborne troops, landing all over the place, some even in Italy, some to rot in inaccessible mountain passes, attacked enemy wherever they found them, and spread alarm in the ranks of the Italians.

The US airborne assault fared no better, but again the widely-scattered paratroops created alarm in the enemy ranks, and while one small and resolute body of men seized a vital road junction east of Gela, others captured Marina di Ragusa. Thus they played an important part in repelling the heavy armoured attack of a German battle group against the landings at Gela.

With these preliminaries at an end, General Montgomery arrived in Sicily on July 11th to play a 'Star' part in the filming on the beaches, his 'rather theatrical' appearances giving rise to 'a good deal of criticism in London'.[1] His visits to his troops, his encouragement to working parties, his distribution of cigarettes, were very popular, while Commando officers ear-marked for an amphibious flanking assault noted with pleasure that the Army Commander had chosen to wear their green beret.

Very little opposition was encountered, the Italians, in Alexander's phrase, being 'driven like chaff before the wind'. The ports of Syracuse and Augusta were soon in British hands, and on July 13th a second airborne assault by the 1st Parachute Brigade attempted to seize the Primosole bridge across the Simeto river, and open the way through to Catania and the Catanian Plain. 'The 8th Army would have to move forward like a tempest to prevent the German defences from being consolidated on a line somewhere between Etna and the sea.'[2]

Montgomery exuded confidence. He would produce the 'tempest'.

Again there was near disaster to the airborne force. Out of 124

[1] Kennedy, *The Business of War*, p. 297.
[2] Hilary St. G. Saunders, *The Red Beret*.

aircraft fifty were damaged and eleven destroyed by 'friendly fire', and twenty-seven were forced to return to base without dropping their troops. Nevertheless a virtual 'handful' of paratroops led by the indomitable Brigadier Lathbury, and his Brigade Major, David Hunter, fought a brave and desperate action for the bridge against enemy paratroops of the highest quality. The demolition charges were successfully removed, but unfortunately the spearhead units of the Eighth Army were slow to reach the bridge, and despite deeds of the utmost heroism a bridgehead was not secured until the 17th. The 'tempest' had never shown signs of developing, and the Eighth Army advance, losing momentum, bogged down in the Catanian plain to be harassed as much by fever as by the enemy.

Predictably Montgomery paused to re-group, to preserve the 'balance' without which he was loath to move, and to begin to develop flanking leverage. At the same time he asked for the 78th Division from the 1st Army to strengthen his left flank and the Canadians fighting northwards from Vizzini.

An unusual feature of the close fighting was the remarkable marksmanship of the German elite troops in the Primosole bridgehead. Men were shot clean between the eyes, and even a hand showing out of the turret of a tank would be hit.

Meanwhile the Americans had done well, having met and repulsed the German onslaught before they had properly gained a foothold, and were expanding to the north and west when Montgomery usurped the Vizzini-Caltagirone road through to Enna, compressing Bradley's corps, and forcing the US 45th Division back to the beaches.

In Bradley's view Montgomery could have, and should have, developed his flanking movement without bouncing this vital highway. 'Having been denied the Vizzini road I had no other choice,' wrote Bradley, 'but to shift the 45th by trucking it back to the beaches . . . I was certain that Alexander could not have known how awkward was this movement into which his directive had forced our corps. For want of a day and a night on the Vizzini road we were forced to disassemble our front and patch it together again.'[1]

Montgomery's brief reference reads: 'There was a danger of overlapping between the two armies in the area Vizzini-

[1] Bradley, *A Soldier's Story*, p. 138.

Caltagirone, but this was put right by orders from 15 Army Group which made the road axis through these places to Piazza Amerina and Enna inclusive to Eighth Army.'[1]

It appears that Montgomery had not only 'bounced' the road, but had also 'bounced' Alexander into sanctioning his action without a word to the Americans. Nothing could have been better calculated to inspire Patton and Bradley to press on to victory. The American role had been visualized as filling the western flank while Montgomery pressed on to Messina to cut the enemy escape route. Accordingly on the 15th Patton was ordered to continue his advance to the north and to cut the coastal road from Palermo to Messina.

'And then,' as one of Bradley's staff expressed it, 'we can sit comfortably on our prats while Monty finishes the goddam war.'

It was almost certainly the intention of 15th Army Group that the island should be 'split into British and American halves', Bradley wrote. 'While Patton limited his effort to the soft Western end, Montgomery's Eighth Army would drive the Germans out across the Messina Straits.'[2]

Montgomery, for his part, was critical of the Americans. 'By wheeling west towards Palermo they had "missed the opportunity" . . . to cut the island in two. And the whole trouble was caused by the lack of a "Master Plan".'

The Americans had ideas of their own, and on the 17th Patton asked Alexander to let him go. There was room for two armies to fight their ways through to Messina. The request was well timed. It was almost at the precise hour when Alexander realized that Montgomery had bitten off more than he could chew, alone.

As soon as Patton was given the 'All Clear', he developed his attacks with rapid improvisation, and a daring justified by the enemy condition. Forming a 'provisional corps' Patton seized Palermo, and while engineers opened the port for supplies his troops pressed on over the coastal road to Messina, putting in amphibious attacks behind the enemy at every opportunity. Meanwhile the 11th US Corps, reorganizing itself as it went along, pushed up the central route on the flank of Leese's British 30th Corps. The power drive of the American and British armies was, therefore, in the centre, and while Montgomery seemed to accept

[1] Montgomery, *El Alamein to the River Sangro*, p. 80.
[2] Bradley, *A Soldier's Story*, p. 140.

a stalemate on the right flank Patton pressed on with all speed over the long northern route determined to beat Montgomery into Messina, whatever the odds.

Patton at this early stage was revealing many valuable qualities. He refused to be chained by 'logistics'. Confronted by the impassable rubble of Troina he called off that kind of bombing. He hated to be held up by anything, and often he felt that the war would end at any moment before he had time to put his ideas into practice. He thought he could do without air strikes, and continued to hold this view right to the end. Of Normandy he wrote, in this context,

> I was also certain that, by pushing harder, we could advance faster. I stated at the time, and still believe, that two armoured divisions, preceded by a heavy artillery concentration using air bursts, and followed by two infantry divisions, could have cut straight down the west coast to Avranches without the necessity of waiting for an air blitz.[1]

Behind Patton's flamboyant exterior was hidden a serious student of war and history. As an army commander in the field he was the complete reverse of Montgomery, and the two men were naturally anti-pathetic. Yet the defensive ability and caution of the one allied to the shrewd dash and genius of the other might produce an irresistible combination.

By the end of July the Germans were already on their way out of Sicily, resolved to save the bulk of their precious divisions in spite of the Allied air dominance over the narrow Straits. It would be tedious to describe in detail the campaign in Sicily. There are some excellent accounts of it, and there were many sound, if depressing, comments from the battlefield at the time. 'Each operation,' wrote Buckley, 'tended to be a repetition of its predecessor.'[2]

The incessant bombing of towns and villages on the routes of advance failed to kill or to stun the enemy and created mounds of rubble for the bull-dozers to clear.

> Villages like Regalbuto and later Randuzzo, were blotted out by bombing from the air on a scale unprecedented in the history of war. . . . I could not help feeling that our pursuit

[1] Patton, *War as I Knew It*, p. 95.
[2] Buckley, *The Road to Rome*, p. 107.

tactics resembled the employment of a ponderous sledgehammer to crush a small but alert reptile which slips away time after time just as the hammer descends.[1]

Many voices would be added to Buckley's long before the end, but the monstrous insanity continued unabated, delaying the advancing armies and destroying the last arts of war.

On August 17th Patton won the race to Messina a few hours ahead of his rival. It had been a 'needle' match, and would be repeated at a crucial hour of the war to change the shape and pattern of final victory.

III

At the end of August General Eisenhower visited General Montgomery at his headquarters in Taormina. Together they looked out across the Messina Straits to the toe of Italy upon which Montgomery was due to effect landings within a day or two. He would have the honour of being the first to land, but he was aware that his was not the glamorous role. He had lost the 7th Armoured Division to the Americans for a landing at Salerno. Two more of his divisions were due for leave, and at a conference in Algiers on the 23rd of the month he had made it clear that he didn't like it. The forces available to him were insufficient for the tasks allotted to him, he argued, and he demanded more. He had been partially successful. He disliked the whole plan intensely, and he was quite right. No clear object had been defined for the assault upon Italy.

Moreover he declined to take an optimistic view of the probable resistance. Very likely the Italians would offer no resistance —indeed, they were about to surrender as a nation—but there could be two German Panzer divisions in the toe of Italy, and Montgomery's patrols, while unable to find any evidence of their presence, were unable to show conclusively that they were not there. Montgomery would, therefore, mount one of his 'colossal cracks' to announce his imminent arrival.

The meeting of the Supreme Commander and Montgomery was informal, relaxed and without a jarring note. Accompanied by his personal photographers the British General met his

[1] Buckley, *The Road to Rome*, p. 107.

distinguished guest at the airfield, and escorted him to the very beautiful palace in which he had established himself. The incident of the Flying Fortress had been happily resolved. Following an awkward landing at Palermo on a visit to General Patton, Montgomery had decided that something smaller would better serve his needs. He had returned the Flying Fortress, and received a Dakota, equipped with a special jeep, in exchange.

Both men were accompanied only by their personal *Aides*, Eisenhower with Captain Butcher, USN, and Montgomery with Captain John Poston. It was one of those rare occasions when Montgomery exercised his great personal charm to dazzle the most junior of his guests, and to make an impression on the Supreme Commander. Dinner that night was a memorable event, the food, the wines, the cigars excellent in spite of Montgomery's personal austerity in these matters. The younger men were encouraged to talk of their less war-like adventures. The Generals listened with the utmost benevolence.

It is unlikely, I think, that there was an ulterior motive in Montgomery's mind, other than the very natural one of making a favourable impression. He was fully aware that he was rather 'unloved' in the American camp; aware also that he was no longer 'principal boy', and that Generals Patton, Bradley and Mark Clark were rapidly occupying the stage. He had received the lion's share of the publicity for his part in Sicily, against the run of the play. It could not be expected to continue indefinitely. Moreover the important Quebec Conference had reached decisions which would almost certainly have an impact upon Montgomery and his guest. Probably the agreement on the cross-channel attack for the early summer of 1944 was briefly discussed, for its impact was immediate in the Mediterranean theatre. The withdrawal of landing craft and troops earmarked for 'Overlord' was already in train.

Montgomery records that he made a bet with Eisenhower that night that the war would not be won by the end of 1944. Both men were destined to be runners in the last race, and each would have an opportunity to hasten the end. Montgomery's pessimism is interesting.

'It was clear to me that it *ought* to be over by then,' he wrote. 'But after our experiences in the planning and conduct of the Sicily campaign I felt that we had much to learn, and I believed in my heart that the Allies would make such mistakes that the war would go into 1945.'

He was highly critical of the Sicily campaign, and Eisenhower refrained from telling him of the British Brigadier Sugden's colourful comment that Patton 'had got the Eighth Army bloody well surrounded.' Montgomery would not have liked it.

> The method by which the campaign would be developed once the armies were on shore, and how the island would finally be reduced, was not decided. In fact, there was no master plan. As a result the operations and actions of the two Allied Armies were not properly co-ordinated.[1]

That his own failure to press on and to maintain momentum to cross the Simeto river before the enemy had had time to harden his defence, might have been the contributory factor in the roles of the two armies, did not enter his head. Everything should have been preordained, and all would have been well. But it is impossible to preordain a campaign.

Yet nothing, it seemed, would shake Montgomery's faith in a 'Master Plan', and as the two commanders relaxed at Taormina with their *Aides*, Montgomery told Eisenhower of how he had found Bedell Smith in an Algerian lavatory, and had put forward the 'final plan' for Sicily.

General Montgomery's belief in his infallibility seemed absolute, as solid as rock, impenetrable and impregnable, without a flaw. No glimmer of humility was evident, and his self-confidence grew with every experience. He lectured on how to win wars at every opportunity in public and private. If anyone, anywhere was in any doubt at any time, Montgomery would be ready to advise. He appeared to be totally incapable of self-criticism, or even of conceiving that his generalship might be less than perfect. He could recapitulate lucidly exactly what his army had done, and how it had been done, but he could not see that it was in any way less than it should have done, or might have done, or that there had been reasonable alternatives. Every set-back was instantly rationalized, and the situation was always as he had foreseen and wanted.

To himself Montgomery was always consistent. He believed in himself as the 'Pope' of the 'Lord, mighty in battle'. He does

[1] Montgomery, *Memoirs*, p. 187.

not appear to have discovered humility even as the chosen instrument of his God.

Eisenhower was always careful and generous in his assessments of Montgomery. He had listened for many months without comment to the widespread criticisms of Montgomery's caution 'when he was conducting his long pursuit of Rommel across the desert'. He had had opportunities in Tunisia and in Sicily of observing for himself, and his comments on Patton may reveal something of his true opinion of Montgomery:[1]

> Patton was a shrewd student of warfare who always clearly appreciated the value of speed in the conduct of operations. Speed of movement often enables troops to minimize any advantage the enemy may temporarily gain, but more important, speed makes possible the full exploitation of every favourable opportunity and prevents the enemy from readjusting his forces to meet successive attacks. Thus through speed and determination each successive advantage is more easily and economically gained than the previous one. Continuation of the process finally results in demoralization of the enemy. Thereupon speed must be redoubled—relentless and speedy pursuit is the most profitable action in war.

Few would be inclined to dispute this statement, and certainly not Montgomery. It was the old 'expanding torrent'.

'Quite right—quite right!' he would say.

Montgomery would continue to play the tortoise to Patton's hare, but he would never know it. In any case he would preserve his undefeated record, along with everyone else, set-backs excluded. He would not take any chances.

---

[1] Eisenhower, *Crusade in Europe*, p. 194.

CHAPTER THIRTEEN

Fortress Europe

I

At times in October and November 1943, the Joint Chiefs of Staff seemed to dislike the thought of an Allied landing at any point to the east of Italy almost as much as the Germans; and while the British welcomed the confusion in South East Europe, the Americans regarded the British attitude with increasing alarm.

Grand Strategy, vol. v.

... the British placed a ... high value on strategic flexibility, in preference to a rigid adherence to a long-prepared plan. To the Americans ... strategy implied concentration of effort, in the Napoleonic sense. Their strategic resource and tactical boldness ... were accordingly exercised in the service of a single strategic target and of a single well-prepared design; and they were quick to note and to fear any sign of an apparent dispersal of force, or of a departure from plans already agreed.

Grand Strategy, vol. v.

THE Italian campaign was the grave of British strategic designs and dreams in the Mediterranean. From the moment of its conception it was subject to variable political and military factors of considerable complexity. It was severely limited militarily, especially in regard to its development, by the insatiable demands of the cross-channel attack, for which the Americans had set a target date of May 1, 1944. This was the overwhelming priority governing all supply. Moreover, from November 1943 the Italian campaign was also, in Alexander's phrase, 'haunted by the ghost of *Anvil*', a landing to be carried out in the South of France, agreed to unwillingly by the British at Teheran, and to coincide with the major assault on Normandy.

In 1943 at Quebec the Americans, in the 'fish or cut bait' mood to which I have previously referred, confronted the

British with a blunt demand for the cross-channel attack in 1944. The demand was accompanied by the lightly veiled threat that they would turn away from the Atlantic theatre. Whether it would have come to that is impossible to say, but that the Americans were resolved henceforth to dominate the Conference tables and to dictate strategy, there was no doubt. They were suspicious of British intentions, of the expertise of the British Chiefs of Staff, and of the prevarications and evasions of which they felt sure they had been the victims.

Fortunately the British had come to the Conference table at Quebec with their preliminary plans for 'Overlord', the new and final name for the operation, in an advanced state. The work of General Paget, Commander-in-Chief Home Forces, and of the varied team of naval and air experts aiding him in the plans known as 'Skyscraper', had been taken over by Leiutenant-General F. E. Morgan and his organization known as 'Cossac', and the results carried conviction of British intent.

There was also a sub or subsidiary plan, known as 'Rankin', which probably reflected British hopes. This plan would go into operation in the event of a German collapse in North-West Europe. Such a remote possibility must not be allowed to catch the Western Allies unprepared, for even to 'walk in' to France un-opposed would be a complex undertaking.

'Had we had our way,' wrote General Kennedy, 'I think there can be little doubt that the invasion of France would not have been done in 1944.'[1]

In short we should have liked to wait for a 'Rankin' situation.

From the moment of the firm agreement on the cross-channel attack any developments arising out of the assault upon southern Italy were ruled out, and severe limitations were immediately imposed. Seven divisions were ear-marked for withdrawal from the Mediterranean theatre, to return to the United Kingdom for training and integration into the invasion force for 'Overlord'. In addition 80 percent of the assault shipping in the Mediterranean would be progressively—and swiftly—withdrawn. The repercussions were even more widely felt, forcing the revision of plans in the Far East.

Thus the amphibious operations essential to a rapid conquest of Italy, or for developments across the Adriatic, would not be

[1] Kennedy, *The Business of War*, p. 305.

possible. If the cross-channel assault in the early summer of 1944 was to be a reality there could be no diversions of any kind. Everything must serve that end. The United States Joint Chiefs of Staff were adamant, suspicious and watchful. The great opportunities opening out in Italy and in the Balkans, hastened by the fall of Mussolini on July 25th, left the Americans unmoved. To them, in General Marshall's words, the Mediterranean was a 'graveyard', and the more it looked like a sea of opportunity, the more it frightened them. The assault upon Italy would take place for little better reason than that the troops were available and should be kept active. Moreover, it would be unthinkable to call a halt, and simply to mark time. A halt could only benefit the German enemy, and gravely discourage the guerillas operating throughout the Balkans, and doubtless, soon, in Italy itself.

There were four main shortages governing all Allied military operations. These were, merchant shipping, assault shipping, transport aircraft, and for the British, men. British manpower was a wasting asset. There were nearly five million men under arms, more and more of them employed in the ever growing 'tails' supporting the 'teeth' of armies and air forces. War production in Britain was already gravely imperilling the trade, the 'peace' life and production, of the nation. Civilian commodities and manufactured goods for export had to keep going, not only to help pay for the enormous imports food bill, but that trade should not wither away. Shipping space was in enormous demand, and shipping losses had been astronomical.

The most tragic shortages threatening the conduct of the war to the very end, were in landing ships tanks (LST), and landing ships infantry (LSI). To these must be added a host of lesser craft, all demanding crews to be trained. These crews could only be obtained by withdrawing men from naval and marine activities, many of which were scarcely less vital.

'In this period in the war,' Churchill wrote, 'all the great strategic combinations of the Western Powers were restricted and distorted by the shortage of tank landing-craft... The letters "LST" are burnt in upon the minds of all those who dealt with military affairs in this period.'[1]

He doubted whether the fact that two great nations were 'so

[1] Churchill, *Closing the Ring*, vol. v., R.U. ed., p. 206.

much ham-strung' by the lack of these vessels would ever be understood by history.

Nevertheless, British opportunism in the Eastern Mediterranean died hard. With the collapse of Italy, as Alexander saw and said, 'the best available alternative' lay in the Balkans. Since the introduction of the British Captain F. W. Deakin to Tito's headquarters in Jugoslavia, the guerilla commander, aided increasingly by the British, and soon to be joined by a military mission led by Brigadier Fitzroy Maclean, controlled the equivalent of twenty-six divisions. Having disarmed the Italians, and added others to his strength, Tito was able finally to seize Istria. It brought 'golden dreams' in prospect as soon as the Allies were in control of Naples and the Foggia airfields. In the German view this was the obvious jumping off point for the Balkans.

As late as November 1943 it was not surprising that General Marshall, the US Chief of Staff, still distrusted British intentions, and told Roosevelt and Hopkins at Teheran that 'the British might like to "ditch" *Overlord* now in order to go into the Balkans.'

The Germans, by that time, had increased their strength from twelve to twenty-four divisions in South Eastern Europe, and from six to twenty-five divisions in Italy. This was proof enough of their fears, and some justification for the long and arduous Italian campaign, conducted with fortitude and invincible humour by General Sir Harold Alexander in the face of difficulties which were not to diminish. At the same time as these developments were taking shape, the Russian advance in the south was gathering momentum.

British strategy in the Mediterranean had been given the *coup de grâce* at the precise moment when it might have become effective. The Teheran conference underlined the United States' predominance made manifest at Quebec three months earlier. The British had become poor relations of the two super powers, and Churchill was casually excluded from private talks between Roosevelt and Stalin. The Americans had begun to bombard the Russians with ideals, as Herbert Feis observed. 'Stalin's delight was marked,' I wrote. 'He had found a great ally, and nothing short of a miracle could stop his armies filling the vacuum in Central Europe.'[1]

[1] Thompson, *The Yankee Marlborough*, p. 60.

The American distrust of the British, revealed to the Russians at Teheran, was decisive for the future of Europe.

'The ultimate effect of this distrust,' wrote Professor Trumbull Higgins, 'appeared at the Teheran Conference in November-December 1943, when after the United States joined up with the Russians to push through the cross-channel invasion, this policy of Russo-American military collaboration tended to continue in the even more delicate realm of politics...'[1]

It was at Teheran that the landing in the South of France, known as 'Anvil', was conceived and agreed, to the obvious pleasure of Stalin, and to add to British discomfiture.

Nevertheless the Americans realized that the only area in which a large scale diversion could take place, helpful to 'Overlord' and to 'Anvil', was in the Mediterranean. The 'object' of the invasion of Italy was negative, that is to engage and contain as many enemy divisions as possible, and to keep them away from North West Europe for at least three months after the landings in Normandy.

Against this shifting background the Italian campaign was planned and fought. Before Sicily had been gained the Germans, realizing that the end of Mussolini would force them to take-over their reluctant ally, had begun to withdraw, and to work out a strategy for holding north of Rome. It became clear, therefore, to Eisenhower and Alexander in late July that they would have to act with great speed. The Italian armed forces were about to become a 'prize' to be contended for by the Allies and by the Germans. It was a highly dubious prize.

On August 15th Marshal Badoglio sent General Castellano to discuss an armistice with Eisenhower and Alexander, and at once 'the stinking Albatross' of unconditional surrender was seen to be fraught with meanings no one could hope to understand. The Western Allies demanded the surrender of the Italian armed forces, but with the Germans increasing their power in Italy how might such a surrender be accomplished? And of what service might Italian troops be? Could they, for example, hold Rome, even long enough for the Allies to drop an airborne division?

The talks dragged on, with Castellano commuting between Rome and Sicily.

[1] Trumbell Higgins, *Winston Churchill and the Second Front*, Ox. Univ. Press.

Meanwhile the planning for initial landings in Italy was well advanced. No one could view with anything but horror a campaign planned to proceed from the toe and grind slowly northwards. The great Byzantine, Belisarius, had advanced from the 'toe' to Naples, and thence to Rome against the whole power of the Goths. Finally he had reached Ravenna. But all that was a long time ago—more than 1,400 years—and Belisarius had been a tactical opportunist and cavalry commander of genius. No one would expect the cautious Montgomery to feel his way forward step by careful step in the footsteps of such a man. The great range of the Appenines backboned the country, with its complex ridges and river like ribs from the central spine to the shores of the Adriatic on the east, and the Tyrrhenian and Ligurian seas on the west.

'We shall not crawl up the leg of Italy like a harvest bug' Churchill said.

But crawl we must, if not much like a harvest bug.

The 'red hot rake of war' would be dragged, as Churchill threatened, from one end of the country to the other. British, American and French troops were the 'red hot' prongs of that unhappy rake. Lack of assault shipping would virtually condemn the invaders to batter their way against a series of almost impregnable ridges, the gaining of one at once confronting the winners with another at least equally severe. Line upon line was drawn across that country, and each one of them is engraved upon the minds of those who struggled grimly north for more than twenty months up from the foot of Italy. It was a wonderful country to defend and throughout August 1943 the Germans were preparing rapidly to defend it.

General Alexander's tactical possibilities in August were limited by the range of his fighter aircraft from his new airfields. This made the Gulf of Salerno the obvious choice for an attack while the shipping and assault craft were still available. Possibly nowhere could have been better. Naples was a considerable prize, and it was good strategy to occupy the country from there to the Adriatic shore about Termoli, north of the 'spur', and thus embracing the valuable Foggia airfields. This would be calculated to keep alive German fears of a Balkan assault. Unfortunately it was not difficult for the enemy to deduce Alexander's intention, and to prepare for it.

Broadly these were the objectives. Montgomery with the 13th Corps, and the 5th Corps to follow, would assault across the Messina Straits, clear Calabria and develop his advance in two prongs, the one towards the 'heel', and the other on the left to drive on with all speed to relieve pressure on the Americans. The US 5th Army, commanded by Lieutenant-General Mark Clark, comprising the US 6th Corps and the British 10th Corps, would assault in the Gulf of Salerno one week after Montgomery's assault in the south.

Meanwhile the negotiations with the Italians dragged on, and it became increasingly clear to Alexander that the military situation was not moving in his favour. To obtain the fullest possible co-operation from the Italians it would be necessary to disclose to them the plans. This the Allies were not prepared to do.

By the end of July the Germans had prepared plans to disarm the Italians, and to seize Rome. They had completed the redeployment of their forces in Italy on the day that Montgomery attacked in the south, the day on which General Castellano would sign the Italian surrender with Eisenhower and Alexander in Sicily.

> The uncertainties of the final events surrounding the Italian surrender prevented its purpose from being achieved. The armed forces in Italy received no warning of their Government's intentions, and the result was a fatal apathy and disorganization.[1]

In fact, by September 10th, the day after Marshal Badoglio announced the surrender in Rome, the bulk of the Italian forces had surrendered to the Germans. Only the Italian navy was to surrender to the Allies. This was a valuable prize, and there were other factors working in the Allied favour. The Germans over-estimated Allied strength, and were prepared to establish their holding line north of Rome, even as far north as the Po. They did not know that the Allied forces in the Mediterranean were ear-marked for another occasion still nine months ahead.

By the time Montgomery landed on the 'toe' at Reggio the Germans had successfully evacuated Calabria, leaving a trail of demolitions, and were able to concentrate without fear to meet

---

[1] Ehrman, *Grand Strategy*, vol. v, pp. 66-7.

the landings which they anticipated in the Gulf of Salerno. Thereafter, according to developments, they might choose to hold a line as far north as Rimini.

Inevitably the Italian campaign was condemned to a dead end.

II

General Montgomery announced the imminent arrival of his army on the southernmost shores of 'Fortress Europe' with the greatest artillery bombardment since the Battle of Alamein. It was September 3rd, the fourth anniversary of Britain's entry into the war, but it is unlikely that Montgomery's great cannonade was intended as a 'salute' to an historic occasion. It had become the General's signature, an inevitable overture and accompaniment to his attacks, irrespective of the opposition. Increasingly the Allied Air Forces were adding the weight of their high explosive to this blasting and bludgeoning.

Pantelleria would lead to Monte Cassino, and on and on.

It had been a formidable task to bring forward 600 guns over the rugged tracks and roads of Sicily, with all their ammunition and transport, to suitable positions upon the heights above Messina. Together with Montgomery's objections to the plans, inasmuch as they concerned him, these endeavours had delayed the assault by forty-eight hours. The guns of the great warships, *Nelson, Warspite, Rodney* and *Valiant* had added to the great din of the night, and bombers and fighter bombers had ensured that nothing should move in safety upon the unhappy toe of Italy.

The barrage had come down upon the beaches, lifted inland before returning to the beaches for a final blast and lifted thereafter at one hundred yard intervals. The Germans had departed. The Italians were about to surrender. The shore batteries were silent. Villagers and townsfolk lay in such shelter as they could find, to meet their conquerors in the dawn with glazed eyes, and in a dazed condition.

One hour before the dawn of September 3rd the leading brigades of the 5th Division of the 13th Corps, landed unopposed, seized Reggio di Calabria and Giovanni, and aided by a Commando landing at Bagnare during the night of the 3rd, moved forward in two prongs as swiftly as the enemy demolitions, and the havoc wrought by their own bombardment, would allow. Their first task was to seal off Calabria across the 'waist' from Pizzo to Catanzaro. It was a 'battle' for engineers.

The crossing of the Straits of Messina, wrote Buckley,[1] 'was just about as hazardous an undertaking as the crossing from Southsea to the Isle of Wight in peacetime.' It was also approximately the same distance. General Montgomery made the crossing a few hours after his assault forces, accompanied by a DUKW[2] laden with cigarettes for distribution to his men. Taking coffee and biscuits on his launch he discoursed upon the Arts of War, and watched the busy scene, 'almost a pantomime atmosphere', wrote Alan Moorehead. Sicilian girls had bidden the General Godspeed with fruit and flowers on the Sicilian shore, but it was still a little early for fruit and flowers on the sore toe of Italy.

Within a week Pizzo and Catanzaro were in Montgomery's hands. Meanwhile, General Alexander, rapidly appreciating the situation in the south and the extent of the German withdrawal, seized the port of Taranto without a shot by a brilliant piece of opportunism. The 1st Airborne Division, awaiting transport to Britain in North Africa to embark upon its training for 'Overlord', was lifted by the Navy without demur and with the utmost speed. Without waiting for any substantial evidence of Italian naval intentions, Admiral Cunningham steamed into Taranto under the guns of warships in the gulf. All was well. Powerful units of the Italian fleet had already sailed for Malta and captivity, and others were on their way.

The 1st Airborne Division was soon reinforced by the 78th Division. Brindisi and Bari were swiftly occupied. Thus powerfully reinforced, and with most of the 'foot' of Italy in his hands, Montgomery could now press on, not only on the Adriatic coast towards Termoli and the Foggia airfields, but also with the 5th Division north from Pizzo to the relief of Salerno.

'My object was now to get forward as quickly as possible in order to pin down the enemy and to initiate without delay a threat to the southern flank of the Germans opposing the Salerno bridgehead,' Montgomery wrote.[3]

---

[1] Buckley, *The Road to Rome*, p. 158.
[2] 2½ ton 6 × 6 Amphibious truck.
[3] Montgomery, *El Alamein to the River Sangro* p. 105.

General Alexander urged him anxiously and emphatically to that end.

The US 5th Army commanded by General Clark had sailed from North Africa on the 3rd, and on September 9th his assault battalions were striving desperately to gain a foothold on the Salerno beaches. Throughout the next eight agonizing days, sustained by massive air support, they gained a bridgehead, and repelled heavy enemy counter-attacks while Montgomery's column dawdled north from Pizzo. 'What was apparent to him (Montgomery),' wrote Moorehead, 'was that he could never hope seriously to buttress the man-power at Salerno in the space of a day or two, and he did not propose to jeopardize his own position hopelessly in trying to do so.'[1]

How Montgomery could have jeopardized his own position hopelessly by pressing forward with his left flank, Moorehead does not say. The General was, as always, concerned with the administrative difficulties in which he was involved.

The Americans at first were confidently expecting Montgomery to 'out-Patton Patton'. 'Patton would have burned shoe leather . . .' wrote Butcher. 'My guess was that Monty will move as he has never moved before. He is the potential hero of a grand melodrama and he will be quick to grasp the possibility of adding further lustre to his name.'[2]

The Americans were soon disillusioned. Daily the BBC gave the impression, 'that Montgomery's army was dashing up the Italian boot to our rescue,' wrote General Clark. 'This eventually proved pretty irritating at times, particularly as the Eighth Army was making a slow advance towards Salerno, despite Alexander's almost daily efforts to prod it into greater speed.'[3]

At about the same time the Public Relations Officer of the US Fifth Army showed General Clark his first cabled censorship instructions: 'First, play up the Eighth Army progress henceforth. Second, the Fifth Army is pushing the enemy back on his right flank. Americans may be mentioned . . .'

Montgomery, however, was well pleased with himself, and with his progress in spite of his grave administrative difficulties: 'We may perhaps never know fully what effect the news of

---

[1] Moorehead, *Montgomery*.
[2] Butcher, *Three Years with Eisenhower*, p. 359.
[3] Mark Clark, *Calculated Risk*. London, Harrap, 1951.

our approach had upon the enemy forces pinning down the Allied bridgehead at Salerno,' he wrote.[1]

General Eisenhower's brief reference is illuminating: 'The fierce fighting in Salerno drew off enemy forces from in front of Montgomery and his advance to the northward speeded up.'[2]

On September 16th, with the Fifth Army beachhead firmly established, a group of war correspondents made contact with the Americans in the vicinity of Vallo, having, it seems, dead-heated with Montgomery's patrols.

Without delay General Clark pushed on to attack Naples, while Montgomery 'is resting his Eighth Army and "winding-up its tail" a process that delays his forward movement for a week or ten days', wrote Butcher, somewhat sourly but truthfully.

Nevertheless by October 1st Montgomery had enveloped the Foggia airfields to clear the way for Fifteenth Strategic Air Force to take over, while Clark's army took Naples. Up to this point the campaign in Italy had been both sensible and satisfactory, but the situation was almost at once to become agonizing, especially to Churchill, working himself into a frenzy, according to General Brooke, and soon to lie ill at Carthage. The enemy had evacuated Sardinia and Corsica, and the long and vulnerable western flank of Italy was laid bare.

The next move was as difficult to take as to avoid. Badoglio, by his hesitancy and his far greater fear of the Germans than of the Allies, had failed to gain Rome. Kesselring worked out his strategy, and on October 6th, having retreated to the Volturno, he decided to move back still further and to stand on the line Garigliano—Monte Cassino—Sangro. He believed the Balkans to be the Allied target, and his decision and his reading of the situation was at once confirmed in a directive from Hitler:

> The enemy may be expected to direct his main operation against the south east area from Italy, possibly with the assistance of forces from Africa. It cannot yet be determined whether he will cross from Southern Italy into Albania, Montenegro and Southern Croatia, or whether he will first try to push further north in order to create a base in central Italy from which to attack Northern Croatia and Istria.[3]

[1] Montgomery, *El Alamein to the River Sangro*, p. 108.
[2] Eisenhower, *Crusade in Europe*, p. 209.
[3] *Grand Strategy*, vol. v, p. 68.

No wonder Churchill was sick with frustration as well as with pneumonia before Christmas. There would be only one way to move Kesselring away from the Garigliano line, and that would be by a flank attack. While the troops on the ground pushed grimly towards the north Churchill won grudging consent for an assault at Anzio to gain Rome, and turn the German line. It was not enough, but it was all he could get.

In December from his sick bed at Marrakesh he fought for landing craft for the Anzio landing. Plans for 'Overlord', and its subsidiary, 'Anvil', bedevilled the issues:

'It would seem irrational,' Churchill cabled to Roosevelt on Christmas Day, 'to remove them (landing craft) from the Mediterranean for the very week when they can render decisive service. What, also, could be more dangerous than to let the Italian battle stagnate and fester on for another three months? We cannot afford to go forward leaving a vast half-finished job behind us . . .'[1]

Together with Eisenhower and Alexander the Prime Minister won a brief reprieve for the assault shipping, and on December 28th Roosevelt gave his consent for the Anzio landing in January. It was cutting things rather fine.

Thereafter the 'Ghost of Anvil' haunted Churchill even more than it did Alexander. In its shadow his dreams of the development of the Italian campaign were doomed. Six months later he would send his lament to Roosevelt:

> What can I do, Mr President, when your Chiefs of Staff insist on casting aside our Italian offensive campaign, with all its dazzling possibilities, relieving Hitler of all his anxieties in the Po Basin and when we are to see the integral life of this campaign drained off into the Rhone Valley in the belief that it will in several months carry effective help to Eisenhower so far away in the North?[2]

III

Before the end of October the fine weather broke in Italy, and a harsh, bitter winter of torrential rains, ice and snow, gripped the land. War conjures its own hellish brands of mud

---
[1] Churchill, *The Hinge of Fate*, vol. iv, R.U. ed., p. 342.
[2] Ehrman, *Grand Strategy*, vol. v. Appendix X, para. 8, p. 577.

from the tortured earth it desecrates, and in the mud of Italy trucks might disappear without trace. Rivers burst into violent flood with little warning, and subsided with a rapidity barely less startling. Bridging became a nightmare testing the stamina and ingenuity of the sappers, and the quality of the Bailey bridging equipment, to the limits. Men, armour, guns, once across a stream often found themselves confined within narrow bridgeheads, without support, and unable to move forward or back. And always there was one more river to cross, one more mountain ridge to be assaulted, won, lost and won again. Villages had to be demolished house by house, barn, sty and stall, before the enemy retreated. Defile after defile had to be penetrated against a resolute enemy giving ground by inches, and threatening a 'stalemate' when he reached the Garigliano.

In these conditions Montgomery strove to bludgeon his army forward with an immense expenditure of high explosive and a consequent strain on petrol supplies and transport. Vehicles were arriving in Italy at the rate of 2,000 each week. The rate should have been 1,300 each day. Montgomery's administrative troubles were always great. He aggravated them by his insatiable appetites, and his inability to break out of his tactical straitjacket. In the Autumn of 1943 these things were serious.

The Fifteenth Strategic Air Force in its hurry to build-up its strength in the Foggia airfieds had consumed 300,000 tons of shipping space in a very short time. Montgomery's unimaginative and extravagant methods added to this immense burden. In his handling of the campaign he was as bankrupt of ideas as the generals of the First World War. His last plan of battle in Italy was very little different from his first. He was the prisoner of a formula, inherited from the First World War, and preached to his disciples at the Staff College. 'The original plan for the crossing of the Sangro, and breaking into the strong German positions based upon that river was likened to that of October 23, 1942, at El Alamein.'[1]

> General Fuller summed up the situation briefly and lucidly: Further still the situation was in no way improved by the command having now become so habituated to the Montgomery tactics that it overlooked that the problem was one of

[1] Liddell Hart, *The Tanks*, vol. ii, p. 274.

mountain warfare. These tactics consisted in: (1) The building-up of such a superiority in every arm that defeat would become virtually impossible; (2) the amassing of enormous quantities of munitions and supplies; (3) a preliminary air and artillery bombardment of obliteration; (4) followed by a methodical infantry advance, normally begun under cover of darkness; and (5) followed by tanks, used as self-propelled artillery, to provide the infantry with fire support.[1]

It is an accurate description of Montgomery's 'Master Plan' for all battles, irrespective of time, space, weather or terrain. War had become for Montgomery and his army simply one 'killing match' after another, until the end. He invariably wished his troops 'good hunting', and it was an unfortunate term to use. He had hunted the weary and grievously wounded Rommel from end to end of the desert, restraining his 'huntsmen' and his hungry 'pack' for the 'kill'. Whenever the quarry went to earth for respite, he called off his hounds, to wait and watch warily.

Would it be always so? Was he capable of the 'kill'—the *mate*—or must it always be 'stalemate', until at last the exhausted and battered enemy resigned?

Methodically, grimly, the Eighth Army crossed the Trigno and the Biferno to the Sangro, fighting demolitions almost as much as they fought the enemy. By night the smoke and flames of burning villages lit the rain filled skies ahead, and throughout all November there was little contact with the enemy as the sappers 'engineered' the way forward. In the first week of November the leading brigade of the 78th Division had cleared the last obstacles, and looked down upon the Sangro. It promised, they knew, a grim battle, for the enemy too had reached a 'destination' on the mountain roads and ridges to the north. It was the first of his winter lines.

On November 8th General Montgomery issued his last battle order in Italy in the phraseology his men knew so well:

The time has now come to drive the Germans North of Rome . . .
The Germans are, in fact, in the very condition in which we want them.

---

[1] Fuller, *The Second World War*, p. 270.

WE WILL NOW HIT THE GERMANS A COLOSSAL CRACK.

He wished them 'Good Hunting'.

Torrential rains made progress impossible. The Germans had two strong divisions blocking the way on the Eighth Army front, and five divisions, with two in reserve, holding the Fifth Army in the West. For seven weeks the British and the Germans fought each other to a standstill.

The armoured regiments involved made their bitter comments upon a battle, 'which, from the armour standpoint was a battle against nature. The ground seemed to turn into a gum-like substance after rain, and during the intense efforts to cross the Sangro thirty tanks got bogged down, seventeen were mined and one was "drowned".'[1]

Before the end of the month a bridgehead had been established, and on December 6th the Sappers built a high level bridge across the river, a magnificent achievement in appalling conditions.

The final assault to gain the lateral road Pescara to Rome was launched on December 23, supported by the 'whole of XIIIth Corps's artillery and five regiments from Vth Corps,' but the enemy held.

Watching these operations from the high ground, Montgomery's Chief of Staff, Major-General de Guingand, found it difficult to understand 'how the enemy could stand much more' of this terrific pounding. At times the whole business reminded him of Passchendaele, and he realised, belatedly, the kind of struggle the British 1st Army had fought in the mountains of Tunisia the previous winter.[2]

In the last days of December Montgomery was forced to call off the battle, having failed to gain the final objective. On December 30th four feet of snow fell upon the sodden land to put an end to the Winter Campaign. It was the end, also, of Montgomery's command of the Eighth Army.

The Prime Minister wrote the Epitaph:

The immortal march of the Eighth Army from the gates of Cairo along the African shore through Tunisia, through

---
[1] Liddell Hart, *The Tanks*, vol. ii, p. 276.
[2] de Guingand, *Operation Victory*, p. 332.

Sicily has now carried its ever-victorious soldiers and their world-honoured Commander far into Italy towards the gates of Rome. The scene changes and vastly expands. A great task accomplished gives place to a greater in which the same unfailing spirit will win for all true men a full and glorious reward.

Winston S. Churchill.

CHAPTER FOURTEEN

A Soldier's Farewell

I

On Christmas Eve, 1943, the War Office signalled General Montgomery the news of his appointment to succeed General Paget in the command of the 21st Army Group, training in the United Kingdom for the assault upon North West Europe. For twenty-four hours Montgomery digested this news in solitude, considering carefully which of his officers he should take with him to these new fields of war. Above all he needed his Chief of Staff, Major-General de Guingand, with whom he had developed an almost paternal relationship. And there were others, the young 'knights', and his personal servants. These had made for him a kind of 'home', sitting round his 'camp fire', warming him with their admiration ,and regaling him with their adventures.

On a junior level de Guingand probably understood his master better than anyone else; on a senior level General Brooke was his nearest guide and friend. But none of these relationships was an easy friendship on a basis of equality, which is the essence of true friendship, and the vital need of adult man. Montgomery had made a 'nest' for himself in which he could be warm and secure, in which there was respect, and affection, and from which intruders were barred. He had grown from youth to manhood within the confines of the military world, and had created for himself a narrower world within it. He had filled the senior command positions in his army with men he had indoctrinated with his ideas in their student days. He had eliminated criticism, and had become incapable of self criticism. He was, in a sense, a 'flat-earther', and this enabled him to simplify all problems in the simple arithmetic of his own mind.

'He knows everything,' old Petain had said about someone. 'But he knows nothing else.'

No one would ever have questioned his authority, but there was no one to say, 'Don't be an ass, Monty!' or, 'What frightful rot!' There was no one to laugh at his pompous, pedantic, trite pronouncements; no one—in his presence—even to smile.

Yet it was his strength that almost everyone smiled 'behind his back.' His every repetition, his every platitude, earned chuckles of delight; his 'Glory to God in the Highest, and Good Hunting to you all', never—or hardly ever—palled, and would echo in the pubs and clubs for many days.

The occasional 'telling off' by General Brooke could not compensate for the lack of adult companionship on his own level; for friends round him; for men he had not trained, and were not friends, but who would have brought with them fresh minds, fresh ideas, fresh approaches, and dared to speak their thoughts. Without such men he would never come to see, or even to imagine, the broad horizons far beyond the rim of his 'flat earth'.

Montgomery inhabited an essentially juvenile world. His affection was for the young. Undoubtedly he was 'fond' of de Guingand, but de Guingand was too junior, too much his master's man and voice to be of service in the growth and development of his command. There is a solitude in command. It begins on a low level, and grows with every step in rank, until the commander of an army, an air force, a battle fleet, is virtually condemned to solitary confinement. It is the problem of power. In making an 'island' of a man it carries inevitable corruption, and condemns mankind to be ruled by those who James Gould Cozzens has called 'Juvenile Delinquents come to man's estate', and Lewis Mumford, 'The Faceless Men'.

As soon as he had discussed his appointment with de Guingand, Montgomery prepared to bid farewell to his Army, and to address his officers down to lieutenant colonels. It would be, not only an 'historic', but also a 'sentimental' occasion. He wrote his farewell message on December 28th in his aircraft on his way back from his first meeting with General Eisenhower in his new role. He prepared for his last appearance with his army with meticulous care. His image had not tarnished at home or abroad, and his popularity had not waned with his troops or with the hosts of the 'common man'. His Eighth Army had enjoyed the lion's share of the publicity in the Italian campaign, although it had performed the lesser role of the two armies engaged. He had been presented with an electrical turntable, and was in the habit of cutting at least two 'discs' of his various speeches and pronouncements, playing them over in the presence of BBC correspondents, and carefully selecting the best to be sent home for broadcasting. As a symbol of victory he was supremely conscious of his role as an actor on a world stage. If he saw himself rather larger than life size, it was not surprising.

De Guingand was entrusted with the stage management of the farewell appearance of his chief. The Opera House in Vasto was not too severely damaged, and would serve admirably for the occasion. De Guingand felt frankly sentimental, and assumed that Montgomery shared his feelings.

'My chief was very quiet," de Guingand wrote, 'and I could see that this was going to be the most difficult operation he had yet attempted."

When they reached the Opera House together, Montgomery said simply:

'Show me where to go, Freddie.'

De Guingand led his chief to the stairs leading to the stage. Montgomery was then on his own to face his audience.

According to de Guingand, Montgomery began to speak 'very quietly', and apologizing for any emotion he might show, 'If I happen to find difficulty in speaking on occasion, I hope you will understand.'

In his *Memoirs* Montgomery shirks a personal account of this memorable event, and prefers to quote de Guingand's sad and sentimental description:

'I felt a lump coming into my throat, and one could feel every one of his audience was perfectly tuned to his mood.'

Denis Johnston of the BBC, a Montgomery man 'warts 'n all', had resolved to be present. He recorded his impressions. He had helped Montgomery to cut his farewell 'discs', ready to be played over 'to those Staff Officers who had not been fortunate enough to be present, and also to the Tac sergeants' mess.'[1]

Johnston decided to face the audience so that he would be able to 'study—not the departing Commander—but the faces in the lines of high-ranking officers as they listened to his lecture on "How to Win Wars".' Of course, as Johnston observes, the lecture was not really about how to win wars, but it always sounded like that. He noted the 'polite and formal expressions on

[1] Johnston, *Nine Rivers from Jordan*, pp. 180-1.

the faces of the corps commanders in the front row, the "glassy smiles" farther back; the frank and open boredom of the air vice-marshal, who was not obliged to register any particular respect.'

'And Monty—talking away on the stage, having the time of his life.'

The General knew, of course, that he was indispensable, but there it was. He had to go. There was only one of him. The army would be in the hands of a good soldier, General Sir Oliver Leese.

Montgomery's genius in part was that he outcrashed with consummate ease all crashing bores. It was as though be broke through the 'sound barrier' in that genre, and brought to his audiences the kind of unbelief, followed by wonder and delight, that they would have felt in the presence of, say, a talking dog, or horse. A vast public swallowed it all, hook, line and sinker.

There had not been laurels for Montgomery in Italy. His army had struck the hard core of bitter German resistance, and those on the Ortona ridge beyond the Sangro on that day of farewell, or in the village of Villa Grande, sensed for the first time something of the meaning of 'total war'. That would be the new Army Commander's headache, but the 600 days of the campaign in Italy, when they were done, would belong to Alexander. It was a long and grim haul for the Eighth Army to the field of Caporetto.

When de Guingand escorted General Montgomery to his car from the Opera House he admitted to tears on his cheeks. Later there was a meeting with the corps commanders.

'As my chief talked to these trusted few I could not help thinking of Napoleon and his marshals.'

I do not think General Montgomery was very sorry to go. It was a bad time, and the Eighth Army did not look much like its old self of those glamorous and exhilarating days of its 'private war' in the desert.

II

General Montgomery had certainly hoped for his new appointment. He had angled for it, and perhaps he expected it. Yet it was remarkable. His failure to collaborate happily and without friction with the Americans was notorious, and a constant anxiety to General Brooke. Moreover Brooke was acutely aware of Montgomery's 'parochial' outlook, and the narrow limits of his horizons. Politically and strategically Montgomery was innocent. He was a soldier, pure and simple, a perfectionist; methodical, competent, and equipped by long application and dedication for the care and management of an army. He had been the ideal soldier in his day, from the First World War and in the years between the wars. While he had been rising slowly, but steadily, to the top of his profession, the military thinkers and innovators of his times had fallen by the wayside, J. F. C. Fuller, B. H. Liddell Hart, and Montgomery's own brother-in-law, Percy Hobart, among them. The works of Liddell Hart, in particular, were in the knapsacks of the great German and Russian commanders, and were not ignored by the Americans. Montgomery did not ignore the great military thinkers, but his nature rendered him incapable of putting their ideas into practice.

Fortunately, Hobart had been lured to fashion the complex and ingenious 'menagerie' of the 79th Armoured Division,[1] and was no longer a corporal in the Home Guard. The others continued to attempt to influence strategy and tactics from the sidelines. Slowly their ideas were having some effect, and Montgomery was not stone deaf to them. He accepted new weapons with pleasure, but tended to use them in old ways. He had not been concerned with grand strategy, and very little with the strategy of the battlefield. He was a simple tactician of the old school.

Montgomery did not give a thought to the reasons why he had been chosen to command the 21st Army Group. He believed himself to be the best man for the job. He thought he was on the best of good terms with Eisenhower, the Supreme Commander; with Bedell Smith, who would continue as Chief of Staff; with Bradley, who would command the US 12th Army Group, and with Patton, who would command an army. Of course, these chaps were all raw and green, but they would have him to keep them on the rails.

A Canadian Army would be under Montgomery's command with the British Second Army, and he was well aware that the

---

[1] Hobart adapted armoured fighting vehicles to many uses, and some of them bore the names of animals.

Canadian General McNaughton would never forgive him for refusing permission for him to visit the Canadian Division in Sicily. The Canadian General had made the journey to Malta with his staff, expressly to see the division in the field. Montgomery's refusal had been bleak, and without grace.

Fortunately General McNaughton had returned to Canada, and General Crerar would command the 1st Canadian Army for the campaign in North West Europe. But the Canadians were less than enthusiastic about the choice of Montgomery. On a high level some remembered that he had been partly responsible for the plan of the Dieppe Raid. It had cost them very dear.

Familiar nicknames were the common currency of address between these men, and may be misleading. They were not indicative of friendship, or goodwill, and at times this custom used between mortal enemies lent a new dimension to jealousies and hatred. Dorman Smith was stabbed in the back by men who called him 'Chink'. The habit was, and is, a carry-over from schooldays, from Sandhurst, from the Staff College, and of innumerable commands, and meetings over many years.

When Montgomery visited Eisenhower immediately after Christmas, before saying farewell to the Eighth Army, he did not appear to be aware of the Supreme Commander's very natural disappointment. No doubt Einsehower disguised his feelings, and behaved with the ease of manner and charm that would serve him so well. Eisenhower had wanted Alexander, and the appointment of Montgomery had come as a chilling shock. Alexander had been the obvious favourite to command the land forces in the cross-channel assault. It seemed natural, the continuation of a fruitful partnership. Alexander had co-operated with the Americans with the utmost ease from the difficult start in Africa. Also he had commanded the 18th Army Group, and then the 15th Army Group, with skill and understanding. His grasp of strategy was sound, and might even have proved exceptional, given opportunities that the peculiar conditions of his command in Italy did not afford. Moreover he was a man of natural distinction, wit and humour.

Montgomery noted the command changes with satisfaction. General Sir Henry Maitland Wilson succeeded General Eisenhower as Supreme Commander, Mediterranean theatre; General Sir Harold Alexander continued in command of 15th

Army Group in Italy. It would have been difficult to see Montgomery in that role. Alexander, vulgarly, was stuck with it.

Perhaps the appointment of Montgomery reflected the British resolution to have a man who would state his military views, not only bluntly and crudely, but with absolute conviction of their rightness. Montgomery's invincible bloody-mindedness and his sense of infallibility may have been just what the British wanted following their changed status after Quebec and Teheran, and their grievous disappointments in the Eastern Mediterranean. Alexander, perhaps, tended to get on too well with the Americans, to be too easy-going, to be too much of a 'gentleman' for Churchill's taste.

Certainly Churchill preferred Montgomery, who amused him, and was 'on the make', rather than Alexander, with whom he was always slightly ill at ease. Like Wavell and Auchinleck, Alexander was incapable of intrigue. Such men tended to stick in Churchill's gullet, and could be a serious handicap in the higher reaches of the power game. Besides, there were certain to be growing divergencies in the political attitudes of the Allies in Europe. The United States' attitude to de Gaulle, reflected in Cordell Hull's contemptuous reference to the 'so-called Free French', their liking for Vichy, and their preference for Giraud in North Africa, had sounded alarums that might, in the end, ring round the world, and would certainly create problems in Western Europe.

General Montgomery could be relied upon to stick to his military last, happily ignorant of such under-currents. For better or for worse, the choice was made.

On the night of December 30th Montgomery handed over the command of the Eighth Army to General Leese, and on the next morning flew off to meet Churchill at Marrakesh. He was to have his first sight of the 'Overlord' plan that night, and of course, since he had had nothing to do with it—so far— it was a bad plan. Montgomery was running true to form.

NOTES

Part One: The Inheritance

Comparison of *Crusader*, November 1941, with *2nd Alamein*, October/November 1942.

Crusader:

    Eighth Army: 118,000 officers and men.
    Armour: 455 tanks, out-armoured and out-gunned by enemy.

The Enemy:

    Panzer Armee Afrika: 100,000 officers and men.
    Armour: 415 tanks.
    Enemy greatly superior in anti-tank guns.
    Total enemy casualties: 60,000 officers and men killed, wounded and missing.
    Own casualties: 18,000 officers and men.

2nd Alamein:

    Eighth Army: 150,000 officers and men.
    Armour: 1,114 tanks, including 128 new Grants and 267 new Shermans, equipped with 75 mm guns.
    Artillery: 1,200 guns.

The Enemy:

    Panzer Armee Afrika: 96,000 officers and men.
    Armour: 600 tanks (half of them Italian).
    Artillery: 550 guns approx.
    Total enemy casualties: 59,000 officers and men.
    Armour losses: 180 tanks.
    Own casualties: 13,500 officers and men.
    Armour losses: 600 tanks.

Equipment: see Appendix 8, *The Mediterranean and Middle East*, vol. iii. Supply position.
    Auchinleck Despatch refers to 'our flimsy and ill-constructed (petrol) container'.

In view of the poor design of our petrol containers a special effort was made to salve as many as possible of the very efficient German petrol and water containers. At Benghazi over two million of them were discovered, but only a few of them could be removed before the enemy made his counter-stroke.

The Alexander Despatch also comments on the equipment of the Eighth Army before he took over.

Eastern Epic, Compton Mackenzie, has many details of faulty equipment.

The following report from a Field Company is typical:

We have only 38 vehicles and we need 100. We have thirteen different types, which makes spares hard to obtain. Thirteen of our lorries are over two years old and completely worn out. Seven are relics which formerly towed trucks up the Keren railway. Their engines are finished, their steering deplorable, their frames out of alignment. The remainder are veterans of Sudan, Syria and Libya. Their mileage over rough desert is in scores of thousands, and they are constantly in the workshops.

The Legend of the two Eighth Armies:

Comment from *Eastern Epic,* Compton Mackenzie.

A legend has grown up that the Eighth Army started its career at the second battle of Alamein, and this legend has been preposterously turned into bad history by those who were responsible for denying to all those who served in it before October 23rd, 1942 the numeral 8 on the ribbon of the Africa Star. The only explanation for such a denial is the guilty conscience of those who were fundamentally responsible for there ever being any need for a second battle of Alamein.

Tributes to the deeds of the Eighth Army prior to August, 1942 may be read in the Official Histories, notably—*The Mediterranean and Middle East,* vol. iii, and *Grand Strategy,* vol. iii, part ii. In *Auchinleck,* by John Connell, *The Desert Generals,* by Correlli Barnett, *The Rommel Papers,* ed. B. H. Liddell Hart, *The Tanks,* vol. ii, by B. H. Liddell Hart, and many other books of distinction.

Achievements and morale of Eighth Army prior to August, 1942, from Playfair, *The Mediterranean and Middle East,* vol. iii.

In retrospect the vital importance of the July fighting stands out clearly, and to General Auchinleck stands the credit for turning retreat into counter-attack. His forecast of mid-September as the earliest date for an 'all-out' offensive may not have been popular in London, but it was realistic and reasonable. In the event this offensive began on October 23rd and its success should not be allowed to overshadow the earlier achievements of those who made it possible.

A special word of recognition is due to those who fought through this period in the most trying conditions, parched by heat and sandstorms and pestered by loathsome swarms of flies. That horrible affliction, the desert sore, was common. These and other forms of the ten plagues had to be endured day after day in cramped or exposed positions or in roasting hot tanks. Small wonder that tempers were short or that strain and malaise set hasty tongues wagging. But it is to the lasting credit of the troops that although they suffered heavily, they none the less responded to every demand made upon them. This could not have happened with a dispirited army.

In spite of the disasters that had befallen his (Auchinleck's) Army he had retained to a remarkable degree its admiration and high regard.

The Battle of Alamein:

Auchinleck alludes to 'The Battle of El Alamein' in July twice in his Despatch, and Dorman Smith wrote 'Battle of El Alamein' in his pocket-book on 1st July.

Montgomery, in his Order of the Day of 5th September, said: 'The Battle of Alamein has now lasted six days.' Only later this battle was named Alam Halfa. Then, in this reckoning came the 3rd Battle of Alamein in October/November.

Montgomery does not mention his Order of the Day of September 5th. See Carver, *Alamein,* p. 72.

MESSAGE 6/7 AUGUST, 1942. PRIME MINISTER TO
DEPUTY PRIME MINISTER
showing passages omitted from Churchill Memoirs

See message 'The Hinge of Fate',
  Grand Strategy, vol. iii, Part ii, p. 654.
  The Mediterranean and Middle East, vol. iii, p. 368.

Our proposal to divide the Command is made entirely on merits. I doubt if the disasters would have occurred in the Western Desert if General Auchinleck had not been distracted by the divergent considerations of a too widely extended front . . . He would have taken direct command of the battle which began at the end of May but for reluctance to become 'immersed in tactical problems in Libya'. This phrase itself reveals the false proportions engendered by extraneous responsibilities. It is in fact the 'tactical problems of Libya' which dominate our immediate affairs.

The two Commands are separated by desert areas of 300 or 400 miles and the only lateral communication between them is by railway through Turkey, which we cannot use for the passage of troops, by motor tracks across the desert and by sea voyage around Arabia, taking nearly fourteen days. Both Commands have entirely different bases of supply. . . . We are all convinced that the division proposed is sound on geographical, strategic and administrative grounds . . .

I have no hesitation in proposing Auchinleck's appointment to the new command . . .

At the head of an army with a single and direct purpose he commands my entire confidence. If he had taken command of the Eighth Army when I urged him to I believe we should have won the Gazala battle and many people here think the same.

He has shown high minded qualities of character and resolution. He restored the battle of Sidi Rezegh and only recently he stemmed the retreat at El Alamein. There is no officer here or in India who has better credentials.

Only the need of making an abrupt and decisive change in the Command against Rommel and giving the Army a sense of a new start has induced me to propose the redistribution of Commands. I should be most reluctant to embarrass Alexander with remote cares at a moment when all our fortunes turn upon the speedy and decisive defeat of Rommel.

Nor can I advise that General Auchinleck should be ruined and cast aside as unfit to render any further service . . . When General Wavell was removed from the Middle East Command to India he in no way lost his reputation . . .

The nation will admire the array of our distinguished commanders, Wavell, Auchinleck, and Alexander, facing their responsibilities on the vast front which extends from Cairo to Calcutta.

There is no difficulty in preserving Air Marshal Tedder's single air command over the existing Middle East area.

I earnestly hope that my colleagues will find themselves able on further consideration of this most difficult problem to authorise me to proceed as I propose. In all this I have the complete agreement of Smuts and C.I.G.S. A decision has now become most urgent, since Alexander has already started and Auchinleck has, of course, no inkling of what is in prospect. I must apprise him tomorrow.

I am most grateful for the agreement of the Cabinet to the other parts of my plan, grave though they be.

Auchinleck's rejection of Persia-Iraq command

Some time between August 11th and 15th, General Auchinleck wrote to the CIGS pointing out that he had at no time been consulted as to the proposed new command:

I have studied the report of the Committee on the implications of setting up an independent command in Iraq-Persia and I consider it makes the best of a bad case. Its conclusions and recommendations make it very obvious that the working of the scheme in practice must depend on compromise in practically every sphere of activity to an excessive degree. It is also clear that the Commander-in-Chief Iraq-Persia will have to depend on the machinery at the disposal of his colleague in Cairo to an extent which cannot fail to place him in a subordinate position to the latter and so bring about again the situation which I understand the scheme is expressly designed to avoid.

I do not think myself that the scheme is workable in practice, and I feel that there is a grave risk of its breaking down under the stress of active operations. I do not therefore feel able to accept the responsibility of this new Command, and I have informed the Secretary of State accordingly.

Quoted from private papers.

Major-General Dorman Smith was Chairman of the Committee formed to report on the proposed Iraq-Persia command. It was on Dorman Smith's direct advice that Auchinleck refused the command.

'Would your advice be the same if I told you that I would take you with me as Chief of Staff?' Auchinleck asked.
'Yes,' said Dorman Smith.

The appointment would have carried the rank of Lieutenant-General. It seems likely that Dorman Smith's adverse report was the direct cause of the ruin of his military career.

Comment from Grand Strategy, *vol. iii, part ii, p. 461, on new Alexander command:*

Auchinleck was the last man to be asked to shoulder the burden of what had been known as 'The Middle East Command'.

The Prime Minister is said to have suggested Sir Harold Alexander to command the Middle East, but his time was not yet come, and when it came he was relieved of responsibility for the Persia and Iraq front.

Alexander's orders were simple:

1. Your prime and main duty will be to take or destroy at the earliest opportunity the German-Italian Army commanded by Field-Marshal Rommel, together with all its supplies and establishments in Egypt and Libya.
2. You will discharge or cause to be discharged such other duties as pertain to your command without prejudice to the task in paragraph 1, which must be considered paramount in His Majesty's interests.

Churchill wrote these orders in his own hand on Embassy notepaper. It gave him the sensation of being a kind of Napoleon.

Comment on situation from The Mediterranean and Middle East, vol. iii, p. 367.

In all the stir of the Prime Minister's visit it was perhaps natural that thoughts should dwell more upon the future than upon the past, more upon the blow that was in store for the Axis forces than upon the mauling they had already received.

Field Marshal Rommel. His condition towards the end of August 1942. From THE ROMMEL PAPERS:

24th August.
Dearest Lu,
I was unable to write again yesterday. I'm now well enough to get up occasionally. But I'll still have to go through with the six weeks treatment in Germany. My blood pressure must be got properly right again some time or other. One of the Fuehrer's doctors is supposed to be on his way. I'm certainly not going to leave my post here until I can hand over to my deputy without worrying. It's not known yet who is coming. I'm having another examination today. It's some comfort to know that the damage can probably all be cleared up. At the rate we've been using up generals in Africa—five per division in eighteen months—it's no wonder that I need an overhaul some time or other.

The Doctor also wrote to Frau Rommel:

Your husband has now been nineteen months in Africa, which is longer than any other officer over forty has stood it so far, an astonishing physical feat. After the rigours of the advance, he has had to carry the immense responsibility of the Alamein front, anxiety for which has for many nights allowed him no rest. Moreover, the bad season has come again.

All this has, in the nature of things, not failed to leave its mark, and thus, in addition to all the symptoms of a heavy cold and the digestive disturbances typical of Africa, he has recently shown signs of exhaustion.

Moreover, the Rommel papers make it clear that the Field-Marshal knew that his task was hopeless, even unaware as he then was of the projected Anglo-American landings in North Africa.

Comment on situation before Alam Halfa by Field-Marshal Kesselring:

> There was no choice but to opt for an offensive solution if there was the slighest prospect of success . . . Everything depended on Rommel's striking as soon as possible . . . Given our knowledge of the full risk of the gamble, the attack ought never to have been begun.
>
> Shortage of petrol was such as to make a sustained battle of more than two or three days impossible.

Comment on situation by reviewer in TLS, October 1, 1964, on publication of Part ii of the diary of Generaloberest Halder, and the Memoirs of General Warlimont:

> By the autumn of 1942 all Halder's worst fears had been realized. Casting to the winds all professional counsel, Hitler had forced his troops forward, both in Russia and in North Africa, into untenable positions. In Russia the wide dispersal of forces led to the disaster of Stalingrad. In the Mediterranean the decision to invade Egypt before the capture of Malta could safeguard Rommel's lines of supply resulted in the destruction of the Afrika Korps and its Italian associates by a slow strangulation, to which the second Battle of Alamein came as a *coup de grâce*.
>
> And finally, with the totally unexpected landings in French North Africa, the Western Allies transformed the Mediterranean from a minor theatre of war into a true second front.

The following note, authorized by Field-Marshal Montgomery, appeared in new editions of his *Memoirs:*

> Since the publication of this book, the author, in a broadcast in the BBC Home Service on November 20, stated that he was grateful to General (now Field-Marshal) Sir Claude Auchinleck and the Eighth Army under his command for stabilizing the British front on the Alamein position, thereby enabling the author to conduct his successful offensive, known to the world as the Battle of Alamein, in October 1942.
>
> The publishers think that readers of this book, who neither heard the broadcast nor read the accounts of it in the Press, might reasonably assume that, immediately before the author

took command over the Eighth Army, General Auchinleck was preparing to withdraw into the Nile Delta, or even beyond, in the event of a determined attack by the enemy.

They wish it to be known that a number of other writers, and notably General Alexander (now Field-Marshal Earl Alexander of Tunis), in a despatch published as a supplement to the *London Gazette* of February 3, 1948, make it clear that after General Auchinleck, commanding the Eighth Army, had successfully halted the enemy's attack in July 1942, it was his intention to launch an offensive from the Alamein position when his Army was rested and had been regrouped.

The Prime Minister's statement in his message of August 21st, 1942 published in *The Hinge of Fate* remains uncorrected.

Under threat of a libel action, and after Lord Shawcross had acted as a go-between, the Prime Minister inserted a footnote in all new editions of *The Hinge of Fate* to exonerate Major-General Dorman Smith from all blame. The general accepted the following footnote, and withdrew his libel action.

Foot of p. 378, vol. iv, R.U. Edition:

The references to the officers whose names figure in this list are factual only. Neither they nor my latter remarks are to be taken as imputing personal blame to any individual. These were the principal changes in Commands and Staff at the time when General Auchinleck was replaced by General Alexander.

Major-General Dorman Smith only became Deputy Chief of Staff on June 16th, 1942; he thus bears no responsibility for the fall of Tobruk or the defeats at Gazala. From June 25th to August 4th, he acted as General Auchinleck's Principal Operations Officer at Headquarters Eighth Army during the operations described in Chapter 24. My appreciation in that chapter of the handling of the Eighth Army is supported by Rommel's remarkable tribute.

General Dorman Smith was still unaware of the reasons for the early termination of a military career marked by unusual brilliance.

The Tanks: The History of the Royal Tank Regiment, vol. ii: B. H. Liddell Hart

> ... in the light of later knowledge and historical examination these sweeping changes were an undiscriminating and unjust conclusion to a crucial month of war. It was left to the enemy to put Auchinleck's achievement in true proportion and be first in paying him due tribute. An ironical sequel to his removal was that the renewal of the British offensive was postponed to a much later date than he had contemplated, and an impatient Prime Minister had to bow to the new High Command's determination to wait—until satisfied that preparations and training were complete, even though the delay meant leaving the initiative to Rommel.

The Mediterranean and Middle East, vol. iii. Playfair. HMSO.

General Alexander upon taking over command found:

> the troops resolute, but puzzled by retreats which they had not understood. 'A more serious cause of discouragement was the knowledge that our defeat had been due in part to inferiority of equipment: there is nothing so sure to cause lack of confidence.' Mr Churchill had expressed the opinion a week earlier that wherever the fault for the present serious situation might lie, it was certainly not with the troops and only to a minor extent with their equipment. But the references in this volume to the performance of British and German tanks and anti-tank guns, particularly in Appendix 8 show that in several respects the British equipment in 1941 and the first half of 1942 was not the equal of the German.

READING LIST

(*This list includes reading for Book Two*)

Alexander of Tunis, Field-Marshal Lord, *Despatch*, London, HMSO.
Auchinleck, Field-Marshal Sir Claude, *Despatch*, London, HMSO.
Barclay, Brigadier C. N., *On Their Shoulders*, London, Faber & Faber, 1964.
Barnett, Correlli, *The Desert Generals*, London, Kimber, 1960.
Bennett, Sir John Wheeler, *King George VI*, London, Macmillan, 1958.
Bradley, Omar P., *A Soldier's Story*, London, Eyre & Spottiswood, 1952.
Bryant, Sir Arthur, *Triumph in the West*, London, Collins, 1959.
Bryant, Sir Arthur, *The Turn of the Tide*, London, Collins, 1956.
Buckley, Christopher, *Road to Rome*, London, Hodder & Stoughton, 1945.
Butcher, Harry C., *Three Years with Eisenhower*, London, Heinemann, 1946.
Carver, Major-General Michael, *El Alamein*, London, Batsford, 1962.
Casey, R. G., *Personal Experience, 1939-1946*, London, Constable.
Churchill, Sir Winston S., *Closing the Ring*, vol. v of The Second World War, London, Cassell, 1952.
Churchill, Sir Winston S., *The Hinge of Fate*, vol. iv of The Second World War, London, Cassell, 1950.
Churchill, Sir Winston S., *Triumph and Tragedy*, vol. vi of The Second World War, London, Cassell, 1954.
Clark, Mark, *Calculated Risk*, London, Harrap, 1951.
Clifford, Alexander, *Three Against Rommel*, London, Harrap, 1946.
Connell, John, *Auchinleck, A Critical Biography*, London, Cassell, 1959.
de Gaulle, Charles, *War Memoirs*, Unity 1942-1944, Documents 1942-1944, London, Weidenfeld & Nicolson, 1959.
de Guingand, Major-General Sir Francis, *Generals at War*, London, Hodder & Stoughton, 1964.
de Guingand, Major-General Sir Francis, *Operation Victory*, London, Hodder & Stoughton, 1947.
Eisenhower, Dwight D., *Crusade in Europe*, London, Heinemann, 1948.
Fuller, Major-General J. F. C., *Generalship, its diseases and their cure*, London, Skeffington, 1933
Fuller, Major-General J. F. C., *The Second World War*, London, Eyre & Spottiswood, 1954.
Hamilton, J. A. I. Agar-, & L. C. F. Turner, *Crisis in the Desert*, London, Oxford University Press.

Hart, B. H. Liddell, (ed.), *The Rommel Papers*, London, Collins, 1953.
Hart, B. H. Liddell, *Strategy, The Indirect Approach*, (with foreword by Major-General E. E. Dorman Smith), (3rd ed.) Faber & Faber, 1954.
Hart, B. H. Liddell, *The Tanks*, The History of the Royal Tank Regiment, vol. ii, London, Cassell, 1949.
Horrocks, Lieutenant-General Sir Brian, *A Full Life*, London, Collins, 1960.
Johnston, Denis, *Nine Rivers from Jordan*, London, Deutsch, 1953.
Kennedy, Major-General Sir John, *The Business of War*, London, Hutchinson, 1957.
Kippenberger, Major-General Sir Howard, *Infantry Brigadier*, London, Oxford University Press, 1949.
Linklater, Eric, *The Campaign in Italy*, London, HMSO, 1945.
Mackenzie, Sir Compton, *Eastern Epic*, vol. i, London, Chatto & Windus, 1951.
Montgomery, Field-Marshal Lord, *El Alamein to the River Sangro*, London, Hutchinson, 1948.
Montgomery, Field-Marshal Lord, *The Memoirs of*, London, Collins, 1958.
Montgomery, Field-Marshal Lord, *Military Leadership*, RUSI pamphlet.
Montgomery. Field-Marshal Lord, *The Path to Leadership*, London, Collins, 1961.
Montgomery, Field-Marshal Lord, *Ten Chapters*, London, RUSI pamphlet.
Moorehead, Alan, *Montgomery*, London, Hamish Hamilton, 1946.
North, John, (ed.), *The Memoirs of Field-Marshal Earl Alexander of Tunis, 1940-1945*, London, Cassell, 1962.
Phillips, Brigadier C. E. Lucas, *Alamein*, London, Heinemann, 1962.
Sherwood, Robert E., *The White House Papers* (Harry Hopkins) two volumes, London, Eyre & Spottiswoode, 1948-1949.
Smuts, J. C., *Jan Christian Smuts*, London, Cassell, 1952.
Young, Desmond, *Rommel*, London, Collins, 1950.

Official Histories

The Eighth Army, November 1941 to May 1943, London, HMSO.
History of the Second World War, *Grand Strategy*
   Vol. III Part I by J. M. A. Gwyer, 1964.
           Part II by J. R. M. Butler, 1964.
   Vol. V   by John Ehrman, 1956. London, HMSO.
Playfair, Major-General I. S. O., *The Mediterranean and Middle East*, vol. iii. London, HMSO.

The Army Air Forces in World War II, Vol. 2: *Europe; Torch to Pointblank.* Air Historical Group, Washington.

US Army in World War II: Mediterranean Theatre of Operations:

George F. Howe, *North West Africa:* Seizing the Initative in the West, Washington Office of the Chief of Military History Dept. of the Army, 1960.

Private Papers

Diaries of Major-General E. E. Dorman Smith (O'Gowan).
Letters, analyses in the archives of B. H. Liddell Hart.

Index

Afrika Corps, at Alma Halfa, 97, 98; casualties, 98, 152, 184; in retreat, 105; ordered to stand firm by Hitler, 115, 116, 119; tank strength, 146; brilliant withdrawal of, 151; reduced to a shadow, 158; mentioned, 152.

Agheila, 158 et seq.; Rommel evades Montgomery there, 161.

Airborne landings, in Sicily, 221; a disaster, 222.

Alam Halfa, Battle of, 95-99; 124, 169; battle foreseen by Auchinleck, 95; described in official history, 106; Montgomery's caution at, 136; victory achieved by sitting tight, 154; sets a pattern of caution, 163; Montgomery compares it to Medenine, 187; Kesselring comments on, 260.

Alamein, 1st Battle of, 40, 42, 63, 66; 2nd Battle of, 81, 106, 111, 115, 163, 170, 203; 119-136; odds in British favour, 119-120; failure of original plans, 134, 140; effect on morale, 136; second part of battle, 136-147; a battle of attrition, 154; Montgomery's failure at, 155; 8th Army's strength at, 253.

Alexander, General Sir Harold, 61, 63, 64, 67, 71, 75, 111, 185, 240; summoned to Cairo, 60; Rommel's defeat his sole duty, 65; his understanding of Montgomery, 80; agrees to Montgomery's dismissals, 81; accepts Auchinleck's plan, 84; replaces Auchinleck, 85; endorses Montgomery's plan, 108; his freedom from political problems, 121; corresponds with Churchill, 121; formulates new plans with Montgomery, 143; his support for Montgomery, 157, 163, 168, 187; impatience at slowness of advance, 158; his tolerance, 163; credit for Tripoli his, 169; message to Churchill, 169; his talents unrecognised, 173; assumes command of 18th Army Group, 180; his good relations with Eisenhower, 182; comments on end of African campaign, 192; commands 15th Army Group, 209; in Sicily, 222, 223; comments on Balkans, 232; his conduct of Italian campaign, 232; appreciates need for speed, 233; and tactical possibilities in Italy, 234; seizes Taranto, 237; urges Montgomery on, 238; the Italian campaign primarily his, 248; favoured by Eisenhower for Europe, 250; but remains in Italy, 251; Churchill's orders to, 258.

Algiers, army conferences at, 219, 225.

Allies, their divergent interests, 26; command structure, 197, 198; evolution of, 200; war methods, 218; strategic conflicts of, 219, 229-230.

America, mistrust of British, 28, 47, 48, 109; clarity of vision, 28; dislike of Churchill's Mediterranean plans, 47; collaboration with USSR, 233.

American Army. 5th Army, in assault on Italy, 235; at Salerno, 237; 7th Army, 211, 213; 1st Armoured Div., 167,

202; 6th Corps, 235; 11th Corps, 169; repulsed, 175; under Alexander, 180; asks Montgomery for help, 184-185; at Mareth, 189, 190; makes contact with 8th Army, 191; takes Bizerta, 193; in Sicily, 223; 45th Div., 222.
Ammunition, complexities of, 217.
Anderson, General, 169, 180.
'Anvil', operation, plan to invade Southern France, 229; conceived at Teheran, 233.
Anzio, plan for assault on, 240.
Arms, British superiority in, 88, 138, 163, 169; Allied superiority in Sicily, 210.
Army Group, 18th, formed, 169; Alexander its commander, 173, 180; reformed, 201.
Arndt, Colonel, 114.
von Arnim, General, 152, 160, 183, 192; attacks British 1st Army, 180; at Mareth, 189.
Atlantic, allied shipping losses, 49; Battle of, 156; 210.
Auchinleck, General Claude, mentioned 60, 62, 63, 65, 79, 84, 107, 115, 124, 132, 210; victor at 'Crusader', 28; appreciates threat to Egypt, 29; wide responsibilities of, 29-30; 43; offensive spirit of, 30; reports on lack of armour, 31; gives order on Tobruk, 33, 37; defies Churchill, 34; given priorities, 35, 46-47; ordered by Churchill to attack, 36; his orders to Ritchie at Gazala, 37; assumes command in field, 39; postpones offensive, 42; at Cairo Conference, 54; integrity of, 54; 8th Army's admiration for, 55, 69; visited by Churchill, 56 et seq.; given new command, 61; receives dismissal notice, 63; refuses Iraq command, 67; shocked by Montgomery's Memoirs, 81; relieved by Alexander, 85; foresees Alam Halfa battle, 95; greatness of, 100; unaware of political issues, 110; burdened by political problems, 120; integrates infantry and armour, 123; his qualities of leadership, 126; insulted by Montgomery, 176; tribute to, 255; by Churchill, 256, 257; his comments on Iraq/Persia command, 257; and on Dorman-Smith's advice, 258.
Australian Army, 9th Division, 123.
Axis, strength in Sicily, 215.

Baden-Powell, Montgomery's resemblance to, 128.
Badoglio, Marshal, 218; discusses armistice terms, 233; announces surrender of Rome, 235; but fails to seize city, 239.
Baruch, friendship with Churchill, 25.
Bayerlein, Colonel, 97; takes over Afrika Corps, 149; amazed by Montgomery, 151; assigned to Italian army, 185; at Mareth, 189, 190, 192.
Beaverbrook, Lord, his friendship with Churchill, 25.
Bedell Smith, General, 249; reports Montgomery a national hero, 202; on 'Flying Fortress' incident, 205; discusses Sicily with Montgomery, 212, 227.
Belisarius, Italian campaign, 234.
Benghazi, 160; 164; 174.
Birkenhead, Lord, 71.
Bismark, General, killed, 97.
Bismark, German battleship, 32.
Brest Litovsk, Treaty of, 114-115.
British Army: 1st Airborne Div., 221; 1st Army, 169, 171, 181, 193, 243; repulsed at Tunis, 175; resents 8th Army, 202; 8th Army in Sicily, 222; 8th Armoured Bde.,

102; at Alamein, 147; occupies Ben Gardine, 182; at Mareth, 187, 189; 9th Armoured Bde., heavy losses at Alamein, 134; further losses, 145; 22nd Armoured Bde., 101, 102, 157, 182; 23rd Armoured Bde., 147; 1st Armoured Div., at Mareth, 188, 193; 7th Armoured Div., at Alam Halfa, 95; leads 8th Army, 157; at Agheila, 161; enters Tunis, 193; assigned to Salerno, 225; 10th Armoured Div., 102, 140; 11th Armoured Div., 102; 79th Armoured Div., 249; 151st Infantry Bde., 188; 154th Bde., 186; 2nd Corps, its former commanders, 80; 92; 5th Corps, in Italy, 235; 9th Corps, 191, 204; 10th Corps, 124; at Alamein, 133; ordered to cut off Rommel, 150; at Mareth, 188, 190; in Italian assault, 235; 13th Corps, 101; at Alamein, 134; in Italy, 235, 236; 30th Corps, at Mareth, 183, 187; in Sicily, 223; 4th County of London Yeomanry, 101; 3rd Division, under Montgomery at Dunkirk, 92; 5th Div., lands in Italy, 236; 44th Div., reaches Egypt, 67, 94; at Alam Halfa, 101; 50th Div., refitting at Alamein, 41; under Ramsden, 127; at Mareth, 190; 51st (Highland) Div., 147, 162-165; advances to Tripoli, 166; parades past Churchill, 171; at Medenine, 184; at Mareth, 190; 78th Div., 171; in Sicily, 222; in Italy, 237; at Sangro, 248; 14th Essex Regt., 101; at Alamein, 135; 11th Hussars, 167; 1st Parachute Bde., in Sicily, 221; 1st Royal Tank Regt., 167; 3rd RTR, 167; 5th RTR, 101, 167; 8th RTR, its losses at Alamein, 147; 40th RTR, 167; 50th RTR, at Mareth, 188.

British people, feelings of at US entry into war, 26; need for a victory, 43.

Bourg el Arab, 67, 68, 70, 72; Montgomery moves HQ there, 83; press conference there before Alamein, 128.

Bradley, General Omar, 226, 249; brushes with Montgomery, 222, 223.

Briggs, General, 127, 142, 147.

Brooke, General Alan, 67, 71, 79, 80, 134, 185, 198, 213, 246; embarrassed by Churchill, 53, 59; dumbfounded by Montgomery, 72; yields command of 2nd Corps, 92; visits Tripoli, 171; comments on Montgomery, 200, 202-203; angered by 'Flying Fortress' incident, 205, 207; recalls Montgomery, 206; misgivings about invasion of Normandy, 219; comments on Churchill's frustrations, 329; rebukes Montgomery, 246; appreciates his outlook, 249.

Buckley, Christopher, war correspondent, 216; quoted, 220; on Sicily, 224; on assault on Italy, 237.

Buechting, Colonel, at Alamein, 139.

Buelowius, General, 158.

Butcher, Captain, Eisenhower's aide, 226.

Butler, R.A., 64.

Canadian (1st) Army, 249, 250.

Carver, Major-General, quoted, 149.

Casablanca, conference, Jan. 1943, 113, 169, 197.

Casey, at Cairo conference, 54.

Casualties: 8th Army's, 34; 188; German, 98, 184, 210.

Castellano, General, sent to discuss armistice terms, 233.

INDEX

Chamberlain, Houston, 114.
Chatfield, Lord, 25.
Churchill, Winston, at low ebb, 23; his responsibility for setbacks, 24; megalomania of, 25; reaction to Pearl Harbour, 26; plans future strategy, 27; wins vote of confidence, 31; obsessed by Middle East, 33; harries Auchinleck, 34, 47; and orders him to attack, 35; effects on of loss of Tobruk, 38; rejects Auchinleck's views, 42; angered by Americans, 49; decides to dismiss Auchinleck, 51; and to visit Egypt, 52; obsessed by Rommel, 53, 65; visits Auchinleck's HQ, 55 et seq., reorganises Middle East Command, 60 et seq.; comments on Auchinleck, 61; dismisses him, 63; leaves for Moscow, 64; enthusiasm for 'Torch', 65; visits Montgomery, 67; on propaganda value of Alamein, 68; as a brandy drinker, 71; is impressed by Montgomery, 72; determined to defeat Rommel by Sept. 15th, 107, 108; tries to persuade Americans to discard 'Sledgehammer', 108; and 'Torch', 109; goes to Moscow, 110; proposes Marshall for invasion command, 110; seeks backing for 'Torch', 111; his strategic thinking, 112-113; harries Alexander, 121; awaits news of Alamein, 134; visits Tripoli, 171; his dislike of rivals, 178; at Casablanca, 197; critical of 'Husky' planning, 209; misgivings about invasion of France, 219; comments on shortage of landing craft, 231; is excluded from Soviet-American talks, 232; on Italian campaign, 233; his impatience with it, 239, 240; illness, 240; on Montgomery, 243, 244; meets Montgomery at Marrakesh, 251; his orders to Alexander, 258; his tribute to Auchinleck, 256-257; exonerates Dorman-Smith, 261.

Clark, General Mark, 226; describes Montgomery's first meeting with Eisenhower, 201; in assault on Italy, 235; at Salerno, 237; visits Montgomery, 238; advances to Naples, 239.

Clifford, Alexander, war correspondent, the voice of 8th Army, 132-133; on Rommel's retreat, 151; quoted, 166.

Cologne, thousand bomber raid on, 24.

Commonwealth forces, right of appeal to own governments, 41.

Coningham, Air Marshall, on bombing of Pantellaria, 220.

Coral Sea, Battle of, 43.

Corbett, Lt. General, 81, 85.

Corsica, 215; evacuated by Axis, 239.

Cramer, General, commands Afrika Corps, 184, 185.

Crerar, General, 250.

Cripps, Sir Stafford, 34.

'Crusader', battle, 28, 39.

Cunningham, Admiral, 199; enters Taranto, 237.

Darlan, Admiral, 199.

Deakin, Captain, with Tito, 232.

Dempsey, General, 80, 81; succesful dealings with Montgomery, 87.

Dieppe, raid, Montgomery's plan, 212; Canadians accuse Montgomery, 250.

Dill, Sir John, angered by Churchill, 178.

Dimoline, Brigadier, 176.

Dorman-Smith, Major-General; 63, 64, 70, 85, 250; his appreciation of situation angers Churchill,

42, 56, 58; confers with Wavell, 60; advises Auchinleck, 258; exonerated in Churchill's memoirs, 261.
Duke of York, HMS, 27.

Eighth Army, 60, 63, 66, 127, 132, 162, 169, 209, 222; inspired by Auchinleck, 28; ill-equipped, 29; at Gazala-Bir Hacheim, 36; its admiration for Auchinleck, 55, 69; casualties, 34, 98, 253; reinforcements, 66; commanders all replaced, 81; has no orders to retreat, 83; at Alam Halfa, 96, 98; is heartened by Alam Halfa, 101; its state of training, 123; Montgomery its mascot, 127; its failure to destroy Afrika Corps, 150; march to Tunisia, 156; curbed by Montgomery's caution, 157; its superiority of strength, 158; frustration of, 160; advances to Tripoli, 162-163, 164; Tripoli, its goal, 167; shares in Montgomery's fame, 170; rests on laurels, 174; continues advance to Tunis, 174, 181; pride of, 175; personality of, 176; its criticism of Montgomery, 180; Americans opinion of, 181; at Medenine, 184; at Mareth, 187-190; reaches end of road, 190-193; arrogance of, 202; enters Sfax, 204; in Sicily, 221, 222; slow advance to Salerno, 238, 239; in Italy, 242, 243; where Montgomery's command ends, 243; receives publicity in Italy, 246; glamour of it gone, 248; its strength at 'Crusader', and Alamein, 253.

Eisenhower, General Dwight, 75, 110, 180, 181, 185, 215, 240, 249; comments on abandonment of 'Sledgehammer', 50; gets on well with Alexander, 182; qualities of, 199-200; meets Montgomery, 201-202; earns Montgomery's approval, 203; comments on Montgomery, 203-204; but angered by 'Flying Fortress' incident, 205; is upset by Montgomery over 'Husky', 206, 213; on Sicilian campaign, 215; visits Montgomery there, 225-227; his generosity to Montgomery, 228; on need for speed in Italy, 233; on Salerno, 239; is disappointed by Montgomery's appointment to NW Europe, 250.

Equipment, faults in British, 253, 254; shortages of, 24; defects in petrol containers, 29.

Etna, Mount, 215, 221.

Fisher, Brigadier, 89, 90.
'Forgotten Army', 32, 170-171.
Fredendall, Major-General, 169; replaced by Patton, 181.
Freyberg, General, 67, 127; meets Churchill, 68; his friendship with Churchill, 123; at Mareth, 189.
Fuller, General, 62, 88, 89, 185, 249; on Montgomery, 154; on policy of unconditional surrender, 198; on generalship, 216; on Montgomery's methods, 241, 242.

Gabes, 162, 169, 189; occupied by 8th Army, 190; Eisenhower meets Montgomery there, 200, 201, 204.
Gatehouse, Major-General, 102, 127, 150; at Alamein, 140; argues with Montgomery, 141, 142; as an armoured div. commander, 147; urges advance on Tobruk, 152.
de Gaulle, General, 199, 251; protects French interests, 26.

Gazala, 36, 83.
German Army: 6th Army, 115; Hermann Goering Div., in Sicily, 215; 90th Light Div., 105; at Alamein, 143, 152; at Agheila, 162; Montgomery's inability to catch it a joke, 170; at Mareth, 191; 164th Light Div,. 152; Panzer Armee Afrika, 120, 152; its strength at 'Crusader', 253; at Alamein, 253; and casualties, 253; 5th Panzer Armee, 180; 10th Panzer Div., 190; 15th Panzer Div., at Alam Halfa, 98, 101; at Alamein, 140; at Mareth, 188, 189, 190, 191; reformed in Sicily, 215; 21st Panzer Div., at Alamein, 143; evades 8th Army, 151; ordered west, 162; at Mareth, 184, 189, 190; Panzer Grenadier Regt., 152.
Giraud, General, 199; US prefers to de Gaulle, 251.
Gott, General, 37, 80, 153; picked out by Churchill, 54; death of, 59, 62; assigned to 8th Army, 61.
Greece, campaign in, 23.
Greek Sacred Squadron, 187.
de Guingand, Major-General, 62, 71, 82, 84, 169, 201; resents Dorman-Smith, 64, 82; misleads Montgomery, 83, 86; on Montgomery, 134; on Eisenhower, 203; promoted, 209; on assault on Rome, 243; his relations with Montgomery, 245; on Montgomery's farewell to 8th Army, 247, 248.
'Gymnast', operation, 28, 48, 108.

Hammamet, 191.
Hankey, Lord, 25.
Higgins, Professor, quoted on US-Soviet collaboration, 233.
Hitler, Adolf, 114; obsessed by Stalingrad, 65, 97; his military decisions, 113; and effects of his beliefs on strategy, 114, 115, 116, 160; orders to Rommel, 119; fatal intervention of at Alamein, 134, 135, 146, 190; his reasons for fighting in Tunisia, 218; his orders to Kesselring in Italy, 239.
Hobart, Percy, military theorist, 249.
Hopkins, Harry, Churchill seeks his support for 'Torch', 111; 232.
Horrocks, General, Brian, 80, 81, 83, 96, 97; Montgomery's opinion of, 85; explains Montgomery's misunderstanding of 8th Army's withdrawal plans, 86; his doubts about Montgomery, 92; commands 13th Corps, 101; pleads for 4th Indian Div., 177; admiration for Montgomery, 181; at Mareth, 188, 189; assigned to 9th Corps, 193.
Howe, author, quoted 109, 111-112.
Hull, Cordell, on Free French, 251.
Hunter, David, 222.
'Husky', operation, 206, 209; forces assigned to, 210; Montgomery's doubts about, 211; uneccessary wealth of information in planning of, 216.
Hutton, Lieut. Colonel, his bold stroke at Mareth, 182, 183.

Indian Army, 4th Indian Div., 167, 178; Montgomery's bad treatment of, 176, 177; at Mareth, 188, 190; 10th Indian Div., 41; 5th Indian Bde, at Alamein, 134, 135, 147; Rajputana Rifles, at Alamein, 135.
Information, excess of in operational planning, 216.
Ismay, General, 27, 209.
Italian Army, Ariete Div., 143; 1st Army, 183, 189; escapes at

Mareth, 190; 62nd Infantry Regt., almost destroyed, 139; Trieste Div., 105.
Italy, surrender of armed forces, 235; campaign, 236; effects of winter on, 240, 241.

Jacob, Colonel Sir Ian, 63.
Johnston, Denis, BBC correspondent, quoted, on minefields, 96; on correspondents' job, 130; on Montgomery, 136; on Montgomery's farewell to 8th Army, 247.
Jugoslavia, 232.

Kasserine Pass, 167, 184; American defeat there, 180; its effect on Eisenhower, 202.
Kennedy, Sir John, author, quoted, on Churchill's intolerance, 178, 207; on invasion of France, 230.
Kesselring, Field Marshal, disputes Rommel's Tunisian strategy, 183; intervenes at Mareth, 189; plans Italian strategy, 239, 240; comments on Alma Halfa.
Kidney Ridge, 134, 140; scene of fierce fighting, 142.
King, Admiral, 108, 109, 110, 111.
Kisch, Brigadier, 70.
Kitchener, Lord, 207.
von Kleist, General, 115.

Lampedusa, saturation bombing of, 219.
Lampson, Lady, 66.
Lathbury, Brigadier, 222.
Leadership, democratic ideal of, 126; Montgomery's 127; military, 164-165; Montgomery's own ideas on, 179.
Le Clerc, General, 187.
Leese, General Sir Oliver, 80, 81; on need for tact with Montgomery, 86; at Mareth, 183; in Sicily, 223; succeeds Montgomery, 248, 251.

Liddell Hart, military historian, 67, 90; quoted, on Alam Halfa, 101, 102, 104; on Alamein, 134; on Montgomery, 141; on his failure to cut off Rommel, 151; on his generalship at Alamein, 154-155; on dismissal of Auchinleck, 262; is read by German commanders, 249.
Long Range Desert Group, 167, 181, 182.
Louisiana, German transport, sunk, 144.
Lumsden, General, 81, 122, 147; accused by Montgomery, 127; protests at Alamein orders, 140; thwarted by Montgomery, 159.

Maclean, Brigadier Fitzroy, 232.
McCreery, General, 67; dismissed by Auchinleck and restored by Alexander, 123.
McNaughton, General, upset by Montgomery, 250.
Maldon, by-election, 39.
Malta, importance of to Churchill's plans, 28; threatened, 29, 35; starving, 32; as a base, 106; relieved, 215.
Manpower, British, 231.
Mareth, Battle of, 187-190.
Mareth Line, 167, 169, 170, 181, 182, 203.
Marksmanship, quality of German, 222.
Marrakech, 240; 251.
Marshall, General, opposes North African invasion, 47; favours Pacific theatre, 48, 49, 50; predicts British defeat, 48; attempts by Churchill to outwit, 108; agrees to 'Torch', 109; proposed by Churchill for cross-Channel invasion command, 110; his opinions on 'Round-Up', 111; as possible Supreme Commander, 198; dislike of Mediterranean

theatre, 231; suspicious of British, 232.
Maxse, General Sir Ivor, 89.
Medenine, German attack repulsed at, 184.
Messe, Lieut. General, 183; at Mareth, 188-189, 190.
Messina, Americans enter, 214; mentioned, 213, 223, 236.
Midway, Battle of, 43.
Minefields, 95, 96; strength of German, 138; not cleared, 140.
Monte Cassino, 236.
Montgomery, General Bernard, 61, 64, 67, 69, 71, 78, 88, 89, 93, 108, 153, 213; favoured by Auchinleck, 54; and summoned by him, 62; eccentricities of, 68, 75, 170; belief in fitness, 70, 93; impresses Churchill, 70, 72; appointed to 8th Army, 75; personality, 76, 78; indiscipline of, 78, 79; at Sandhurst, 80; he dismisses Ramsden, 80, 83; dislike of Auchinleck, 82; addresses staff, 84; misunderstands plans, 83, 86; dislike of losing face, 87; generalship, 89 et seq., 192; writes to Liddell Hart, 90; his orthodoxy, 91, 123, 249; Great War experience, 91 et seq., in 1940 campaign, 92; his poverty, 93; his challenge, 94; at Alam Halfa, 95-99; limitations of, 100, 172; failure to exploit Alam Halfa, 103-104; prepares Alamein, 105; at Alamein, 119 et seq., 133, 134; crisis at Alamein, 140; overrules generals at Alamein, 141; makes new plans, 143, 144, 146; romanticism of, 121, 179; authority of, 122, 124; training methods, 123; adopts Auchinleck's plan, 124-125; symbol of 8th Army, 126, 148; compared to Baden-Powell, 128; meets press, 136, 148; love of publicity, 130-131, 136, 170; his tank beret, 148; entertains von Thoma, 149; overestimates Rommel, 152, 153, 159; his weaknesses, 154; his objectives, 155, 157; holds back 8th Army, 157, 159, 162; fails to catch Rommel at Agheila, 161; predictability of, 162; his anxieties, 163, 165; his triumph, 167; new tasks, 169; reputation, 170-171, 173; dislike of Indian Army, 176-177; resents criticism, 178 et seq., fails to impress Patton, 181; in Tunisia, 184; plans Mareth attack, 185-187; order to army, 186; Mareth plan fails, 188-190; Mareth, his last chance, 191; on Alexander's visit, 192; difficulty of working with, 200, 202-203, 248; meets Eisenhower, 201; on his victories, 203; 'Flying Fortress' incident, 204, 205, 206-208, 226; bedevils Sicily planning, 206, 209, 211-212; popularity of at home, 207-208; responsibility for Dieppe raid, 212; in Sicily, 216, 216, 221, 222; favours mass bombardments, 217; brushes with Americans, 222, 223; meets Eisenhower, 225-226; pessimistic, 226, 227; on himself, 227-228; in Italian landings, 235, 237; in Italy, 238-239; lack of ideas, 241-242; leaves 8th Army, 243, 246-248, 251; appointed to 21st Army group, 245; his liking for young people, 93, 246; unpopular with Canadians, 250; Memoirs, quoted, 82, 166, 179, 184, 189, 192, 227, 247, 261.
Morgan, General, 'Overlord' planner, 230.
Moorehead, Alan, war correspondent, on Montgomery, 94,

96, 208; on Montgomery's failure to pursue Rommel, 103; on his anxieties, 164; on his opposition to Sicily plans, 212; on the Italian assault, 237.
Morshead, General Sir Leslie, 41.
Moscow, Churchill's visits to, 52, 64.
Mussolini, 68, 160; fall of, 231; effects of fall, 233.

Napoleon, 157, 248.
Naumann, Friederich, 114, 115.
Nehring, General, 97.
New Zealand Division, 96, 101, 102, 105, 157; bears brunt of fighting, 123; at Alamein, 142; at Agheila, 161; at Mareth, 187-188.
Nye, General, 201; confirms Auchinleck's appreciations, 34; briefs Montgomery, 78.

O'Connor, General, 127, 210; his victories, 27; at Beda Fomm, 167.
Oil, threats to, 29, 35, 46; Auchinleck's responsibility for, 36, 46; its importance superior to to defence of Egypt, 46, 53.
'Overlord', operation, 28, 233; material demands of, 210; Sicily, a curtain-raiser for, 214; planning of, 216; its impact on Mediterranean, 226, 230; Montgomery's reaction to it, 251.

Paget, General, 75, 198; works on 'Overlord', 230; succeeded by Montgomery, 245.
Pan-Germanism, 114-115.
Pantellaria, saturation bombing of, 219, 220, 236.
Passchendaele, compared with Alamein, 119; and with Italy, 245.
Panzers,—see under German Army.
Patton, General, 169, 182, 190, 201, 206, 211, 226, 249; replaces Fredendall, 181; eccentricity of, 200; seizes Messina, 214, 225; his enterprise, 217, 223-224; opposite of Montgomery, 224; Eisenhower's opinion of, 228.
von Paulus, General, at Stalingrad, 115; defeat of, 160.
Pearl Harbour, 26.
Petain, Marshal, quoted, 245.
Pile, General, 78, 79.
Poston, John, Montgomery's aide, 226; death of, 179.
Prinz Eugen, the, 32.
Prince of Wales, HMS, 23.

Quattara Depression, 138, 144; minefields there, 95, 96.
Quebec, conference, 219, 226, 232; invasion of France discussed there, 229, 230; changed status of British, 251.

Raeder, Admiral, 32.
Ramsden, Lieut. General, 62, 108, 122, 127; dismissed, 80; cross-examined by Montgomery, 83; ordered to plan attack, 124.
'Rankin', operation, 230.
Rees, Goronwy, author, quoted, on meeting Montgomery, 76, 77.
Repulse, HMS, 23.
Renton, Major-General, 102.
Ritchie, General, 62, 83; generalship of, 29; sacrifices Tobruk, 33; squanders his armour there, 37; succeeded by Auchinleck, 39.
Roberts, Brigadier, 102.
Roberts, Lord, 207.
Rome, 235.
Rommel, Field-Marshal Erwin, 65, 66, 81, 107, 108, 110, 185, 191, 228; opposing Auchinleck, 28; reinforced, 29; attack of May 26, 1942; 36; on British tactics, 37; ill-health of, 41, 66, 84, 97, 182; Churchill obsessed by him,

53, 65; inadequate forces of, 66; myth of, 72; at Alam Halfa, 96-99; asks to be relieved, 97; mistaken to cross Egyptian frontier, 106; at mercy of 8th Army, 107; hands over command, 121, 136; wants to withdraw at Alamein but is prevented by Hitler, 135, 146; resumes command, 140; disturbed by situation at Alamein, 142, 143; withdraws, 143-146; moves fast, 150; describes retreat, 152; and battle of Alamein, 153, 155; gains time, 158, 159, 162; comments on Montgomery's caution, 159, 162; visits Germany, 160; at Agheila, 161; at Mareth, 167; survives long retreat, 168; in Tunisia, 180; faces two fronts there, 182; shortens front, 183; leaves Africa for good, 184; but intervenes in Mareth battle from Rome, 188-189.

Roosevelt, President F. D., 198, 232; surprised by Churchill, 26; supports Churchill's Mediterranean plans, 28; informs Churchill of fall of Tobruk, 38; considers Middle East situation, 48; favours pre-eminence of European theatre, 49; supports 'Torch', 50, 111; offers Sherman tanks 104; Churchill tries to win his support, 108, 109, 110; at Casablanca, 197; agrees to Anzio operation, 240.

'Round-up', operation, 28, 108, 110; Churchill tries to cancel, 111.

Royal Air Force, Churchill's faith in, 23; supports army, 169; at Mareth, 188-189.

Royal Navy, 169, 204.

Royal Tank Corps, annoyed by Montgomery's adoption of beret, 148.

Russia, campaign in, German threat to Caucasus, 29, 35, 46, 65; Stalingrad, 65; how situation there affected allied planning, 109-110, 113; ties down huge German army, 209.

Salerno, 225, 237; Germans anticipate attack there, 236; assault, 238-239.

Sardinia, 215; evacuated by Axis, 239.

Saxe, Marshal, quoted, 157.

Scharnhorst, the, escapes from Brest, 32.

Sfax, 'Flying Fortress' incident, 204.

Sicily, 198; invasion plans, 200; planning bedevilled by Montgomery, 206; invasion of, 214; effects of conquest of, 214-215; 219; airborne attack on, 221, 222.

Simpson, General Sir Frank, 93.

Singapore, loss of, 23.

'Skyscraper', plan, 230.

'Sledgehammer', operation, plan for attack on continent in 1942, 28, 38, 48, 111, 197; Roosevelt ready to discard, 49; plan is abandoned, 50; Churchill's efforts to obtain cancellation, 108.

Slim, General, 32; leadership of, 126.

Smuts, Field-Marshal J. C., 48; summoned to Cairo, 54; doubts about cross-channel invasion, 219.

Stalin, J., 110; meets Churchill, 64; Churchill cables to him, 109; his delight in Roosevelt, 232; pleasure at Operation 'Anvil', 233.

Stalingrad, 65, 115; defeat there comparable to Tunisia for Germans, 180.

Strategy, Churchill's grasp of, 27; difference of British and American concepts, 28, 113-114, 199,

229; German errors of in Tunisia, 180; Italy, graveyard of British Mediterranean, 229, 232; American determination to dominate allies, 230.

Strategic bombing programme, Churchill's faith in, 23; endangers Britain, 115; lengthened war, 156; excuse for, 219.

Stumme, General, succeeds Rommel, 121; his difficulties, 137, 138, 139; death of, 139-140.

Sugden, Brigadier, 227.

'Supercharge', plan, 143; put into effect at Alamein, 145-147.

Tanks, 119; at Alamein, 134, 135; at Tel el Aqquaquir, 146; Afrika Corps' strength in, 146, 153, 163; concentrated for advance to Tripoli, 162.

Tedder, Air Chief Marshal Sir A. W., 199.

Teheran, conference, 229; US dominance at, 232; American distrust of British revealed at, 233; status of British changed at, 251.

Tel el Aqquaquir, German tank success there, 119-120; battle, 134, 146.

Thoma, General von, captured and entertained by Montgomery, 149.

Tirpitz, the, 32.

Tito, Marshal J., 232.

Tobruk, 139, 152; loss of, 37; Auchinleck's orders concerning, 33, 37; effect of loss on Churchill, 38; re-occupied by British, 158.

'Torch', operation, 61, 64, 75, 108, 110, 121; Roosevelt supports, 50; Churchill's enthusiasm for, 65; American's reluctant acceptance of, 109; dependent on Russian situation, 109, 110; timing of with Alamein, 125.

Tomes, Major, 89; his affection for Montgomery, 93.

Tripoli, advance on, 163-167, 169; visited by Churchill, 171.

Tuker, Major-General Francis, 127; is outraged by Montgomery, 177.

Tunis, 169; British and Americans thrown back before, 175; entered, 193.

Unconditional Surrender, declaration of, 113-114; 197, 198; meaning disputed with Badoglio, 218, 233.

Vichy, government, American liking for, 251.

Voss, Lieut. Colonel, commands German delaying group, 151.

Wadi Zigzaou, 187, 188.

War, art of, 99-100, 216; Hitler's concept of, 115; Montgomery's lectures on in Italy, 236.

War correspondents, 129-130, 131; Montgomery, a gift to, 148; exhilaration of, 164; opinions of during advance to Tripoli, 166; link up with Americans at Salerno, 239.

Wavell, Field Marshal Sir A. P., 29, 122, 210; is dismissed, 25, 33; summoned to Cairo, 54; confers with Dorman-Smith, 60; supports Montgomery, 79; burdened by political problems, 120.

Wellington, Duke of, 136.

Whiteley, Brigadier, 64.

Wilson, General Sir Henry, Iraq-Persia Commander, 67; succeeds Eisenhower in Mediterranean theatre, 250.

For Product Safety Concerns and Information please contact our EU representative GPSR@taylorandfrancis.com
Taylor & Francis Verlag GmbH, Kaufingerstraße 24, 80331 München, Germany

www.ingramcontent.com/pod-product-compliance
Lightning Source LLC
Chambersburg PA
CBHW070555300426
44113CB00010B/1268